GODCAST

Transforming Encounters with God;
Bylines by Media Journalist and Pastor

Dan Betzer

GODCAST

Transforming Encounters with God;
Bylines by Media Journalist and Pastor

Dan Betzer

First printing: September 2008

ISBN-13: 978-0-89221-689-1
ISBN-10: 0-89221-689-5
Library of Congress Catalog Number: 2008934674

Unless otherwise noted, all Scripture is from the King James Version of the Bible.

Cover and interior design by Diana Bogardus

Printed in the United States of America

Please visit our website for other great titles:
www.newleafpress.net

For information regarding author interviews, please contact the publicity department at (870) 438-5288.

New Leaf Press
A Division of New Leaf Publishing Group

Fifty-two years ago, my wife, Darlene, committed her life to me. Throughout all these intervening years, through the proverbial "thick or thin," she has been my strength and inspiration.

Her words have always been encouraging. Never once has she "rained on my parade," even when my "parade" meandered off course.

She has been my constant intercessor before God's throne.

I am blessed beyond measure to have her at my side. I dedicate this book to her with deepest love, respect, and admiration.

INTRODUCTION

I have been in media all my life. Well, almost. At the young age of 71, I still have some years to go, God willing. My first "appearance" in media was on a church radio program at age three. It was 1940. The station was WNAX, a powerful AM station at that time with twin locations, Sioux City, Iowa, and Yankton, South Dakota. This is the station where Lawrence Welk and his orchestra performed for many years, and later it would be the start of the news ladder for Tom Brokaw. Every Saturday (a children's program) and Sunday (the church hour) I continued broadcasting for the next dozen years or so.

By the time I was in high school in Springfield, Missouri, I found myself in the television news business in both radio and television. My TV newscasting was during those local five-minute cutaways on NBC's *Today Show*. Those were the old black-and-white days. Dave Garroway was the host of the *Today Show*. Remember him? He was a genius! We didn't have color TV then and certainly no video tape. But how I loved that business! On radio, I announced live country music shows with Red Foley, Porter Waggoner, Brenda Lee, Gene Autry, Slim Wilson, Billy Walker, Wanda Jackson, and many others. When God called me into the ministry, my wife Darlene and I pioneered churches in Ohio. To put bread on the table, I earned my way again in the media, primarily in news and play-by-play sportscasting.

In 1977, I received an invitation to join the headquarters of the Assemblies of God in Springfield, Missouri, to be the director of the media department. The Assemblies had a major syndicated radio broadcast on about 700 stations in over 80 nations weekly called *Revivaltime*. We had the same agency as Billy Graham's *Hour of Decision*, the Walter Bennett Agency. In the early days, both of our broadcasts were on the ABC radio network. Later, when ABC sold, the new proprietors refused religious broadcasting, so both of our programs went into syndication. Our speaker on *Revivaltime* was the legendary C.M. Ward. I always believed that he and Paul Harvey were the two premier radio broadcasters in media history. Ward surprised us all by retiring at the age of 69, and to my enormous shock, the leaders of the Assemblies of God asked me to become the speaker on *Revivaltime*.

I held that position for 17 years. Dr. Ward was the speaker for the 25 years prior to that so, all in all, the broadcast was on the air with a new, fresh program every week (never a repeat!) for 42 years. When the leadership of the Assemblies decided to pull the broadcast and opt for a more contemporary version, I received a call from Brandt Gustafson, then president of the National Religious Broadcasters. He said, "Dan, we are so shocked about the decision to pull *Revivaltime* because, after 42 years, *Revivaltime* is still the fourth-rated weekly religious broadcast in the world." In my 17 years as speaker, I received over 1.25 million letters. (This was before the days of e-mail.)

Out of the *Revivaltime* broadcast came the radio, TV, and Internet series called *Byline.* I was on radio and television every day, Monday through Friday. The radio program was heard about 250 times daily in America, and the TV version was seen on many religious television cable systems, including TBN, CTN, Family Net, Cornerstone, and others, with releases of several thousand programs around the world five days a week. They originated from our TV studios at headquarters as well as on-location spots such as the Kremlin in Moscow, the White House, the Knesset in Jerusalem, the jungles of Africa, the frozen plains of Siberia, all over China, South America, and many other venues as well. The radio script (which was different from the television script) was released as well on the Internet to hundreds of subscribers.

In December of 2007, *Byline* was set aside by the Assemblies of God leadership to facilitate other ministries. I had calls, e-mails, and letters from around the world, "Please, Dan, continue to make these daily *Bylines* happen." Hence — the book you hold in your hand. Some of these daily devotionals are new, and some are rewritten from the radio scripts.

You must remember as you read them that I spent years in media journalism. That was my college training as well. So even though I am a pastor, I don't think like one (I've been told). I still think as a reporter of news. So the *Bylines* you will read in this volume are observations, insights, and thoughts on scores of different subjects. Some of the pages will have humor, while others are dramatic. Some will be biographical, even autobiographical. Some of these columns are caustic, some are strong, some are just plain old private opinion. But they won't be dull.

I hope this volume will bring you a few hours of reading enjoyment and spiritual strength. May God bless you.

— Dan Betzer

STUFF

Exodus 36:7: "For the stuff they had was sufficient for all the work to make it, and too much."

What a Scripture! What a realization of eternal truth! Just weeks out of 400 years of Egyptian slavery, the Israelites, led by Moses, were able to erect the tabernacle in the wilderness. One commentary places the value of the structures at $13.5 million. Enabled by the Lord, the Israelites had not only sufficient resources, but even more than enough.

Many church members (and church leaders) poormouth themselves and the Lord. They moan, "We can't do this — we can't do that," especially in the areas of evangelism and missions. Many times when they build necessary buildings, they go into unnecessary debt. Are you aware that the resources available in the average congregation just stagger the imagination? I had lunch recently with a pastor who claimed his church was about on its last legs, that they had no money, no resources. I asked him what time he thought God had toppled dead off His throne. He snapped, "How can you ask such a foolish question?" I replied, "Well, I was just responding to your implication that God lied when He promised to provide all our needs."

I cannot tell you how many times I have seen the Lord provide the absolutely unexpected "unprovidable"! God commanded Moses and the Israelites to build the tabernacle. When they implicitly obeyed their Lord's directive, His limitless resources were at their beckon. When we obey the Lord's direction in both our private lives and the corporate life of the church, the resources are there. If the resources are *not* there, check your premises. Something is amiss. If we are in God's plan, the "stuff" we have is enough. In fact, it is more than enough!

PRAYER: O God, open my eyes of faith to behold the wonders of Your provision that my natural eyes cannot comprehend. May I always do according to Your will and purpose and so see Your hand at work in all the dealings of life. **Amen.**

There used to be a church house right here

Acts 26:19: Whereupon, O king Agrippa, I was not disobedient unto the heavenly vision.

I enjoy taking big band pop songs and re-writing the lyrics so I can sing them in church rallies. This devotional is about one of those songs.

Recently I got to thinking about my joyous childhood, which was centered around three institutions: my home, my school, and my church. Of the three, only the house still stands. I loved my church beyond words to tell you. It was perhaps at that time the strongest evangelical church within a three-state area. Recently I drove by it. A chain-link, locked fence surrounds the structure. The grounds are covered by weeds. The site frankly broke my heart, and — thinking about it — I wrote these lyrics for a song prompted in my thinking by Joseph Rapozo's song, "There Used to Be a Ballpark Right Here."

> And there used to be a church house / in my childhood and my teens / where the people sang and worshiped with a joy I've seldom seen / and the place was filled with wonder / from the platform to the rear / yes, there used to be a church house right here.
>
> And there used to be a vision of those things God wanted done / now there's no one still attending of those saints, not even one / and the sky has got so cloudy when it used to be so clear / and the glory left so quickly one year.
>
> Now the children try to find it / and they can't believe their eyes / for the old folks don't remember, so no one really tries / but I'll never stop recalling / those days still seem so near / that there used to be a church house right here."

It's a sad song. I pray it never happens to your home church.

Prayer: O God, please help me do my part to keep the vision burning brightly in the church I attend. In generations to come, may it continue to be a tribute to the power, mercy, and glory of Your name. *Amen.*

WHEN RELIGION BECOMES COUNTER-PRODUCTIVE

> **1 Corinthians 13:13**
>
> And now these three remain: faith, hope and love. But the greatest of these is love (NIV).

Recently a 40-year-old Pakistani man decided that his 25-year-old stepdaughter had committed an immoral act. She hadn't, but he thought otherwise and killed her in cold blood. Then he killed his three young daughters.

According to the Independent Human Rights Commission of Pakistan, male relatives murder hundreds of girls and women each year in this conservative Islamic nation. Speaking to the Associated Press in the back of a police truck, the man showed no contrition, only dismay that he didn't murder the stepdaughter's alleged lover as well. He added, "I thought my younger daughters would do what the older girl did, so they should be eliminated."[1]

Authorities report the murdered woman actually did nothing, except flee her brutal husband who had forced her to work in a brick-making factory. To get even with her for running away, the husband accused her falsely of adultery. A human rights worker said, "Women are treated here as property." Here we find another major difference between Islam and Christianity. Throughout history, Christianity has elevated the status of women — and rightly so! Followers of Christ in general honor human rights, and the dignity of the individual is upheld. Jesus called upon His followers to "follow peace with all men, and holiness, without which no man shall see the Lord" (Heb. 12:14). That is often not the case in religions where there is blind hatred, often fomented by so-called clerics who call for their congregations to kill and destroy. The equipment of the follower of Christ is love. Unfortunately, equipment for some other faiths is often a sword.

> **PRAYER**
>
> O God, help me to ever remember that the uniform of a Christ-follower is love. May I always react to those around me, drawing from the very love of Jesus who dwells within me. May I never give reason for reproach upon the lovely name of my Lord Jesus. Amen.

1. Khalid Tanveer, The Associated Press, January 1, 2006.

SAINTS IN CAESAR'S HOUSEHOLD

Philippians 4:21–22; NIV

Greet all the saints in Christ Jesus.
. . . All the saints send you greetings,
especially those who belong to Caesar's
household.

When our Lord was born, Augustus
was the caesar of Rome. He was
followed by Tiberias (about whom it
was said that he liked not one single
human being and that not one single
human being liked him). Tiberius was
followed by the depraved Gaius Caesar,
better known as Caligula — Little
Boots. He ruled for four years and was
a monster of cruelty and vice. He was
finally assassinated in the year A.D.
41. The Praetorian Guard, fearful of
a return to a republic, forcibly made
Claudius (officially Tiberius Claudius
Drusus Nero Germanicus) the
emperor. And for the next 13 years, this
strange man of handicapped body and
slow speech was the monarch of the
Roman world. Claudius was followed,
in turn, by Nero, who
ruled for 14 years
until his suicide
in A.D. 68. All these decades were
splotched with immorality, depravity,
and insanity such as the world has
rarely witnessed.

But think of it! In those years between
A.D. 40 and 60, there were men and
women who were followers of Jesus
Christ who managed to thrive while
working in the very palace of Caligula,
Claudius, and Nero! Paul, who was
under house arrest in Rome, testified of
this reality in the letter he sent to the
church at Philippi, "All the saints send
you greetings, especially those who
belong to Caesar's household" (Phil.
4:22; NIV).

Today, we sometimes find professing
saints who complain about the
pressures of serving God in the free
world. How do they think they would
have fared in ancient Rome where
their witness for Christ could have
made them fodder for the lions? But
on the other hand, some of the most
courageous saints ever are serving God
this very day. Are you one of them?

Byline #4

PRAYER

O God, let me by Thy Spirit serve Thee well this
day! May there be no pressure or circumstance
that would cause me to grieve Thee. Let my
thoughts, words, and actions please Thee! Amen.

GOD'S LOVE TAKES AWAY ALL FEAR FROM OUR LIVES

LEVITICUS 20:24; NIV: "You will possess their land; I will give it to you as an inheritance, a land flowing with milk and honey."

Israel has been my "home away from home" since 1971. The first trip there was still two years away from the infamous Munich Olympics massacre, offering entry to the shadowy and bloody world of terrorism. I am often asked if I worry about safety in the Holy Land. Frankly, no. We are all well cognizant of the dangers that face the world today; however, I refuse to cower in the corner when there is so much living to do.

Some of my life's greatest adventures have come in Israel. I think of climbing into the ancient guard tower in the Jericho ruins, believed to be the oldest man-made structure on earth, even predating the pyramids by thousands of years. I remember that tiny, open-sided helicopter that whisked me from one end of Israel to the other, our feet hanging out as we swept over Nazareth, Haifa, the Sea of Galilee, and Jerusalem. I often reminisce about the prayer meeting with the Greek Orthodox priests early one morning in the cave of the nativity in Bethlehem. I can still hear the laughter ringing from my friends on Yehuda's wooden boat as we filmed a documentary in the middle of the Sea of Galilee. And I positively drool when I remember a tiny hole-in-the-wall restaurant in Jerusalem where my friend David Assael took me late one night, where the bread is "to die for." I think often of the late-night dinners with Palestinian friends overlooking the Herodian and the tiny village of Tekoaha.

Life is so fulfilling and rich! But not if one shrinks into the shadows of presumed safety. Yes, life can offer danger in many cloaks. But somehow it's realized more often by the fearful. God's love casts out all fear, my friend! So enjoy living.

Prayer: O God, by the word of Thy mouth, strike all fear from my life. May I walk in joy and the security of knowing You. You promised life abundant! And You have delivered it to those of us willing to reach for it. Thank You. Amen.

Forget post-modern and remember Pentecost

Acts 1:8 But ye shall receive power, after that the Holy Ghost is come upon you: and ye shall be witnesses unto me both in Jerusalem, and in all Judaea, and in Samaria, and unto the uttermost part of the earth.

According to a recent poll, the church in America is growing rapidly, and thoughts of a "post-Christian" America are just not true. People who never went to church or went only occasionally are now signing up as official members in growing numbers across the nation. Well over half of Americans are connected to the church in one way or another. My friend, that's a clear majority!

In my own part of the world, southwest Florida, churches that fervently declare the old-fashioned gospel of the Bible are the ones that are flourishing. Those congregations that entangle themselves in politics or even social issues alone (good though they may be) are declining. Jesus promised us His power to fulfill His divine redemptive mission on this earth; therefore, the mission is possible by His Spirit.

Church growth is not rocket science. Decades ago I heard Dr. Robert Schuller teach three principles I have never forgotten. He claimed that every pastor and church leader needs to be able to answer these questions: (1) What in the world am I trying to do here? (A recent poll indicated that 90 percent of church leaders cannot clearly articulate the vision of their church.) (2) How in the world do I plan to do it? (3) Why in the world do I do the work? Decades ago, in our church, we clearly concluded and stated what our church goals were. Then we prayerfully and painstakingly laid out the plan of how we believed Jesus wanted it done. Through very hard work, fervent prayer, and vision, we have seen miracles of every kind. Post-modern, indeed! This is the day of the Holy Ghost!

Prayer: O God, may our church faithfully reflect Thy majesty, compassion, and wisdom. Empower us by Thy precious Holy Spirit to do Your work on earth, occupying until You return. ***Amen.***

SPRING IN YOUR HEART

Proverbs 23:7: For as he thinketh in his heart, so is he.

A friend up north just called me to report brutal weather, including ice and snow. I live in the tropics, so I just patiently smiled and said somewhat sardonically, "Oh, really. . . ." He snapped back, "Yeah, well, you have to deal with humidity!" I retorted, "Yes, but in 21 years of living here, I've never had to scrape humidity off my windshield." He hung up on me.

But, you know, our daily attitude is not dependent upon weather. Honestly, it's not! We can have spring in our hearts 12 months each year. The other day I was in the airport in Little Rock, Arkansas. It was about six a.m. I was preparing to go through security. I approached the lady at the entry point and said, "Good morning, ma'am. Are you having a good day?" She looked me straight in the eyes, grinned, and responded, "Sir, this is going to be the best day of my entire life!" I thought to myself, *Hey, it probably will be.* She had already pre-determined that in her mind.

The Bible itself teaches us that as a person thinks, so is he. "She," too. God's promises are generic, you know. You cannot always control your circumstances, but by an act of your will, you can usually determine how you are going to react to them. If you woke up this morning determined to somehow grouse your way through the day, it's probably not going to be too scintillating for you or those around you. If, on the other hand, you woke up knowing this is the day the Lord made and you're going to rejoice and be glad in it, you're probably going to have a wonderful day. Look at the opportunities for real living extant all around you, thank the Lord, breathe in deeply, and say, "Yes, Lord, it's gonna be a great day!"

PRAYER: O God, this day let every thought that goes through my brain and every word that comes from my mouth be worthy of You and pleasing in Your sight and hearing! You truly did make this day, so let me make the very best of it, by Your grace. Amen.

THE BLESSINGS OF A GENEROUS SPIRIT

Luke 6:38

Give, and it shall be given unto you; good measure, pressed down, and shaken together, and running over, shall men give into your bosom. For with the same measure that ye mete withal it shall be measured to you again.

The Bible teaches that it's more blessed to give than to receive. That would be a great verse for a prizefighter, wouldn't it? But seriously, the way to gain is to give. However, here's the hitch: we don't give just to get. In all my years of pastoring, I can make an air-tight case for the joy of giving, both scripturally and in actual life occurrences. Giving churches are invariably receiving churches. Giving individuals are invariably those who receive bountifully. Jesus taught it. Look at the Scripture above. Our Lord promised, "Give, and it shall be given unto you!"

I often tell young pastors and church leaders, "If you want your church to be blessed, you must be a blessing yourself." I love Proverbs 11:24 that promises, "One man gives freely, yet gains even more; another withholds unduly, but comes to poverty" (NIV). The wealth spoken of here is not necessarily money (although God certainly blesses in that area as well). The receiving is primarily the bounty of God's provision in your life in basically every area of existence. Church leader, if you want more people in your church, be willing to give or send some of the people you do have to work in other vineyards. If you want financial strength, undergird missions around the world. Scripture emphasizes: "Give! Don't hoard!"

It truly is more blessed to give than to receive. Try it! Yes, this goes against the teachings and understandings of the world system, but we're not in that system anyway.

Be a giver today! And every day!

Byline #8

PRAYER

O God, You loved me so much that You gave. You freely gave Jesus to us so that we could have eternal life. You have taught us that loving leads to giving. May we, as Your servants, learn that lesson well and having learned it, practice it in everyday life. Amen.

THE SINGIN' COWBOY

2 Corinthians 5:17: Therefore if any man be in Christ, he is a new creature: old things are passed away; behold, all things are become new.

Probably no convert to Christ ever caught so much attention of the church crowd as did Stuart Hamblen. He committed his life to Christ in 1949. The young preacher who so influenced him by God's Spirit was Billy Graham.

Hamblen began his career in radio in 1926 on station KAYO in Abilene, Texas. He may well have been that media's first "singing cowboy." Hamblen soon went to Hollywood and was known to the radio audience as "Cowboy Joe." For 21 years thereafter, Hamblen stayed in front of the West Coast public with his radio show, "King Cowboy and His Woolly West Review." He also made a number of western films with such stars as Roy Rogers and Gene Autry. He wrote quite a few hit songs. In 1945, Stuart became the first man to "fly a horse" when he flew his race horse Lobo by plane, of course, to a distant racetrack. He became as well-known for his racehorses as for his music. But when he met Christ, Hamblen turned away from radio and films in order to devote his life to Christ. He was married to his wife Suzy for 55 years prior to his death in 1989.

I met Hamblen several times, one of them the night I gave my life to Christ as a 13 year old. He sang in that very service. It was Stuart Hamblen who gave us the classic song, "It Is No Secret What God Can Do," recorded by Elvis, the Andrews Sisters, Jo Stafford, and Bill Kenny and the Ink Spots (my own personal favorite rendition of that song).

The last time I met Hamblen (in an elevator of all places!), I shook his hand and thanked him for his role in bringing me to Christ. You know, old Stuart was right: "It's no secret what God can do!"

Prayer: O God, I thank Thee that I'm not what I used to be. And, I'm not yet what I'm going to be. I am a "becomer," one who is "becoming" a child of God. Thank You for new life in Your Son Jesus. Amen.

When you're up to your ears in . . . iguanas!

Job 4:8 Even as I have seen, they that plow iniquity, and sow wickedness, reap the same.

This whole wild scenario in our county got started when a few folks grew weary of their pet iguanas. They took the critters out in the countryside and just let 'em go. No, that certainly was not cruelty to a reptile, not here in warm, tropical southwest Florida! The iguanas would do just fine. Boy . . . would they ever do fine!

Just north of my house rolls the mighty Peace River, one of the hot spots for tarpon angling on the planet. And iguanas. Lots and lots of iguanas! In fact, in one little town alone, authorities estimate there are at least 10,000 iguanas. Residents are not happy. They say they often find the creatures inside their homes, nesting in crawl spaces, shredding attic insulation, scratching holes in pool screens, and eating prized gardens. These iguanas are a far cry from the kazillion chameleons we have everywhere that are three or four inches long. No, these big guys get four feet long or longer. They can reproduce in their second year of life, with the females laying an average of 35 eggs per nest. So you can see that we are about to be inundated with lizards. Here's what we've learned: it's easier to not release the original iguanas than it is to stop them once they start mass-producing themselves.

The Scripture that opens this devotional warns of that which we incubate within us. If we sow iniquity and wickedness, that's what we reap. In life, you and I need to be very careful what we release in our minds and hearts. It's easy to get started but often impossible to stop. Don't even think about looking at porn on your computer or TV screens. Don't even think about taking that first drink. Tell the drug pusher to go away and leave you alone. If you don't, you may soon be wading through life's iguanas. And, brother, sister, that's not fun!

Prayer: O God, I pray the cry of the Psalmist today: "Let the words that I say and the thoughts that I think be acceptable in Thy sight, O Lord, my strength and redeemer." Help me to guard carefully those things I allow in through the eye and ear gates of my soul. I look to Thee today, O King of my heart! Spare me from hell's iguanas. *Amen.*

THE STAR WHOSE LIGHT WENT OUT

Byline #11

For that ye ought to say, If the Lord will, we shall live, and do this, or that.

A few decades ago, I spent a somewhat dreadful year traveling with a gospel-singing group. I wouldn't say we were bad, but I didn't even buy our records! One night we sang in Detroit. Our tenor singer was a good friend of one of the best-known pop singers of that day who had four huge hits, two of them hitting number one on the pop charts. Our tenor heard that the star was singing in a nightclub in Windsor, just across the river in Canada, and called him. The star, who happened to be a real gentleman, invited us to his show that night and to sing some gospel songs with him. So we did.

I had never been around that sort of thing before and was intrigued by the acclaim the fellow got from his audience. He told us that he had a brilliant career mapped out and there was no telling how far he could go. Well, his plans never materialized. Several months later, the singer was accosted by somebody and beaten almost to death. He recovered, thankfully, but never again reached such a pinnacle of success.

It made me think of James's writing in the New Testament. He warned us through the Holy Spirit never to say, "I will do this or that" or "We intend to do this or that." Why? Because we don't know what the next breath will hold. And so we ought to preface our predictions by saying, "If God wills, I will do this or that." This devotional is most certainly not a condemnation of the star singer. He was a truly nice man, a delight to join in song. These words are merely a reminder that none of us should ever discount God and His plans for our lives. With Him we move and have our being. Without Him? Well, let's not even contemplate such a thing.

PRAYER

O God, I know my entire being this day is in Your hands. Your plans for me are good. I will trust You with every action, word, and thought so that You may be glorified and my life enriched. Amen.

No! I don't want to!

Exodus 36:2 And Moses called . . . every wise hearted man . . . whose heart stirred him up to come unto the work to do it.

My friend Michael and I were stranded in a patented Russian blizzard. We had been filming in Volgograd (that's the famed Stalingrad of World War II days). If you think airline service can be confusing in America, you should get isolated sometime in a Russian airport. We actually didn't mind the first couple of days because we were able to visit the famed Stalingrad War Memorial honoring the million or so men and women who died in that awful, freezing maelstrom of human suffering in the war.

But on this day, Michael and I ventured back to the airport and approached the "Information" (or lack thereof) center. Mike speaks fluent Russian. He approached the dour lady sitting behind the desk and politely asked, "Can you help me?" She never broke her intimidating countenance and snapped, "No!" Several times she and Mike went over that dialogue. Finally Mike asked her, "Well, do you have the information about outgoing flights that I am requesting?" "Yes," she grunted. Mike pushed on: "Well, ma'am, if you have that needed information, would you give it to me please?" "No," she repeated, even more loudly. Totally frustrated, Mike asked, "Why won't you tell me?" Her answer put me on the floor in laughter. She stared right at him and said, "Because I don't want to."

Oh, we've all met lots of folks like that in Christian churches. They could be great assets to Christ's kingdom on earth. They just don't want to. "Would you be an usher, one of God's gatekeepers in His house?" "No." "Why?" "I don't want to." "Are you a tither?" "No." "Why not?" "I don't want to." "Do you witness to people about Jesus?" "Uh — no." "Any reason why not?" "Don't want to." Now the lady in Volgograd made me laugh. But folks who could be an asset to God but refuse to are not funny. In fact, they're rather frightening when you start thinking of eternity.

Prayer: O God, may my heart be willing today, joyfully so, to accomplish by Your Spirit all You have planned for me. I don't want to be a foot-dragger but a front-runner for Your glory. ***Amen.***

THE JOY OF GIVING

Exodus 36:5: And they spake unto Moses, saying, The people bring much more than enough for the service of the work, which the LORD commanded to make.

Based on well over 50 years of marriage, Darlene and I can testify to the blessings of giving. We do not "give to get"; however, there truly is a law of sowing and reaping. Are you aware that the average Christian gives away less than 3 percent of his or her income? What about tithing, God's 10 percent that should come right off the top of all income? Only 4 percent of all Christians are known to actually tithe. It has been observed by those who should know that the average *Christian* in our churches today gives less than the average *American* (saved or unsaved) gave in 1933 in the midst of the Great Depression. Of course, Christ's church suffers for this spiritual Scrooge mentality; but the one who suffers the most is the non-giving Christian.

A half-century of marriage has taught my wife and me that we live far, far better on the 90 percent of our income that remains after tithe than we ever could have spending God's 10 percent on ourselves. Most followers of Christ I know will give the same report. Proverbs 11:24–26 gives us the reason: "There is that scattereth, and yet increaseth; and there is that withholdeth more than is meet, but it tendeth to poverty. The liberal soul shall be made fat: and he that watereth shall be watered also himself. He that withholdeth corn, the people shall curse him: but blessing shall be upon the head of him that selleth it."

The blessings of giving come from (1) honoring God with our income, (2) seeing God's work thrive because of our faithfulness, and (3) having our own lives enriched with our Father's supernatural blessings. If you're not giving to God on an ongoing, regular basis, don't just "try it for a while," but make generosity to God and your fellow man a lifestyle. Yes, you'll be blessed!

PRAYER: O God, give me faith to believe Your Word, all of it, yes, even those parts that admonish me to be a giver. As John prayed, prosper me even as my soul prospers and I will always honor You with my checkbook. Amen.

ARE WE STILL TENDING GOD'S GARDEN?

Genesis 1:28

And God blessed them, and God said unto them, Be fruitful, and multiply, and replenish the earth, and subdue it.

The earth's environment and the responsibility of God's people concerning it are touchy subjects to Christians for some reason. Tensions grew measurably recently as reported by Reuters when a group of 85 well-known evangelical Christian leaders lent support for legislation combating global warming. This group included mega-church pastors, Christian college presidents, religious broadcasters, and writers. The campaign by these evangelicals coincided with a call by a leading U.S. think tank for the United States to take immediate steps to fight global warming. The Pew Center for Global Climate Change reported that America has waited too long to seriously tackle the climate-change problem. The Center also outlined 15 steps the United States could take to reduce emissions it spews as the world's biggest energy consumer and producer of greenhouse gases.

As a resident of Florida, I add my "amen" to those who voice such concerns. I have sat through three major hurricanes here in recent years, one that did over a million dollars' worth of damage to our church. The Gulf of Mexico, a mere 15-minute drive from our church, had temperatures in the mid-90s, an all-time record, which simply added "fuel" to the rage of these storms. The hurricanes surged through our part of Florida, ripping up homes, churches, and businesses. Thankfully, our home (a 50-year-old, well-constructed ranch-style) was spared except for minor damage. Many experts are convinced that global warming was a major factor in the escalation of storms here.

God challenged Adam and Eve to be "dressers of the Garden" of Eden. It was their responsibility to take care of their part of the earth. Are we believers today less responsible? We have a mission to reach the souls of humanity, but also to have concerns for this earth for the sake of future generations.

Byline #14

PRAYER

O God, I will not take this earth for granted. May Your people feel a definite and personal responsibility to take care of what You have provided. May those who follow us in life be blessed with the same surroundings as those who greeted us when we were physically born. Amen.

COLSON'S CONCEPT OF CHORUSES

Isaiah 5:1: Now will I sing to my wellbeloved a song of my beloved touching his vineyard.

Few subjects elicit such a storm from both sides of the issue as church music. In all the years *Byline* appeared in international radio, television, and Internet, I received stacks (literal stacks!) of e-mails, letters, and phone calls regarding the decline of meaningful music in some churches today. So many reported having been subjected to having to stand in church, sometimes for nearly an hour, singing repetitive musical phrases, all too often to tunes that are virtually non-melodic.

In one of his thought-provoking Internet columns, "Breakpoint," Chuck Colson reported reaching the end of his endurance in such a service. He wrote, "When church music directors lead the congregation in singing some praise music, I often listen stoically with teeth clenched. But one Sunday morning I cracked. We had been led through endless repetitions of a meaningless ditty. The song had zero theological content and could be sung in a nightclub for that matter. When I thought it was finally and mercifully over, the music leader beamed at us and said in a cheerful voice, 'Let's sing that again, shall we?' 'No!' I shouted loudly. Heads all around me spun while my wife cringed" (Feb. 6, 2006, column).

I laughed out loud when I read Colson's reaction. But I also add my hearty "amen" to it. Yes, certainly there are some praise choruses that have both solid biblical content and lovely melodies. They can often assist us in our musical worship. Thank God for these helps. But other choruses are much less worthy. So we sing such choruses one time through. Okay, I'm still with you. The second time? Maybe. The third time? No, I don't think so. Worship leaders (whatever that title means), have mercy! Don't expect folks my age to stand the whole time while you and your band of merry guitarists, eyes tightly shut, drill our hearing with your personal concerts. Surely God deserves better! Why not allow us to lift our voices in some hymns that have proven theologically worthy for decades? We would all be blessed, not just the drummer.

Prayer: O God, let the songs we sing prove acceptable in Your most holy presence. Do not allow us to reduce the majesty of Your glory to a modified ecclesiastical karaoke hour. Thank You! Amen.

But what about the weeping?

Psalm 30:5: "...weeping may endure for a night, but joy cometh in the morning."

Christians frequently suffer loss. Yes, they even grieve. It is a fact that Christ's followers often weep. Death visits their families. Let's talk about it.

It is true that Romans 8:28 promises that all things work together for good to those who love God. But that joyful revelation does not erase anxieties and frustrations and hurts we feel when we experience some big losses. Like health. The doctor looks at you sadly and gives you the sorry report that the disease is not reversible and time is the only unknown ingredient. And you start going through the denial, anger, bargaining, depression, and finally acceptance. And you weep.

Yes, even believers trudge through that valley. "Oh, but, Dan — I know Christians who just sail through all those trials." Perhaps, but that doesn't mean every saint will. "But, Dan, the Bible promises joy in the morning!" Yes, but don't forget the preliminary clause in that Psalm, "Weeping may endure for a night." You see, we don't all respond the same way to life's ebb and flow. This is why Jesus commanded us to be nonjudgmental toward others. We don't all wear the same sandals. We don't experience the same depths of emotion as everyone else.

Don't ever let anyone condemn you because your heart is aching or broken. A lady called our home Thanksgiving night. Her husband had just walked out the door and was not coming back. He said he had found someone else. She was stricken with overwhelming grief. I can still hear her crying in the night. Someone might say, "Oh, if only she knew Jesus!" But she *did* know the Lord. That didn't take away the pain, though. Here is God's promise: "I have heard thy prayer, I have seen thy tears: behold, I will heal thee" (2 Kings 20:5). And then, dear friend, joy truly does come in the morning.

Prayer: O God, my voice is lifted to You today on behalf of the one who is suffering so terribly in this hour . . . that one whose health is terminal . . . that one whose mate has just left . . . that one whose child is dying. May Your divine presence envelop these precious brothers and sisters today so that they truly feel Your concern. Thank You. *Amen.*

NOT READY FOR HARRY

Matthew 24:42

Watch therefore: for ye know not what hour your Lord doth come.

A few decades ago I was working as a TV newscaster for a local NBC affiliate. I did the early news during the two five-minute local slots on the *Today Show*, then starring Dave Garroway. I was only a teenager at the time. I was painting in our home one afternoon when the phone rang. It was my boss. "Dan, we need you in the studio in 15 minutes." I wasn't due in until much later in the day for an evening newscast. I asked why I was needed so early. "Dan, we've scheduled you to do a one-on-one interview," my boss informed me. "Oh ... with whom?" I asked. My boss blindsided me: "With President Harry Truman." I had paint all over me and was dressed in jeans and gym shoes, but I replied with a gulp, "I'll be there!" And I was!

An engineer in a mobile unit met me, and we raced out to a park where the president's caravan was waiting. A huge guy, I guessed a secret service man, hustled me to a huge black Lincoln sedan. The back door opened and out stepped the president of the United States. My goodness, less than a half-hour earlier I had been painting my house. Now — there he stood, the most powerful man in the world. My interview was very poor. How in the world does one prepare to meet the president within just a few minutes? It's impossible! And the interview reflected that impossibility! My boss was understanding. He said, "We asked you to do in a quarter-hour what veteran newscasters prepare for many days."

Here's my question: If I couldn't be ready to meet the president with 15 minutes notice, how do people expect to meet King Jesus in the "twinkling of an eye"? That's how quickly He is coming back. Small wonder the Bible teaches, "Today is the day of salvation" (2 Cor. 6:2; NLT). How ready are you for the King? If He came today, would you be prepared? If not, this very moment, why don't you ask Him into your life?

PRAYER

O Lord, You reminded me in that Matthew text that we do not know ahead of time when You are returning. I must be ready at all times. Even now I ask You to be in control of my life. May all my sins be covered by Your precious blood. And even so, come quickly, Lord Jesus. Amen.

WILL THERE BE CELL PHONES IN HEAVEN?

Galatians 5:22

But the fruit of the Spirit is love, joy, peace, longsuffering, gentleness, goodness, faith. . . .

In today's world of cell phones, one needs all those Galatians 5:22 spiritual virtues, fruit of the Holy Spirit! Case in point: I love golf and take it seriously. I was on the 16th green in a very tight match, facing a critical downhill four-foot putt for a desperately needed par. I figured out the line, carefully lined up the shot, and drew the putter back. Suddenly came this jarring sound: one of the other players' cell phone went off. The suddenly misdirected putter drove the ball off the green. Ha! That's just a minor case. Now read this: My wife and I were in Africa perched in a viewing stand high over a water hole in the jungle. To our right, not more than 30 yards away, the tall grass was parting and we could hear the coughing grunt of an approaching lion. My video camera was humming, aimed right at the spot where a lion would emerge. It would have been the video shot of my life! Then —

then the fellow sitting next to me? You got it! His cell phone went off. The lion was last seen somewhere miles away. "O God, I need Your gentleness and longsuffering to surface in my life right *now!*"

Have you grown weary of having to endure unwanted cell phones ringing? Like in church? Tired of being in a restaurant and having to hear the guy in the next booth giving some long-winded and quite loudly annoying response to his unseen communicant? Tired of being nearly hit by the oncoming driver of a car glued to his or her cell instead of watching the road? I can remember a time, not all that long ago either, when we didn't need to be talking on the phone all the time. When one could attend a concert without hearing someone's cell ringing some interminable jangling. Ah, those were the good old days, weren't they?

Well, use your cell if you must. But if your phone goes off in our church, we will gladly confiscate it. Then neither of us will have to worry about it anymore. (Lest you think I'm cruel, on Broadway, if your phone goes off during the play, your cell is confiscated, you are fined 50 bucks, and you are escorted from the theater! Think ye on that!)

Byline #18

PRAYER

O God, I need patience. And I need it now! Amen.

TOO MUCH MONTH LEFT
AT THE END OF THE MONEY

Matthew 6:20–21: "But lay up for yourselves treasures in heaven, where neither moth nor rust doth corrupt, and where thieves do not break through nor steal: for where your treasure is, there will your heart be also."

While having breakfast in a Russian hotel recently, I read the daily *Moscow Times*. The paper is kind of their version of our *USA Today*. An article captured my attention that stated that Russians are among the world's leaders at having expendable income after paying their bills. In fact, they are in the top five. In the meantime, the United States was near the bottom of the list. How can such a thing be? How can Russians, who make far, far less per week than Americans and have a cost of living, especially in Moscow and St. Petersburg, that rivals, if not exceeds, the cost of living here, have more money left after paying bills?

Pretty simple. They don't spend as much because they apparently don't need — or want — as much. In their major cities they have almost as much stuff to buy as we do (although that's not the case in rural areas). It appears that we Americans just have a voracious appetite for "stuff," an appetite often fed by television commercials. We see it on the screen and think we just have to have it. Then we have to rent storage places to keep the stuff. And all too often we can't afford the stuff we buy and have purchased on credit and thus are faced with impossible bills each month.

The consumer debt of us Americans is dumbfounding. So along comes the need on the mission field. "Well, we can't do anything for that," we say, "because we still have eight payments left on that automatic turtle shell polisher we bought." Or, "Well, I can't pay my tithes because I've got all these payments on my car." We haven't learned well Jesus' teaching that a person cannot consume more than he produces. Pathetic, isn't it? So much money comes in, yet there's so little, if any, left. Sometimes not even for God's work.

PRAYER: O God, teach me well the lesson to be content with what I have and not to covet that which others have. Teach me to be very thankful for the blessings I now enjoy. And make me a good steward of all that You have given me. Amen.

No, my phone call is not important to them

1 Samuel 3:4: That the LORD called Samuel: and he answered, Here am I.

Have you ever made what you consider to be an important phone call, only to be answered by a machine? Recently I called a church where I was scheduled to speak in a few months. I needed some information about the event. The phone was answered by a machine. The cold, metallic "voice" welcomed me to the automated answering service and then proceeded to give me the entire schedule of the church services for what seemed to me an interminable length of time. Then the "voice" informed me that if I knew my party's extension number I should enter it "now." I wondered how I was supposed to know that number. Then the "voice" began to read all the extension numbers for virtually everyone in that church and finally assured me that — get this! — my call was "important to them." Well, having received the extension number, I dialed it and got — you guessed it! — another machine: "I am not at my desk now but your call is important to me." Etc. Etc. I just hung up and wrote the pastor a very kind letter canceling my date there in a few months. I had this inner fear that if I ever actually got to that church and walked out on the platform, I would be looking at rows of phone-answering machines.

Now here's the kicker: We are told that our call is "important" to them. No, frankly, it is not. If my call were important, there would be a live human being there to answer the phone, at least during business hours. On a whim one day, I called a half-dozen major *successful* churches across the country and on every occasion the phone was answered by a live, and apparently caring, person. I got the feeling from them that, yes, my call really was important to them.

So what happens when God tries to call you? As Samuel, do you instantly respond, "Speak, Lord — I'm listening"? Or do you put God on some automatic answering device that makes it very clear to Him that His message to you really is not all that important? Oh, one more question: who answers your church phone?

Prayer: O God, let my heart always be open to receive Your call upon my life. May You know, from my instant response, how vital Your voice is to me. May You say, "I believe that person really does believe that My 'call is important.'" ***Amen.***

RUSSIA BECOMES ONE OF MY FAVORITE PLACES

MARK 16:20: And they went forth, and preached every where, the Lord working with them, and confirming the word with signs following.

At the end of World War II in 1945, the world waited for the battle to begin between the United States and the Soviet Union. Without a shot ever fired, the cold war ended and wonder of wonders, the great nation of Russia opened to the gospel. If you would have told me even ten years ago that Russia would become one of my favorite places, I would have suggested some kind of treatment for you. Yet that is precisely what has happened. Moscow's Red Square is in my top ten list of all the places I've traveled, which is over 60 nations now. That familiar bricked expanse lies along the eastern wall of the Kremlin and sits on about five acres. Think of Red Square and you will remember photos of past May Day parades when the Soviet military displayed its might, passing dutifully before the Soviet leadership standing atop Lenin's Tomb. You might also think of magnificent St. Basil's Cathedral with its multi-colored onion domes. Czar Ivan IV, also known as Ivan the Terrible, commissioned that facility nearly 500 years ago. And of course, there is the tomb of Vladimir Lenin, where his body lies encased in glass. The name Red Square came about because of a Russian word that can mean either "red" or "beautiful." Boy, is that place aptly named! It defines the word "beautiful."

So why have I gone on these occasions to Russia? Because since detente several decades back, the doors for evangelism have swung open there. The Russian people, as I have seen firsthand, show overwhelming interest in God and activities of the Holy Spirit. There are now thousands of churches all across Russia that are on fire and actively spreading the gospel. How long will this door remain open? Who can tell? We see intermittent signs that some authorities there want that door shut once again. What we do know for sure, though, is this: While that door remains open, we are going through it! Whatever you can do in prayerful intercession, or even financial support, for Russian ministries, do it! It's eternal harvest time there.

Prayer: O God, thank You for this golden opportunity to obey Your Great Commission mandate in so many areas that were formerly closed. Joel was right when he wrote that in these last days You would pour forth of Your Spirit upon all flesh. We are thankful to be a part of it! Help us to always take our place in Your front line. Amen.

THE LOST ART OF INFILTRATION

1 Corinthians 9:22

To the weak became I as weak, that I might gain the weak: I am made all things to all men, that I might by all means save some.

Ask the average church leader his or her purpose for ministry and you'll hear the lofty "Reach my city for Christ." The typical church member will rephrase that somewhat perhaps, but with the same general intent. Well, right on! That's what our purpose should be. But when one follows up with this question, "How do you plan to do that?" eyes glaze over. Then comes the patented, standard response, "Well, we pray for open doors." My goodness, the much-sought open doors are already there and have been for a long time. It's like praying for the Holy Spirit to "move" over the face of the earth when He's already been doing so since Genesis 1:2. So what's our problem?

The Christian art of infiltration into our society is missing. It takes more than Sunday services. Yes, even more than Christian media. Reaching our communities requires day-in, day-out relationships with those who don't know Christ. Infiltration demands innovative outreach. During the course of a given week, here are some avenues of infiltrating ministry we pursue in our church: Sports leagues yield a good return of new people; I can think of a number of families now following Christ in our congregation because of them. I think of the ladies who invade the exotic dance clubs here in town. To date, over 60 of those dancers have left the clubs to follow Christ and live normal lives. (Our ladies had to go to them; the dancers did not initially come to us!) I think of the neighborhood clean-ups accomplished by our young people. There are now over 40 elderly care facilities that receive weekly visits and services from our teams. The regional symphony orchestra performs here twice a year, bringing in hundreds of first-timers to our sanctuary. We are in the prisons every week, and every two months I am with prisoners on death row in the Florida State Penitentiary. Friend, this is *planned infiltration*. It's light in the darkness. The hunger for Christ in our society is just incredible! The open doors are already here. Let's just go through them! Infiltrate!

Byline #22

PRAYER

O God, all around us are people in desperate need of You. Give me a sensitivity to their plight. And beyond that, intentionally put me in their path somehow to say and be what they need for their lives to be changed. We are the salt of the earth, You said. Salt is useless when it remains in the shaker. Let me be an infiltrator. Amen.

THE KEY TO GOD'S BLESSING YOUR CHURCH

> **Mark 16:17**
>
> And these signs shall follow them that believe. . . .

A pastor in Tallahassee, Florida, called me recently, inviting me to address his congregation on behalf of missions. This good pastor pulled out all the stops, taking the banquet to the Florida State University football stadium where we met in a sky restaurant overlooking the field. Several hundred attended. The food was superb, the sound system actually worked well, and we did not eat off paper plates, using plastic knives and forks. The pastor told me that last year his church gave $50,000 to missions and requested that I receive the missions faith commitments and offering for the year. I did as he asked. A few days later he e-mailed me to report that the offering that night exceeded a quarter-million dollars!

He is one of those fortunate church leaders who understand that missions enhance everything in the church. Supernatural provision follows obedience to Christ's Great Commission. Read Mark 16. I contrast this pastor with yet another who hauled me out to his church and said, "Now, Dan, don't be taking faith promises; we're doing the best we can." I wondered why he brought me clear across the country for a night of absolutely nothing.

If you would take time to carefully observe the top churches in your town, the fastest-growing, the most relevant, you would see that these churches are missions-minded. Their pastors have a worldview. We just must stop hoarding for ourselves those provisions God gives us. We are conduits from God's supply, all of which is to be freely poured around the world to redeem the lost. Proverbs 11:25 promises that the liberal soul shall be made fat. Now there's a lesson that all church leaders must learn.

> **PRAYER**
>
> O God, teach me Your way in encompassing the world with compassion and ministry. May I always understand that You give me Your divine supply that I may bless the nations. Make me liberal and thus spiritually fat. Amen.

Instead of desperately clutching tightly what God has given, give it away in return. Invest it in the world harvest. Then watch what happens to both yourself and your church.

The danger of an unforgiving spirit

Matthew 6:12: "And forgive us our debts, as we forgive our debtors."

How many professing followers of Christ harbor bitterness or unforgiveness in their hearts? It's a dangerous way to live. For one thing, answered prayer depends upon our having forgiven those who have hurt us.

I spoke at a convention in the Midwest some time ago. A fellow remained in the altars, asking for my attention. As I knelt beside him, he told me — and remember that this was a professing believer! — that he had hated a man for 20 years. He hated him so much, in fact, that he said he would kill the fellow if he had a chance and knew he could get away with it. I was taken back by his vehemence and asked him, "What in the world did this man do to you all those long years ago that elicited such hatred within you?" He looked stunned at my question and I asked it again. "What did this person do to you?" Finally the fellow stumbled an answer, "I — I don't remember." Can you even imagine such a boil in the spirit of this man? He lived in bondage to the past to the point of jeopardizing all his future, and for something he could not even recall. I would not be at all surprised if the man he hated was not even aware of the situation.

Bitterness is the most counter-productive emotion known to man. I often tell our congregation that holding unforgiveness or bitterness in your heart is like eating a pound of rat poison and then waiting for the rats to die. My friend, God has forgiven you for infinitely more than you could ever forgive someone else. As He has forgiven you, so must you forgive the one who wounded you in some way. It's your eternal future that is at stake, not the one who harmed you. Once again the classic question surfaces, "What would Jesus do?" Why, He would forgive, of course.

Prayer: O God, I don't want a cancer of bitterness to reside in my spirit. No matter what I feel was done wrongly to me, I will not live in the dark shadow of that which I cannot change. Soften my hard heart and quicken my mind to fully comprehend the tragedy to come if I fail to come to grips with this blot in my life. Thank You for forgiving me for all I have done against You. Now I will forgive the one who has harmed me, in Your Name. *Amen.*

PRAYERS UNANSWERED? WHY IS THAT?

Hebrews 10:23: Let us hold fast the profession of our faith without wavering; (for he is faithful that promised).

Does God really answer prayer? Or is it just wishful thinking on our part? Jesus promised, "Whatsoever ye shall ask in prayer, believing, ye shall receive" (Matt. 21:22). So what happens when prayers are not answered?

Did you ever notice that when we truly don't know the answer to a tough question we like to make one up? Such as: "Well, the reason that person's prayers are not answered is because of lack of faith." Or: "There is probably sin in that person's life." Oh, really? And exactly how do we know that? Especially in light of Christ's command to His followers not to judge others. Because of all the scriptural promises of answered prayer, perhaps we should take careful inventory of our prayers and ask ourselves some tough questions.

Such as: Am I currently living in the center of God's will for my life? I can know if I am there through determined talking to the Lord, through the thorough study of His Word, and through hearing God's Spirit bearing witness with my spirit. If I detect any flags in such introspection, perhaps then I have begun to discover reasons for unanswered prayers. Such as: Since Jesus has commanded that we must forgive as we have been forgiven by Him or our prayers are hindered, I have to ask myself, do I harbor a grudge or unforgiveness in my heart toward someone? Do I have something against another, even someone who is not a follower of Jesus? I also need to question my own motivation. Why do I want this prayer answered? Will it bring glory to me or to the Lord?

I need to understand that God will answer any prayer that Jesus would pray. Now there is a criteria for me: I have prayed, yes . . . but . . . would Jesus pray that same prayer?

PRAYER: O God, I am instructed in Your Word to pray according to Your will. So let those things that are important to You always be important to me as well so that I never ask You for something I should not. I am grateful that You hear me. Amen.

DON'T TITHE?
DON'T GRIPE!

Matthew 23:23

"Ye pay tithe ... these ought ye to have done...."

A pastor told me recently of a strange phone call he received from a lady in his congregation. "She was irate," he said, a knowing look in his sad eyes. The woman complained at some length that the church seemed to give to missions but the area of ministry that concerned her personally did not get funded all that well, at least according to her estimate. She demanded to know why.

The pastor paused and then plunged in: "Let me ask you ... do you tithe?" There was silence on the other end of the line. "Well?" persisted the pastor. "Do you tithe?" Finally the lady responded, "Pastor, you need to understand. There is a family we know who has need, and we give our tithe to them." The pastor replied, "I am sure you believe that your gesture is noble and good. But let's think it through.

"Suppose you have just received an overdue notice from your utility company. They warn you that they'll cut off your electricity unless you pay the overdue bill. You respond, 'I appreciate your concern about this bill, but you know, there's a family nearby that needs help and we have been giving our utility money to them.' Or to the bank people who call you, 'Well, we've been paying our mortgage payment to a village overseas.' See, lady, you would not do that to a utility or bank. You'll lose your home and utility service. So why do you do that kind of thing to God?"

My pastor friend was right. The tithe, the first ten percent of one's income, is not that person's money to spend. It is God's. End of story. God tells us plainly in His Word that the tithe belongs in the storehouse, the place where you are given regular spiritual food. I am often shocked by people who wonder why their church can't do this or that but yet they themselves don't tithe. My friend, if you are a registered voter and don't vote, don't complain about the government. By the same reasoning, if you don't tithe, don't gripe about your church. You have no right to.

Byline #26

PRAYER

O God, forgive me for taking Your money to spend on my own needs. Teach me to see You first and then all these other things will be added to me. Amen.

PRAY FOR EUROPE!

Revelation 2:4: Nevertheless I have somewhat against thee, because thou hast left thy first love.

More and more I am spending time in Europe. No, not to sightsee. I am spending time with pastors and church leaders there who are trying to reach what many consider to be the darkest continent spiritually on the face of the earth. I once told a church group that Western Europe was the least-touched continent for Christianity, a remark that was greeted with hooting laughter. "Why, haven't you ever seen those great cathedrals in Europe? What in the world are you talking about? There are steeples everywhere." Steeples, yes. Peoples, no. Those churches are for the most part mere museums.

A story coming from Sweden from the Associated Press illustrates my point. "A punk-rock style, trendy tight fit and affordable prices have made [certain] jeans a hot commodity among young Swedes. But what has people talking is the brand's ungodly logo, a skull with a cross turned upside down on its forehead." The logo's designer told the AP, "It is an active statement against Christianity," which he called "a force of evil."[1] Such a remark might incite outrage or prompt retailers to drop the brand in more religious countries. But not in Sweden, where the churchgoing has been declining for decades. Even the country's largest church, a mainline denomination, reacts with a shrug. One of the church's leaders said, "I don't think it's so much to be horrified about." He's kidding himself.

As a person who has raised a lot of money for missions over the decades, I can tell you that raising money for reaching Europe is a tough assignment! It is hard to get Americans to "feel a burden" for that continent. Yet it is so spiritually dark there. Many scholars believe that Western Europe will be the power base for Antichrist. No one knows who that person is going to be, but the spirit of this evil one is already at work on this sophisticated continent. Pray for Europe!

Prayer: O God, our voices and hearts are raised to You today on behalf of that continent from which we have received so many blessings through the centuries. Let there be another spiritual renaissance, we ask in the name of Jesus! Amen.

1. Associated Press, "Anti-Christian Jeans Are a Trend in Sweden," December 30, 2005; Foxnews.com

Byline #28

When the Church becomes something God never meant it to be

Ephesians 5:25: Christ also loved the church, and gave himself for it.

In his excellent book *Off-Road Disciplines*, Earl Creps observes that missions is the very reason for the Church. He wrote, "To remove missions does not just make the Church less effective, it changes the Church into something else, something that does not resemble the New Testament account of our identity as a sent people."[1]

Someone once fancied that when Jesus re-entered heaven after His ascension, the angels gathered around to hear His account of being on earth as a man. Jesus concluded by saying that after His crucifixion, burial, and resurrection, He had commissioned all His followers to be witnesses around the world, empowered by the Holy Spirit. One of the angels ventured, "But, Lord, if the people fail in this mission, what is your fall-back plan?" Jesus looked at the angel for a moment and softly replied, "There is no other plan."

As a pastor, I know how easily we can get sidetracked in our work of evangelizing the world. So many things are on our plate: buildings, general fund, needs of parishioners, births, deaths, staffing needs, and so forth. Yes, all of these things are important. But the primary mission of the Church is to win the world for Christ. Jesus made that abundantly clear in His last recorded earthly statement: "But ye shall receive power, after that the Holy Ghost is come upon you: and ye shall be witnesses unto me both in Jerusalem, and in all Judaea, and in Samaria, and unto the uttermost part of the earth" (Acts 1:8).

Do we think Jesus was just kidding? Do we understand that the role of the Church in global redemption is the absolute and only plan God has given for evangelizing the world? Sometimes church leaders tell me, "We're praying about it." Praying about what? Whether to obey Christ? Last we heard, Jesus' Great Commission is still in the Bible: "Go ye into all the world, and preach the gospel to every creature" (Mark 16:15). Anything less than obedience to that reduces the Church to a civic club.

1. Earl G. Creps, *Off-Road Disciplines* (San Francisco, CA: Jossey-Bass, 2006).

Prayer: O God, although I may not be a missionary on the actual field, make me a missionary of supply and intercession. May I be faithful to Your call. **Amen.**

STOPPING THE FLOW
OF THE HOLY SPIRIT

1 Thessalonians 5:19: Quench not the Spirit.

Computers drive me crazy! My mind does not function in computerese. I have no comprehension whatsoever of what makes these machines work (or not work, as the case may be). Frankly, I really don't care. I just want to strike a key and have the thing turn on and function.

Yesterday is a good case in point. I had just installed a new color cartridge in my printer. When I tried to print a project, nothing happened. I checked the control panel and the printer installation. Nothing! Then something caught my eye near the bottom of the screen. In effect it read, "Peel the tape off the cartridge so the ink can flow, stupid!" (The message didn't actually use the word "stupid"; it's just how it made me feel.) So I took out the cartridge, peeled off the tape, reinserted it into the computer, and — it worked! Amazing what happens when one follows directions. It's ridiculous how little gets done when one doesn't allow the ink to flow.

It's kind of like the Church. Nothing much happens if the Holy Spirit isn't allowed to flow. We church leaders like to meticulously plan a service (and of course, there should be some kind of plan, as long as it doesn't restrict what God wants to do). And being an old radio/TV guy, I used to be really fussy about the timing and planned each part of the service to the minute. One day the Holy Spirit spoke to my heart and said, "Dan, I'm getting really tired of you telling Me what I can or cannot do in My house. Leave Me alone and let me do My work!" Now that doesn't mean I don't study anymore, or pray and truly prepare for each service. I spend hours in that pursuit. But each service is now given to the Lord for whatever He wants. See, I just pulled off the tape, so to speak, to allow the ink to flow. Well, that makes all the difference in the world in a computer. Think of the difference it makes when we allow God to flow.

PRAYER: O God, convict my heart for ever attempting, even innocently, to restrict You in what You want to accomplish — and the way in which You choose to do it. Your ways are not our ways. Your ways are infinitely better! Help us to remove all restrictions or barriers and to simply allow Your Holy Spirit to work among us each day. Amen.

LIGHTEN UP!

Judges 19:6

. . . let thine heart be merry.

Do you like to laugh? I love it! Yes, I know there are those who protest, "We see no place in Scripture where Jesus ever laughed." Perhaps. But we know Jesus was present at creation, out of which we got such creatures as chimpanzees. How could the creator of chimps not have a sense of humor? If God created everything, which He most certainly did, then humor is one of His gifts to mankind. Let's use it.

You are doubtless aware of a growing number of men and women who call themselves "Christian comedians." While I am not a member of that troop, I do appreciate what they are attempting to do, which is to lighten the load from the saints. Someone taught me decades ago to take God's work seriously but to never, never take myself seriously. It was good advice then and now. It has probably saved me ulcers. We need to learn how to enjoy life.

Byline #30

I have spent a lot of time over the years with "The Swan," Dennis Swanberg. I have appeared on some of his television shows, and he has been in our church on a number of New Year's Eves. This man with an earned doctorate in theology is just simply funny. His impressions are "dead-on." His Billy Graham impression is shockingly accurate — and very amusing. He once introduced me in his Billy Graham voice, and I almost had to leave the platform from laughing.

Honestly, sometimes we believers need to just lighten up. I know I am very intense in my work, and I truly do take it seriously. But there come times when it's just good to let your hair down (or take it off, as the case may be) and just laugh. God gave us that ability, so why do we think He's uncomfortable when we use it? Earlier in this byline I wrote I don't take myself very seriously. I can't afford to. Too many people are laughing at me. So I might as well laugh with them.

PRAYER

O God, I believe that heaven is going to be a place of joy and liberty of spirit. Even now, on this earth, we can begin to practice the atmosphere of Your celestial city. Teach me, Lord, to continue to be earnest in my zeal for You, but also to recognize that at times life is just — just plain funny. Thank You for the gift of laughter. Amen.

THE WONDERS OF GOD'S GRACE

"...he...had seen the grace of God, [and] was glad, and exhorted them all, that with purpose of heart they would cleave unto the Lord."

Do you recall the classic hymn from the heart and pen of Fanny Crosby, "Rescue the Perishing"? One of the stanzas has this remarkable observation on the grace of God:

"Down in the human heart / Crushed by the tempter / Feelings lie buried that grace can restore." Is there a point beyond which the most degenerate human monster can no longer be reached? Is there some invisible line drawn in the sand of a person's life which, if crossed, is irrevocable? Beyond which reason, love, and redemption are impossible?

This very page could be read at this moment by someone whom society has written off completely. This person is (what's the word we use here?) "untouchable." Society shakes an accusing finger at such a person when his or her vitriolic behavior reaches a new depth or depravity, and we all recoil at such behavior. As a pastor, I know the feeling when confronted by someone altogether unlovable. I almost walk away and then — then I see tears slip down the cheek and hear the voice tremble. I catch the desperate look in that person's eyes searching for help, for understanding and just a little compassion. Society says, "Forget that person. He or she is beyond any human sympathy whatsoever." Humanly speaking, society may well be right. But redemption through the marvelous grace of our loving Lord comes into play.

Was Fanny Crosby prophetic that grace can restore those buried hopes and dreams? Oh, let's hang on tightly to that probability. None of us are appointed judges, are we? No, we are merely the messengers of God's grace. We are to take the "good news" to the hopeless, the dying, and the graceless. That's the gospel, bringing hope to those who are simply hopeless. Yes, that's hard work, isn't it? But through the power of God's very Spirit, lives touched by Him are changed so magnificently!

O God, I don't want to be a condemner. I want to be a lifter of people's hopes and dreams. Through Your Spirit, may I show someone Your grace today. Amen.

Tried by a Committee?
Or tried by Christ?

2 Corinthians 4:9: Persecuted, but not forsaken; cast down, but not destroyed.

Let's think about committees for a moment. Although I am on more committees than I can probably name off the top of my head, I view them all with suspicion. Why? Because committees tend to operate by consensus, which is all too often a barrier against inspiration. Let's face it: committees are known to make mistakes. Case in point: When Oswald J. Smith died in his late 90s, Billy Graham preached his funeral and told the large, assembled crowd, "We are here to honor the greatest missionary mind of the 20th century." Yet, when Smith, in his early 20s, applied to his denomination for missions appointment, that committee rejected him out-of-hand, reporting, "Sorry, you are not missions material!" All of watching heaven must have greeted that decision with a resounding "*Ha!*"

Who has ever been a greater preacher than G. Campbell Morgan? Yet, at age 25, when he made application to his denomination for ordination, they denied him, saying, "You show no promise for preaching." Well, that's what the committee said. Here's what history records: Morgan linked arms with D.L. Moody and preached across England. The church he pastored in England, Westminster Chapel, was peerless among congregations of that day. Later, Morgan came to America, where he pastored other historic churches. When asked his secret, he replied, "Work. Hard work. And again . . . hard work." He was called to his last pastorate when he was 72! He retired at 80. G. Campbell Morgan passed away in 1945. What a preacher! What a man of God! What a powerful force for all eternity! *Yet an ecclesiastical committee rejected him completely.* You see, he didn't fit their guidelines.

I have learned in all these decades of ministry not to be too concerned by any critic who doesn't have nail prints in his hands. When I need mid-course correction, the One with the prints will do it. If He wants to reward me, that will be His option. Not some committee's prerogative.

Prayer: O God, don't let pride fill my heart when I am appreciated, but on the other hand, don't let me fall apart when I'm not. My allegiance is to You, not some sociological group. I thank You for Your support. *Amen.*

GOD HAS GIVEN US THE GIFT OF READING

1 Thessalonians 5:27: I charge you by the Lord that this epistle be read unto all the holy brethren.

Did you ever stop to consider how blessed you are if you have the ability to read? Books open up the universe to us. What a gift!

For 47 years, the pastor of the historic First Baptist Church in Dallas was George W. Truett. I have a number of his sermons in print, but my friends who are into church history tell me it was one thing to read his sermons, but quite another to hear them. Some who actually heard him preach said that Truett was one of the most exciting preachers to hear but one of the most disappointing to read. That being said, it should be reported that when Truett died in 1944, Dallas came to a standstill and no auditorium could hold the crowd wanting to attend the memorial service.

Truett was a man of books. His home looked like a public library. He had over 10,000 books on many subjects, despite the fact that he constantly gave books to other people. He read quickly, and it is said that when he started a day's journey by train, he would take three or four books with him and finish them before he reached his destination. He especially loved biographies.

For any person who is going to be a public speaker (or even an interesting conversationalist) and who plans to have fresh content on a constant basis, reading is mandatory. Learn to read with speed and retention. Many kids today are taught to read a syllable at a time despite the fact that the human brain is just as capable of absorbing a full sentence line at a time.

I am grateful for teachers who spent hours with me when I was a young student, teaching me grammar and encouraging me to read. Reading has been the "open sesame" portal to me, as it is for anyone who will take the time to pick up a book and actually read it.

Prayer: O God, You have equipped Your creation with so many abilities. Forgive us when we do not expand our horizons of experiencing life. Thank You for the gift of curiosity and the reading ability to satisfy it. You are wonderful to us! Amen.

THE DANGER OF BEING STEPHEN

Acts 7:59

And they stoned Stephen, calling upon God, and saying, Lord Jesus, receive my spirit.

As a small boy, growing up in the huge town of Climbing Hill, Iowa, my best buddy was a kid named Denny. We were both four years old as this little story opens. Denny and his parents attended a small church right in Climbing Hill while my folks and I drove into Sioux City, 25 miles away, for services in our church. On Mondays, Denny and I would compare notes.

One day he asked me what I had learned in Sunday school the previous day. I could hardly wait to tell him. "Oh, Denny," I began, "we learned all about Stephen. He was the first guy to ever be killed for loving Jesus!"

Denny was impressed. "No kiddin'? So — how did Stephen die?"

I gave my buddy a superior smile and answered, "Well, Denny, my teacher told us that some people picked up rocks and threw 'em at him 'til he died."

Byline #34

"Wow," said Denny, "that would be a great story for you and me to act out. Let's play Stephen!"

"Great," I replied. "It's my story, so I get to play Stephen."

Denny agreed. He reached down and picked up one of those hard-clay Iowa clods, wound up, and let it fly. He had good aim! He hit me right between the eyes and split my forehead wide open. I went home screaming and the town doctor, Dr. Glen, stitched me up.

I learned a vital lesson in life that day. *Pick the part you want to play very carefully!* If you make a bad choice of parts, you can get clobbered! I know! Well, Denny and I never played Stephen again. Or any other Bible story where there were dangerous parts.

Not long after that, Denny and his family moved to California, where he was killed in a car accident. I look forward to seeing him in heaven. It will be quite a reunion. See, I've always wanted a pet lion in heaven. So I'll say, "Hey, Denny, whaddya say we play Daniel in the lions' den? You can play Daniel!"

PRAYER

O God, on a very serious note, let me follow Your choice of "parts" You want me to play in life. My choices can be dangerous for me. You know what's best. And tell Denny I'm comin'! Just tell him to get ready! I owe him one. Amen.

THAT MEDDLING CAMERA!

Psalm 139:1–4: O LORD, thou hast searched me, and known me. Thou knowest my downsitting and mine uprising, thou understandest my thought afar off. Thou compassest my path and my lying down, and art acquainted with all my ways. For there is not a word in my tongue, but, lo, O LORD, thou knowest it altogether.

Our church held a missions golf tournament recently. Someone brought in a photographer who went from foursome to foursome taking shots of each of us swinging the club. I received my copies of the pictures several days later. I am still depressed. See, in my mind's eye, I feel that I must look a lot like Tiger Woods when I swing. The pictures revealed something altogether different. Like Tiger Woods' great grandmother. In the picture I saw this slightly heavy fellow with the rusty, over-the-top swing that was truly a disgusting sight to behold. Yes, it was I! What can I tell you? What a revelation!

Perhaps that is one reason many folks never read the Bible. Scriptures are God's camera and show us precisely the way we look to Him. Frankly, some of it is negative (no pun intended there). But on the other hand, some of the pictures are pretty good. After all, we are God's handiwork. That part of Him within us that we allow to be conformed to the image of His Son Jesus always looks healthy and invigorating. It's that dreaded sin part, uncovered by the blood of Jesus, that is revolting.

Isaiah made it clear that "all we like sheep have gone astray" (Isa. 53:6). While you and I should never set ourselves up as judges of others, we must judge ourselves in the light of Scripture. For example, when we take communion, Paul writes, "Let a man [woman] examine himself [herself]" (1 Cor. 11:28). God's photographer, the Holy Scripture, is taking shots of us this very day. So . . . do you want to look at the proofs?

PRAYER:
O God, let me see myself as You see me. And then, by the power of the Holy Spirit, allow me to see myself as I could be by Your redemptive power. In every word, thought, and deed today, let me be conformed to that latter photo. Amen.

The impact of a good mentor

2 Corinthians 4:11: . . . that the life also of Jesus might be made manifest in our mortal flesh.

Over the past half-century of ministry, powerful and profound spiritual mentors have blessed me. A half dozen or so have been even more influential than the rest. Of that half dozen, two shine forth the brightest: Leonard Ravenhill, author of *Why Revival Tarries,* and Oswald J. Smith (who at his funeral Billy Graham called "the greatest missionary mind of the 20th century"). While I loved them both dearly, I would not have invited either one to a party. These men were living definitions of the word "serious." Ravenhill once said to me, "Many pastors criticize me for taking the gospel so seriously. But do they really think that on judgment day Christ will chastise me, saying, 'Leonard, you took Me too seriously?' "

My wife and I often visited the Ravenhills in their home near Lindale, Texas. On two separate occasions, Ravenhill preached extended revival meetings in churches I pastored. He mentored me in discipleship matters in a way no one else ever did. He once said to me, "Dan, if Jesus preached the same message that many ministers preach today, He would never have been crucified." The great Christian and Missionary Alliance writer A.W. Tozer (Ravenhill's close friend) observed this about him: "Such a man [as Ravenhill] is not an easy companion. He is not the professional evangelist who leaves the wrought-up meeting as soon as it is over to hurry to the most expensive restaurant to feast and crack jokes with his retainers. He cannot turn off the burden of the Holy Ghost as one would turn off a faucet. He insists upon being a Christian all the time, everywhere. And again, this marks him as different."

Tozer was right. I once complained in a letter to Ravenhill about a tough time I was going through and he replied, "Dan, you are quite possibly the greatest martyr in the history of Christianity." I could have walked upright *under* a door! Thank God for mentors who not only tell it like it is, but live it the same way!

Prayer: O God, I thank You for sending men and women into my life who stretched me spiritually. They were not always easy to be with, but oh, the difference they made in the way I live! May I, too, be a mentor to someone for Your sake. ***Amen.***

THE JOY OF RECEIVING HELPFUL AND FRIENDLY SERVICE

Luke 12:37

> Blessed are those servants, whom the lord when he cometh shall find watching: verily I say unto you, that he shall gird himself, and make them to sit down to meat, and will come forth and serve them.

Jesus was a willing servant. He expects you and me to be servants as well. Recently, my wife and I had lunch at a local restaurant. It was certainly not a fancy eating establishment; in fact, it was a franchise place. But the food was acceptable and the building was clean. What I remember about this restaurant was the waitress, a middle-aged lady of quiet but efficient manner. Her concept of service was remarkable. She knew when to approach the table to help, and she knew when to stay away. It was as if she could sense when we needed something, and she anticipated us every time. When we asked for something, she smiled and reacted as if filling our need was her greatest pleasure for the day. She didn't make us wait for the check either, drumming our fingers on the table. She watched us carefully and knew exactly when to present the bill. I said to her, "Ma'am, I must tell you that you are an incredible waitress! Thank you!" And I reinforced my comments with a more-than-ample tip.

Service is so vital in any enterprise. I have eaten at fancy places where the food was good but the service was awful. I won't return to those places. But I will return to the restaurant just described again and again — if we can have that lady as our waitress. I don't remember the food so much or even the decor, but I remember the service!

How important it is for a church to give good service! I have often visited one of the largest churches on the West Coast. I enjoy going there for many reasons, chief of which is that before I ever get to the door I am made to feel as if I belong there. On the other hand, I have visited churches where it was made obvious they could not possibly care if I was there. How about help from the parking attendants? Helpful ushers? Clean restrooms? Service! This is not rocket science. It's just plain common sense, not to mention scriptural.

PRAYER

O God, help me to remember that Jesus came to serve, not to be served. As a follower of our blessed Lord, may I be of service to all those around me. May others see Jesus in the way I address myself to their burdens of life. Amen.

THEY WEREN'T REAL...ONLY MYTHS

John 1:14

And the Word was made flesh, and dwelt among us, (and we beheld his glory, the glory as of the only begotten of the Father,) full of grace and truth.

Recently a book was released titled *The 101 Most Influential People Who Never Lived*,[1] written by Allan Lazar. Catch the phrase, "Who never lived." Mythical people. Make-believe personages. Here are a few of the entries who, according to Lazar, most impacted society: number one was the Marlboro Man. Lazar contends that this lanky cowboy reigns as a global symbolism of capitalism. He didn't indicate how the Marlboro Man impacted once-healthy, pink lungs. Number two on the list was Big Brother, Orwell's creature from the novel *1984*. Number three was King Arthur. Santa Claus grabbed the number four spot and Hamlet was number five. Frankenstein's monster also made the top ten. Others in the 101 included Dr. Jekyll, Robin Hood, Scrooge, Mickey Mouse, King Midas, and Archie Bunker.

Byline #38

But all of these figures were mere figments of someone's fertile imagination. They never actually breathed or did a single heroic thing. Jesus Christ, on the other hand, split the ages with His very real life. Dr. James Allan Francis was profound when he preached a message in 1926 about the actual Christ of God and concluded: "... of all the armies that ever marched, all the navies that were ever built, all the parliaments that ever sat and all the kings that ever reigned, put together, have not affected the life of man upon this earth as has that one solitary life." Yet "... he never wrote a book, never held an office, never went to college. He never traveled 200 miles from the place He was born." Not a myth, dear friend! The greatest reality of all time was Jesus Christ, the Messiah, sent by God, the Word who became flesh and dwelt among us full of grace and truth.[2]

The wonder is that we can know Him, Jesus, personally. We can talk to Him constantly. He dwells within us. You have that privilege today of an intimate daily walk with the greatest One of all, the Lord Jesus Christ.

1. Allan Lazar, *The 101 Most Influential People Who Never Lived* (New York: Harper, 2006).
2. James Allan Francis, *The Real Jesus and Other Sermons* (Philadelphia, PA: The Judson Press, 1926), p. 123–124.

PRAYER

O God, what a privilege to be indwelt by Your Holy One, not a myth, not a legend, but the living Christ. I am blessed today. Amen.

KEEP SOWING THE SEED OF GOD'S WORD

Luke 8:11: Now the parable is this: The seed is the word of God.

A critic of my preaching once complained, "Ah, you're just a story teller." I said, "Thank you." I doubt if he caught the irony. Jesus used parables to communicate. Basically, a parable is a story about ordinary life that contains eternal truths. Jesus was the Master Storyteller! In fact, Scripture informs us that Jesus rarely spoke without the use of telling stories.

In Luke 8, Jesus told the parable of the sower. He talked about the wayside soil, the stony ground, the thorny ground, and the good ground that yielded a great return. As I was reading this chapter again recently, my mind raced back to the early 1950s when evangelist Billy Graham held his first crusade at Haringay Arena in London. Despite early criticism of his going there, the crusade was a mammoth success. One night, as Graham gave the invitation to accept Christ, a striking young actor, well-known on Piccadilly Circus, strode forth. His stage name was John French. He had already done command performances before the queen and Sir Winston Churchill, as well as Hollywood movies. When French said yes to Jesus, he meant it! God called him into the ministry. Until the day he died several years ago, John was on the front lines for Christ, preaching, writing, and acting in Christian drama. I knew him very well. He was often a guest in our home and spent a number of Christmases with us. I asked him once, after dinner, "John, why did you leave the theater?" He looked at me for a moment and replied softly, "Why, Dan, I never left the theater; the theater left me!"

John French was a prime case of the seed of the Word finding fertile soil. Here's the principle: the more of the seed of the Word we sow, the more it finds good fertile ground. Let's be faithful sowers today!

Prayer: O God, I am so thankful the seed of the Word was sown in England so my friend John could know You. I am thankful that he sowed so much in his life. Now we continue the cycle of being faithful sowers to the next generation. Let the soil I find today be truly fertile for eternity. Amen.

Should old acquaintance be forgot

2 Timothy 4:11 Only Luke is with me.

The apostle Paul wrote those words while languishing in Emperor Nero's dungeon in Rome. There he awaited execution by beheading. Many of his friends had vanished into the crowded streets, terrorized by what might possibly happen to them if they were associated in some way with the condemned man. But on some kind of regular basis, Luke, the beloved physician, would appear through the iron grate at the top of the dungeon to greet his dear friend Paul. Think of the pathos in those five short words: "Only Luke is with me." I have stood in that dungeon, wondering about the impact of Luke's visits on this great man of God.

Is there anything as priceless as an old friend? I was on the phone the other day with a fellow I haven't seen in a long time. When I began pastoring in northern Ohio in the early 1960s, this man and his wife were so helpful to me. I remembered his contribution to the ministry with such great joy. I told him how much I'd just love to sit in front of his fireplace and talk about those fascinating "old days." Then the same day I received an e-mail from the fellow who was my very first youth pastor. What a delight to renew that friendship!

Acquaintances are one thing, but friends are quite another. As a kid, I used to hear songs about heaven and spending times with those who'd already gone on. I'd think, "Man, that place will be dull." But I don't think those thoughts anymore. Perhaps one of the most delightful aspects of glory will be having friends all around and spending a few thousand years just reminiscing.

Perhaps some young person reading this might think, "How dull is that!" But wait a few years. There will come a time when you will say, "Of all earth's treasures, I value my lifelong friends the most! They are simply irreplaceable."

Prayer: O God, You have blessed me with countless friends all my days. Even as my days grow shorter on this earth, those acquaintances grow even fonder. And You above all are a friend that stays closer than a brother. Today help me to be a friend to someone whose life will be changed because we have met. ***Amen.***

SO LONG, ROSALIE

1 Corinthians 6:19 What? know ye not that your body is the temple of the Holy Ghost?

My dear friend Rosalie Bradford is now with the Lord. Her name may strike a familiar chord to you. She at one time was the Guinness Book record holder for weight loss. Her weight exceeded 1,200 pounds. Can you even imagine that? She eventually lost 950 pounds, which she kept off, by the way. She credits God first of all for giving her the will to discipline herself, and she also credits her close buddy Richard Simmons for telling her how to do it. At her heaviest, Rosalie had lost all self-respect and got to the point where it just didn't matter to her how much she weighed. When they first met, Simmons challenged Rosalie by saying, "God doesn't make junk, and you are worth the effort to change your situation!" Rosalie told me several times that the great secret to her weight loss was a change of heart and lifestyle.

I remember clearly our first encounter. I was speaking in a church north of Philadelphia when a very lovely lady came up to say hello. Her pastor introduced us and said, "Dan, I want you to meet Rosalie, who listens to you regularly on radio. She has one of the most incredible testimonies you'll ever hear!" Boy, was he ever right about that! Rosalie had a passionate love for Christ and traveled across America telling her story, encouraging people to take care of their bodies, which are the "temple of the Holy Ghost," and adding, "But your soul is even more important!"

I hadn't seen Rosalie for several years when I got the word that she had slipped into glory. Ah, but I'll see her again at the Marriage Supper of the Lamb! I can hear her even now as I reach for the pie: "Uh, uh, Dan — not even in heaven! No pie for you!" Then I'll explain, "Rosalie, we now have glorified bodies, so it doesn't matter." I can see her big smile and hear her laughter as she responds, "Yeah? Well, touch that pie, pal, and we'll see if your glorified body feels pain!"

PRAYER:
O God, thank You for letting me know Rosalie and learning the extent to which You enable us to live disciplined lives, both physically and spiritually. Tell Rosy I miss her and remind her how much she blessed my life. Amen.

ANTAGONIZING ALLIGATORS IN A SWAMP AT FOUR IN THE MORNING

2 Corinthians 10:5

Casting down imaginations, and every high thing that exalteth itself against the knowledge of God, and bringing into captivity every thought to the obedience of Christ.

Sometimes I'm asked where I get the stories I tell, and some have even ventured that perhaps I might even make them up. Well, I don't make them up. You have to remember that in my younger days I was a newscaster, and I'm a careful watcher of humanity. Sometimes it's hilarious. Read your newspaper every day and you'll understand why one does not have to make up unbelievable stories. They are happening all around us — every day. Here's an example of a story I picked up on the AP wire service not too long ago:

"Florida deputies pulled a naked man from the jaws of a 12-foot alligator that nearly severed the victim's arm. Four deputies waded through thick mud about 20 feet into Lake Parker to find [the man who shall be nameless here

for *Byline*], age 45, around 4 a.m. They were responding to multiple reports about a man screaming for help. Deputies pulled the victim's arms while the gator gripped the man's lower half and the officers eventually pulled the man free. Deputies said they couldn't shoot the alligator because it was too dark and they might have hit the victim." Now note this next line; it's unbelievable! "Deputies said it was not clear why the victim was in the water at such an early hour. The victim told the officers he had been smoking crack."[1] Well . . . duh! Are we living in a crazy generation or what? The deputies can't figure out why this guy is in the water with a 12-foot gator even though he tells them he's been smoking crack?

People often get what they ask for in life. Play with booze or drugs that mess up your mind, and don't be surprised at anything that happens. Paul warned the Corinthians to bring every thought into captivity. People who've done that don't go into alligator-infested swamps, naked or clothed. Of course, imprisoning your thought life requires some obligation on your part, doesn't it? No one can do it for you.

1. CBS/AP, November 30, 2006.

Byline #42

PRAYER

O God, forgive me for allowing impure thoughts to remain lodged in my mind —- or any thought that is unworthy of You and Your creation. Let the thoughts I think today bring glory to You. Amen.

CHAINING? OR LOOSING?

John 11:44

> Jesus saith unto them, Loose him, and let him go.

It would have done Lazarus little good to be resurrected had he been forced to stay in those awful grave bindings. Jesus made sure that living nightmare would not occur by commanding, "Loose him, and let him go!" That's an edict that many authority figures have trouble understanding.

Each year Americans bid "Happy Birthday" to Abraham Lincoln, believed by many to be our greatest president. Despite the decades that have passed since he died, Lincoln's legacy continues. "Honest Abe" is remembered for many reasons, but two stand out principally: He led this nation through the Civil War, and he proclaimed the Emancipation Proclamation in January of 1863. While the document was not the cure-all when it came to civil liberties, it certainly set the tone for what would happen in future decades.

It takes an ego-driven leader to chain people. It takes great leaders to set them free. Leaders such as Jesus! The Scriptures promise that when Jesus sets us free, we are truly free! Think about folks who are imprisoned by drugs, pornography, and other bondage. Hopeless? No, indeed, for Jesus delivers. It's a proven fact! There are so many examples. I think often of my good buddy Gary S. Paxton, the pop songwriter who gave the world such "classics" as "Monster Mash" and "Alley Oop," as well as many really sane songs. For 22 years, Gary lived under substance abuse dominion. Then, one night in a little church in Nashville, Gary met Jesus. The bondage was smashed! Shortly thereafter, Gary wrote the gospel classic "He (Jesus) Was There All the Time."

PRAYER

O God, I proclaim my liberty through Christ Jesus! I am not a prisoner of the enemy, nor am I under his boot to obey him. I am free to live, free to celebrate creation, free to enjoy every day of life. Including today! Amen.

We followers of Christ celebrate liberty. Not necessarily freedom to do what we always want to do, but liberty to do those things that we ought to do. In pursuing that course, we find the fulfillment and joy God meant for us to have all along.

The riches
of Egypt

Genesis 41:42–43: And Pharaoh took off his ring from his hand, and put it upon Joseph's hand, and arrayed him in vestures of fine linen, and put a gold chain about his neck; and he made him to ride in the second chariot which he had; and they cried before him, Bow the knee: and he made him ruler over all the land of Egypt.

The Book of Genesis relates the marvelous story of the young Jewish man who saved the world from starvation. God put him on the throne, second in command to the pharaoh, in the land of Egypt. His name was Joseph. The plan God gave Joseph saved the known world at that time from starvation. You will note from Scripture that it was not Joseph's money that made the provision; it was his personal relationship with God and *Pharaoh's* money. I believe that you and I are in a very similar situation. You and I have been called to reach the world in the name of Jesus. Over and again we hear believers wail, "We can't do this because we don't have money." Okay. So we don't. Then let's use Pharaoh's money!

Do you have any idea at all how much money there is in this world? Recently I played golf with a fellow who belongs to one of the most beautiful country clubs in America. Homes along the fairways are 10–15 thousand square feet and cost a minimum of $500 per square foot to build on million-dollar lots. There are hundreds of those houses! Our local paper recently relayed the story of a home that sold in our town for $14.5 million! No, of course not everyone has that kind of money. But it's a proven fact that there are *billions* of dollars in investments in our county alone. Proportionately, your county has unbelievable funds as well, even in difficult economic times.

Part of our job as Christian leaders is to be Joseph. There must be a way to channel those funds into God's work. Of course, the local church is supported by the people giving God His tithes. Every professing believer should be a tither. That being said, it still remains there are fortunes to be legitimately and morally mined everywhere. Church leader, never say, "There's just no money." There *is* money! God help us to become good, creative miners!

Prayer: O God, help me to see Your divine resources all around me, not to be used for my own comfort, but to impact the world for Christ! Teach me Your stewardship. ***Amen.***

SPIT BALLS AND BATTLESHIPS

Matthew 5:11–12: Blessed are ye, when men shall revile you, and persecute you, and shall say all manner of evil against you falsely, for my sake. Rejoice, and be exceeding glad: for great is your reward in heaven.

You may remember the late, famed sportscaster Howard Cosell. He verbally could hold his own with anyone, especially his critics (and there were some severe ones). A celebrity roast was held in his honor during which the speakers had a field day ribbing Cosell for everything from his very bad hairpiece to his vitriolic way of broadcasting. Their broadsides were hilarious and everyone waited to hear how Cosell would respond. When he finally took the podium, he said, "You roasters have hit me with the best you've had. But it was like throwing spitballs at a battleship." Oh, I love that line! Talk about putting critics in their place!

So let me ask you: how do you deal with the "roasters" in your life? Yes, we all have them! Well, first of all, understand that for every person who would vilify you there are probably a dozen or more who would praise you. Ah, but we don't remember the dozen or more, do we? No, no, we remember the spiteful people. You know, critics concern me. I sometimes read critics' reviews of movies. Rarely do these geniuses agree with each other. I have wondered, "Hey, if these critics are so smart, why aren't they out there making the movies and the big bucks?" Simple answer. They can't. They just criticize those who can.

I have had probably more than my share of critics, primarily because I've been in front of the public for a half century. I want to please as many people as I can, but if that isn't possible, I can be satisfied with a day's activities if I know I've pleased Christ. Always check for the nail prints in your critics' hands. If they don't have those marks, then their verbal jabs are nothing more than spitballs against a battleship. Please the Master. If He says, "Well done!" then you've got it made.

Prayer: O God, let me be like the apostle Paul, always looking to Jesus, the author and finisher of my faith. Let me not be deterred by those who don't understand or are misinformed. You are my defense, my shield. I rest in that knowledge today. Amen.

CRACKED ECCLESIASTICAL BOTTLES

Matthew 9:16–17

No man putteth a piece of new cloth unto an old garment, for that which is put in to fill it up taketh from the garment, and the rent is made worse. Neither do men put new wine into old bottles: else the bottles break, and the wine runneth out, and the bottles perish: but they put new wine into new bottles, and both are preserved.

Have you ever heard of a fellow named Jonas Hanway? I hadn't either until the other day. He's the fellow who introduced American society to a gizmo he called an umbrella. I am told by one historian that when Hanway first walked down a public street, holding the opened umbrella over his head, he was subjected to a barrage of things, including insults. Why? The "throwers" had never seen an umbrella before.

The dislike, or distrust, of the new enters into every sphere of life — unfortunately, even into church life. The fact that we are born again, or saved, does not automatically mean our old nature has been crucified with Christ that day. So often, in church, if a new idea or a new method — or any change — is suggested, even when the change is vital, various objections are raised, usually to the tune of, "We never did it that way before." Yet Jesus himself opened the door for change in the Scripture that heads this column, taken from Matthew 9.

I know, I know. There are some who will howl when this text is used in any treatise encouraging acceptance of change. "Improper exegesis," they cry. This howl usually comes from those who are inextricably welded to the past. The fact is, Jesus was perfectly aware of how difficult it is to get a new idea into people's minds. No, we never change the timeless message of the gospel. But the delivery system generally used by churches often grows moldy and ineffective. In this day of ever-changing technology, linked with the desperate need of mankind for Christ, we need some new ecclesiastical bottles!

Byline #46

PRAYER

O God, forgive me if I cling to old ways that are now counterproductive simply because I am obstinate about or afraid of change. Amen.

HAS ANYBODY SEEN THE APOSTLE PAUL?

2 Timothy 4:6: For I am now ready to be offered, and the time of my departure is at hand.

Many years have passed since I stood on the stone floor of the dungeon in Rome's ancient Mamertine Prison. It was believed to be here that the great apostle Paul was incarcerated in Emperor Nero's death row 2,000 years ago. He was beheaded for the sake of Jesus and his missions work. Guards took Paul to the third milestone on the Ostian Way north of the city. It is believed that the execution party stopped at a place called Three Fountains, where an abbey stands today in Paul's honor. The following morning Paul paid with his very life for his walk with Christ and the ministry God entrusted to him.

Now news sources report that Paul's actual grave may have been located beneath Rome's second-largest basilica (the largest, of course, is St. Peter's at the Vatican). The second largest is St. Paul's Outside-the-Walls, a truly magnificent structure. A marble sarcophagus has been found that some believe may contain Paul's bones. The coffin dates from at least A.D. 390, although Paul died three centuries earlier. I am always somewhat leery about such proclamations of historical findings. For example, in my travels I have been shown two skulls purported to be that of the apostle John. Having two heads would *not* be better than one, not even for this man Jesus called a "son of thunder."

Of course, Paul himself won't be found in that sarcophagus, even if his bones are. His spirit and soul have been with the Lord since the moment the axe descended on the back of his neck. And just this warning: if the rapture takes place before the experts secure their findings in that coffin, those bones won't be there either. They will have risen at the trumpet sound, reunited with Paul's body and spirit. As he would have said, ". . . and so shall I be in the presence of the Lord" (see 1 Thess. 4:16–18; NIV).

PRAYER: O God, always let me keep fresh in my thoughts that this world is not my home. I truly am just passing through. Let my values be eternal in their nature and scope. Let me make investments in forever this very day. Amen.

Standing on a glass deck — 4,000 feet up!

Psalm 139:3: Thou compassest my path and my lying down, and art acquainted with all my ways.

Recently a spokesperson for the Hualapai Native American tribe in Arizona announced a startling construction project that now graces their reservation. In order to bring in needed revenue, the tribe has built an observation deck 4,000 feet above the Colorado River in the Grand Canyon. The visitor walks out about 70 feet from the canyon wall and stands nearly 400 stories above the river on what will seem like — nothing. You see, the floor of the deck is GLASS!

I saw something similar, but not quite as spectacular, on a trip to Macau, China. There is a 65-story observation tower there from which you can stare into mainland China. One exits the elevator of the tower on the 65th floor and steps out onto the large observation deck that circumnavigates the entire structure. As one walks to the railing, some 40 feet away, he or she notices that the last 20 feet of the deck floor are glass.

The spectator looks straight down nearly 700 feet — nothing between that person and the ground far below but that allegedly safe glass. I made it clear to the rail, but not easily. I had to make myself do so because a person's mind plays terrible tricks. In your brain you know that glass is very thick and would hold an elephant probably, but your eyes tell you that you're just simply stepping into empty space. Now the observation deck at the Grand Canyon is over five times that high and will have people clutching for skyhooks. From that height, the Colorado River far below will look like a tiny, meandering ribbon.

Think of God's view of this planet. Small wonder David wrote in Psalm 139 that there is nothing hidden from His view. Why, not even the darkness hinders His vision. The darkness and the light are both alike to Him. On a clear day, God can see forever. On an overcast one, too.

Prayer: O God, the fact that You can see me at this very moment does not trouble me but rather brings me blessed comfort. You see every circumstance of my life, yes, even how it will all finally culminate. My trust is in You, my Father! ***Amen.***

MULE TRAIN CHURCHES IN A SPACE STATION SOCIETY

Matthew 28:19

Go ye therefore, and teach all nations, baptizing them in the name of the Father, and of the Son, and of the Holy Ghost.

On January 20, 1937, Franklin Delano Roosevelt gave his second inaugural speech as president of the United States. John Garner was his vice-president. On the very next day, my mother gave birth — to me! Boy, was it ever a different world from today! The nations were gearing for the global maelstrom fomented by Hitler, Mussolini, and Tojo. Sixty million people would die because of war-related causes within the next eight years. The average annual American income in 1937 was $1,788. A new car could be purchased for $750. A new home could be bought for around $4,000. At the grocery store, you'd find a loaf of bread for 9 cents and a gallon of milk would set you back 50 cents. A gallon of gas? A dime. Remember, America was just emerging from the Great Depression. Life expectancy in the United States was a mere 59 years. The shifting of social sands has almost blotted out remembered yesteryears.

Now we come to this day and time. This is the era of space travel, of computers in every home, of iPods, of criss-crossing interstate highways, of cars that sell for tens of thousands of dollars and homes that cost at least 50 times more than they did when I was born. It's a different world, my friend! Face it! Yet many churches still operate as if we were still in the '30s or '40s.

It has been observed by social scientists that the typical church shows change in methodology every half century while the average business changes every three to five years. I do not refer here to tinkering with the timeless message of the gospel; I speak of the antiquated delivery systems still employed by far too many churches.

PRAYER

O God, as I grow older, don't allow me to grasp tenaciously to things of the past that are no longer relevant. I will enjoy their memory even as I go from victory to victory through the power of the Holy Spirit, grateful that You have allowed me to live to see this very day — and to be a participant of it. Amen.

"This is the way we've always done it," comes their cry. Small wonder the percentage of Americans attending church regularly is in decline. We're in mule-train methodology in a space-station society.

SHAMMI, OUR HAIRLESS "ATTACK" CAT

Genesis 1:25

And God made the beast of the earth after his kind, and cattle after their kind, and every thing that creepeth upon the earth after his kind: and God saw that it was good.

On my 70th birthday, my church family got me a most extraordinary gift: a hairless (Sphynx) cat. I had seen one several years earlier at the home of a family member and just loved it. What a strange and quite wonderful creature! Some folks don't like these cats because they have no hair. None! They have enormous ears and luminous green eyes. They are just magnificent. Hairless cats have the temperament of a dog; that is, they come running when you call, like pampering, and develop quite unusual personalities. So here came this four-month-old critter into our lives.

Holding a hairless cat is not unlike holding a chamois — you know, the animal skin used for drying a car. So that's what we called him: "Shammi!" His official name on the breeder's docket is Chamois Suede Betzer. Honest! Now Shammi is an attack cat, somewhat like Peter Seller's weird helper Kato in the Pink Panther movies, if you remember. He pounces at you from the strangest places. He's not much of a "guard cat," though. At night, while we watch television, Shammi jumps up on one of our shoulders, curls himself around our necks, and is gone for the night, sound asleep. Strangest thing — Shammi craves human touch. How can you not like an animal like that? And weird looking or not, I think he's just gorgeous with his tuxedo markings.

You know, God created a magnificent world. Little Shammi has helped me just slow down a bit to enjoy it. We go so hard that we sometimes miss the wonder all around us. We tend to forget or neglect many aspects of life that can bring us joy and laughter. Like the purring of a hairless cat, draped sound asleep over your shoulder.

Byline #50

PRAYER

O God, don't let me get so busy today that I neglect Your creation all around me. Help me be observant to all the wonders You have made: a grove of trees, a garden of bright flowers, the marvel of a flying bird, the touch of a snowflake, the laughter of a child. And let me remember that You made me and redeemed me — and You love me. Amen.

FAITH, THE ABSOLUTE INGREDIENT TO PLEASING GOD

Hebrews 11:6: But without faith it is impossible to please him.

Read that verse again and again. Let its truth sink into the bedrock of your soul. The verse doesn't mention charisma, talent, money, or prestige. It mentions only faith, and that without it, it is impossible to please God. This verse does not refer to "saving faith." It refers to the ability to trust God for everything, even though there isn't even a hint of the divine provision materializing. (Hebrews 11:1: Now faith is the substance of things hoped for, the evidence of things not seen.)

I grew up in a home where my parents were people of remarkable faith. My earliest pastor was a man named Willis Smith. I remember him so clearly and dearly. He was a man of faith who preached faith, who lived by faith, and as a result, over 70 of my relatives eventually came to know Christ as Lord. Pastor Smith walked into St. Vincent's Hospital in Sioux City, Iowa, in 1936 and was led by the Holy Spirit into a cancer ward. There he saw a 20-year-old woman dying. She was already in a terminal coma, according to her physician. Pastor Smith prayed a simple prayer, anointed the woman with oil (according to James 5:14) and walked out of the hospital. Several days later . . . Faye walked out, too. She lived another almost 50 years of active and effective work for her healing Lord. How do I know this story? Faye was my cousin. Pastor Smith's faith was contagious, and like falling dominoes, one after another of our family came to know Christ through that miracle, either directly or indirectly.

Faith is not some "wizard of Oz" experience. Faith is based on substance (again refer to Hebrews 11:1). We learned from our beloved pastor that we can do anything God calls upon us to do through Christ who strengthens us. In your world today, all things are possible. Faith is the key to unlock God's provisions. Together, let's ask the Lord to greatly increase our faith today.

Prayer: O God, if I truly cannot please You without faith, then increase my faith, I ask. My faith is bolstered by Your Word, either reading or hearing it. So I saturate my soul today with the Scriptures that my faith be built up and in so doing I please You. Amen.

You're going to be *where* on the Lord's Day?

Hebrews 10:25: Not forsaking the assembling of ourselves together, as the manner of some is; but exhorting one another: and so much the more, as ye see the day approaching.

Do you plan to be in church this Lord's Day? You ought to be there, you know. The Scriptures say so. It's to your benefit. There are so many blessings to be received by the person who faithfully attends a solid, Bible-preaching church. Let me tell you a for-instance story.

In my state of Florida, people often rid themselves of exotic pets they can no longer handle because of their size. More often than not, they release them in our nearby swamps. As a result we have a veritable plethora of various creatures here not native to our region. We have monitor lizards, for example, by the thousands. Folks thought they were cute when they were a foot long, but once they reached six feet, they weren't so much fun, and they were let go in the wild. We have lots of big snakes not indigenous to this area either. The other day, a fellow ran over a 12-foot python. The way police gathered around, including camera people from the news media (the picture made our front page!), you'd have thought it was the Loch Ness monster. The python was actually harmless to any adult. He just looked scary. In our annual Noah and the ark drama, I have often hoisted a 16-foot python onto the ark. Now *that's* a beast that can hurt you if you don't know what you're doing. But see, I know a lot about animals, so they are not frightening to me. You don't fear what you know!

In church we study God's Word, which tells us over and again, "Be not afraid." And "God has not given us the spirit of fear." We don't fear because in church we learn the nature of our enemy, Satan. We learn how to deal with "his devices." We learn that God is infinitely stronger than any foe on earth. We fear only those things about which we are not informed. So you see, there are many reasons for being in church faithfully each Lord's Day. Why not make it this weekend — and every one thereafter? You'll be so much better for it.

Prayer: O God, thank You for the body of Christ, the Church, on this earth. I want to be a contributing, faithful member of that congregation near me. I will not forsake the assembling together with brothers and sisters in Christ. Count on me! *Amen.*

JOHN WILKES BOOTH AND
THE END OF THE MATTER

Galatians 6:7: Be not deceived; God is not mocked: for whatsoever a man soweth, that shall he also reap.

It was the middle of February 1869. America was still licking its wounds from the bloody and deadly Civil War. Nearly four years had passed since President Abraham Lincoln had been assassinated. His killer, actor John Wilkes Booth, had been shot through the throat in a burning barn and died a paralyzed, agonized man. His convicted cohorts in the assassination plot had been hanged at the Old Arsenal in Washington, D.C. The president, Andrew Johnson, had sent orders of pardon for others implicated in the assassination: Dr. Samuel Mudd, Samuel Arnold, and Edward Spangler.

On that cold, wintry day in '89, a broken man from New York wrote the president an imploring letter. The writer was Edwin Booth, the brother of Lincoln's assassin. He asked for the body of his brother to be returned to the family for proper burial in Baltimore. The president acquiesced to the request. Five days later, a sturdy wood crate was unloaded in Washington and temporarily stored in a stable. Even the *Washington Evening Star* newspaper commented on the irony of the situation. The remains of John Wilkes Booth had been temporarily deposited in a stable behind . . . Ford's Theater! It was the exact stable where Booth had tethered his getaway horse the night he shot President Lincoln. Now his withered and skeletal remains lay in a rough wooden box at the very same site.

It was a real-life fulfillment of Eliphaz's terse line from Job 4:8 so long ago: "Even as I have seen, they that plow iniquity, and sow wickedness, reap the same." History has proven again and again that God is not mocked and that whatsoever a man sows, that shall he also reap. That divine principle is as valid as the law of gravity. A person who sows to the wind will reap the whirlwind.

PRAYER: O God, as Paul recognized, may Your Spirit help me keep "my body under" so that at the last I myself am not removed as a castaway. Your laws can be broken, but only at unsurmountable cost. Thank You for your warnings in Scripture. Those warnings will keep me safe at all times. **Amen.**

THE WONDER OF GREAT BOOKS

John 21:25

I suppose that even the world itself could not contain the books that should be written. Amen.

John's reference to books in this Scripture referred to all the works of Jesus on this earth, known and unknown, which would fill all the existing libraries. We are aware of only a tiny portion of the knowledge available. Curiosity alone demands disciplined reading. I try to read three books each week, not counting daily encounters in the Bible. Do you think there might be a Barnes and Noble in heaven? Just asking. My goodness — great books and strong coffee! Sounds like heaven to me.

I suspect that my choice of books, for a pastor, is quite eclectic. Yes, there are the requisite rows of commentaries and research books. How valuable they are! I also have a pretty good collection of sermon books, many of them written by me on the *Revivaltime* radio network around the world. I enjoy reading sermons by others, but I can't — or won't — preach them. The styles differ too widely from my own, which become "Saul's armor" to me. My two preferences in reading material are biographies and history books. What richness in delving into the lives of the famous and infamous through the centuries! Sprinkled into my reading list are current event books. And a number of newspapers. Not all my volumes are serious. For example, shortly after acquiring a hairless cat, I was given a book by Stephen Baker called *How to Live with a Neurotic Cat.*[1] Funny!

Reading is essential if you plan to grow mentally and spiritually. Try stretching your mind by occasionally reading books that are counter to your own thinking, but only if you possess some spiritual maturity. If you are new in the Christian faith, read books and periodicals that will bolster your walk with the Lord. The bottom line is this: Books can be great friends to you. Why not get acquainted with some this week?

1. Stephen Baker, *How to Live with a Neurotic Cat* (New York: Gramercy Books, 1999).

Byline #54

PRAYER

O God, I am thankful for the ability to read, to comprehend, to learn, to expand my personal universe. Thank You for all the great authors who have increased my faith and vision through all these years. Somehow, bless each one of them, I pray. Amen.

WHERE DID WE LOSE OUR WAY?

Byline #55

2 Timothy 4:5

> But watch thou in all things, endure afflictions, do the work of an evangelist. . . .

There's an old saying, "It's hard to remember when you're up to your ears in alligators that your original purpose was to drain the swamp." Our task from the Lord is to preach the gospel to every person on earth. But very often, the "machinery" of church administration and polity reminds me of that alligator/swamp business. Christ made it very clear that our job was evangelism and discipleship. Ah, but then came the alligators.

Such as politics (including national, regional, and church). Many clergymen feel they are to be spokespersons for a political cause rather than being spokespersons for Christ. The apostle Paul said his message was "Jesus Christ, and him crucified" (1 Cor. 2:2). Who authorized preachers of the gospel to change subjects in the pulpit? There is another 'gator I call middle management. That includes those safely ensconced in church business offices, either elected or appointed, who attempt to direct the activities of the "marines" invading the beachhead. It's like oiling a Rolex watch with maple syrup. Middle management will clog any corporation, secular or religious. How about the alligator of fads? Music seems to be the big one at the moment. Get an electronic keyboard, a couple of gyrating guitar players, some strobe lights, and you're "in." The question is this: If religious hip-hop is the answer to reaching our nation, then why aren't our churches exploding with growth? God knows they surely are exploding with sound! The sad fact is that most churches are not growing. Many are actually in decline.

Where did we lose our way in this whole business of evangelism? We have the greatest "product" in the world, and that's Christ's precious gospel. Let's get back to our primary assignment of preaching God's Word, truly caring for the lost and downtrodden, and being the light of the world that Jesus always intended for us to be.

PRAYER

O God, I have a divinely given commission to preach and live Your gospel to everyone. Help me recognize my responsibility in missions and personal evangelism and never think for even a moment that anything else is acceptable to You. Amen.

What about the future of our grandchildren?

2 Timothy 1:5: When I call to remembrance the unfeigned faith that is in thee, which dwelt first in thy grandmother Lois. . . .

The apostle Paul wrote those words to his protégé son in the faith, Timothy. Paul reminded the young evangelist of his heritage, which included a precious grandmother full of faith in God! My wife and I have seven grandchildren. The other night I came home and found one of them curled up on the sofa, watching cartoons on TV. She was giggling. Our cat was purring contentedly at her side. What a beautiful sight!

Thoughts of our grandchildren ought to fill our minds. What kind of a world will they know? We have lived to see many societal changes all around us, many of them far from good. Will the boundaries of decency be irrevocably crossed in the future? Will our grandchildren see a nuclear attack in this country? Will some deadly strain of virus be unleashed on unsuspecting innocents? Will some deranged killer slip into their school, guns in hand, prepared to unleash a deadly barrage against them? Will America still stand firm and tall with liberty and freedom for all? Will churches still be vibrant and relevant? Will they even be open? These are legitimate questions that concern our progeny. None of those queries will be answered by a somnambulant body of believers with a "whatever-will-be-will-be" attitude.

We, as followers of Christ, must be about our Father's business. If current events don't matter much to us now, they will most certainly matter to our precious grandchildren in the decades to come. One of the most vital foundations we can build for our offspring is a solid Christian education. A person saturated with the Word of God stands a far better chance not only of survival but also of success in the future. So for all our grandchildren, let's stay on the front line of all these key issues and make sure these kids have a future!

Prayer: O God, how can I ever thank You enough for the joys of our grandchildren? May we as grandparents always be cognizant of our responsibilities to them in love, respect, and impartation of spiritual truths. May each of them become giants for God. *Amen.*

JOEY MEETS JESUS

2 Corinthians 5:17: Therefore if any man be in Christ, he is a new creature: old things are passed away; behold, all things are become new.

Atlantic City in the '50s was the home of a famous nightclub, "The 500 Club," operated by Skinny D'amato. His enterprise was extremely profitable, making millions. It was here that Dean Martin and Jerry Lewis launched their entertainment careers. A guy named Sinatra loved the club and Skinny so much that legend, at least, has it that he worked there for nothing. But it was a young kid from York, Pennsylvania, who was stealing the show, a kid whose stage name was Joey Stevens.

At the age of 19, he was a headliner in the club. There was never any question about his singing talents. The only unknown was how long Joey could last. In his early 20s, he was already boozing and popping pills. But Stevens had something going for him that most entertainers did not: a praying preacher father who pastored a church in York. His dad never gave up on his son, always interceding for his total redemption. The singer's extracurricular activities were threatening his marriage. Finally, on the cusp of suicide, the prodigal son at last felt the impact of his father's prayers. Like the prodigal son, Stevens fell on his knees and asked God to save him. God did, of course. He is always faithful and just to forgive us of our sins. Stevens left showbiz and began singing for Christ, using his real name, Dave Boyer.

Dave has been a buddy of mine now for well over 40 years. He and his precious wife, June, are constantly on the front lines for Christ, bringing people to the knowledge of personal salvation. Boyer's story is one of hope, redemption, and the overwhelming grace of God. If this page is touching your heart, perhaps it is dawning on you that it isn't too late for you, just as it wasn't too late for the singer. God loves you as much as He did Joey Stevens. Why don't you call out to Him today?

Prayer: O God, thank You for praying moms and dads who keep on interceding for their children, even when they don't know where they are. Your Word promises us that You hear us when we pray! We receive hope in our hearts today. Amen.

THE SET OF
THE SAIL

Proverbs 22:6

Train up a child in the way he should go: and when he is old, he will not depart from it.

In December of 2006 two famous men died. One was former president of the United States Gerald Ford. He died at age 93 of natural causes and was mourned by Americans. The other was the former dictator of Iraq, Saddam Hussein, who was hanged at the age of 69. Millions reviled him, even in his death.

Years ago, one of my favorite poets, Ella Wheeler Wilcox, wrote: "One ship drives east and another drives west / with the self same winds that blow / 'Tis the set of the sails, and not the gales, that tells us the way to go." How profound! What set of the sail would make Gerald Ford become a leader, healer, and example for good? And what set of the sail would form "the beast of Baghdad," as Hussein was sometimes called? My late friend, the marvelous

and dramatic evangelist Jack Shuler, wrote, "In his formative years, man is stronger than his choice; but in the years of maturity, the choice is master and he is slave. Let him cast the vote of his discretion early against God, and the unfolding years will produce a riptide, sweeping upon its giant crest both body and soul into hell. Let him direct his young will toward God, and all the forces of earth and hell shall be powerless to dissuade him in his ever-increasing velocity toward heaven."[1]

How about your children or your grandchildren? To which direction is their sail set in these formative years? And to what extent have you "set the sail" for them? I cannot comment forcefully enough on the positive virtues and impact of Sunday school! It may be that the very Sunday school class to which you failed to take your child last week would have set his or her sail for life.

You were sleeping in.

1. Jack Shuler, *Short Sermons: Thirty-eight Selected Sermons* (Grand Rapids, MI: Zondervan Publ. House, 1952), p. 35.

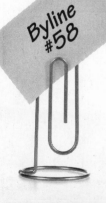

Byline #58

PRAYER

O God, You have lent me the precious life of a child. You expect me to exhibit strong stewardship in the raising of that youngster. Help me to set the sail of that young life in the right direction! It's a matter of life and death. Amen.

BURMA SHAVE REVISITED

Acts 4:31: . . . and they spake the word of God with boldness.

One of my earliest and fondest memories is of riding through the northwest Iowa countryside with my father, who was driving our 1932 Chevrolet Cabriolet. Boy, that was some snazzy car! If the weather was nice, Dad let me ride in the rumble seat. (And all the young readers are saying to themselves, "What in the world is a rumble seat?") The trouble was that Dad drove that machine for 17 years. After the tenth year, it was just an old tub of bolts. Then a drunk driver hit us head-on, and that was the end of the Chevy.

The Iowa country roads in those days had quasi-curbs, which certainly channeled the runoff of melting snow and ice water, but they made driving somewhat perilous. As a result, Dad never drove too fast, which would let me read the Burma Shave signs along the roadway. Remember them? Oh, they were classics! There would be five of them, spaced about 50 feet or so apart, and would read like this: "Don't lose your head . . . to gain a minute . . . you need your head . . . your brains are in it . . . Burma Shave." Here's another: "Brother Speeder . . . let's rehearse . . . all together . . . good morning, nurse. Burma Shave." I liked this one: "The midnight ride . . . of Paul for beer . . . led to a warmer . . . atmosphere . . . Burma Shave." One more: "Around the curve . . . lickety split . . . beautiful car . . . wasn't it? . . . Burma Shave." I wonder if there has ever been a product so identified with its advertising as that shaving cream.

Far and away, the best advertising a church has is its parishioners. A local newspaper columnist, not a believer, once talked to me about one of our church members. He said, "Reverend, if all Christians were as fine as that guy, I'd be a believer, too!" As far as he was concerned, our church member was a positive advertisement for Christ. So a Burma Shave-type ad for the Lord today might be, "Following Jesus . . . that's my style . . . He's made my life . . . so worthwhile!" Oh, go ahead — you can add "Burma Shave" if you want to.

1. George L. Johnson and Cleavant Derricks, "Let the Beauty of Jesus Be Seen in Me."

PRAYER: O God, let me be a true advertisement of You this day. As the old chorus says, "Let the beauty of Jesus be seen in me / all His wonderful passion and purity."[1] Refine me for Your glory today, I ask. **Amen.**

Byline #60

Goodbye, Son

Acts 13:2: As they ministered to the Lord, and fasted, the Holy Ghost said, Separate me Barnabas and Saul for the work whereunto I have called them.

Tuesday, March 20, 2007, was not an easy day for my wife or me. On that morning, we went to our local airport to see our son David and his wife Janis off to Africa, along with the younger two of their four children (the older two are in the States living on their own now). David and Janis have been missionaries in South Africa since 1994. The first time they left was very painful, yet somehow bearable, knowing they were doing the work to which God had called and ordained them. But every four years, when they would come home on furlough, it was that much harder to see them leave for Africa again.

A normal term of duty on a foreign field for our missionaries is four years. As I watched our precious family board the KLM flight that morning, I had to ponder, "Dan, you and Darlene are 70 years old. Your chances of seeing your family again in this life diminish every time they leave for another term."

What makes these partings acceptable is the passion my wife and I have for missions. When I was a kid, I really believed I would be a missionary myself one day. Several years back, while in India, I prayed, "Lord, You know my heart for missions. Why have You never allowed me to be a missionary?" The Holy Spirit responded gently in my heart, "But, Dan, you *are* a missionary — a missionary of supply." My heart pounds for missions. It is the priority in my life. It always has been. But, you know, it's easy to give money. Darlene and I have annually given more to missions than the amount of our tithe. No problem. That's easy — it's just money. How much "stuff" do we need? But giving your children? Oh, my friend, that's another thing altogether. Yes, there is the joy of fulfillment that your progeny are expanding the front lines for Christ on foreign soil. But somehow that morning in question it didn't ease the deep ache in this father's heart when I watched that flight leap off the runway and disappear into the far eastern sky. Then I remembered: God gave His Son. . . . Can I do less?

Prayer: O God, thank You for the joy and privilege of having children establishing beachheads for the gospel in faraway lands. Keep them safe and well. Prosper them even as their soul prospers. And let us see them again. *Amen.*

MISSIONARIES ARE HEROES, DON'T YOU THINK?

> **Acts 14:27**
>
> And when they were come, and had gathered the church together, they rehearsed all that God had done with them, and how he had opened the door of faith unto the Gentiles.

In the previous Byline, I wrote of our son David and his family, who are career missionaries in Africa. I have worked with them there on numerous occasions, as well as with other missionaries in 60 nations. The workload of these soldiers of the cross is extensive and exhausting. All productive missionaries could tell you the same story. Missions is not "National-Geographic-Take-a-Picture" time; it's "Lay-Down-Your-Life-for-Jesus" time. In our son's case, he pastors a church he founded in South Africa. He and Janis also founded and operate the Lighthouse Children's Shelter in which hundreds of little children, orphaned by the AIDS pandemic, have been rescued, nurtured to full health, and adopted by loving, Christian parents. It's a job that keeps them busy around the clock, even with a good staff of hardworking helpers.

Our church has an ongoing love affair with missionaries. We usually see at least 70 or 80 of them in our pulpit annually. Every Wednesday night and quite a few Sunday mornings feature a ten-minute window with a real, live missionary. As a result, many from our church are in missions somewhere around the world, hundreds of them each year in short-term projects and dozens full-time. The priority of Christ's church is global evangelism. If you don't believe that, read the Gospels of Matthew, Mark, Luke, and John once again. Read the Book of Acts. These books are about missions! As a pastor whose church has given literally tens of millions of dollars to missions through the past 20 years, I cannot understand how churches can have hundreds of thousands of dollars in savings reserves while the world all around them is going into eternity. I ask such pastors, "What are you saving the money for?" I usually hear, "Oh, for a rainy day." Really? Look around you! It's raining!

> **PRAYER**
>
> O God, may I ever be true to the missions call, either by going myself or helping to supply the needs of those who have gone! Amen.

Do we really think God will be impressed on Judgment Day by our bank reserves? Or do you think He might be more favorable if we can show we've obeyed the Great Commission?

BUREAUCRACY
— THE BANE OF
GOD'S WORK

Matthew 23:13

But woe unto you, scribes and Pharisees, hypocrites! for ye shut up the kingdom of heaven against men: for ye neither go in yourselves, neither suffer ye them that are entering to go in.

What strong words to come from our blessed Lord! There is nothing kind or compassionate about them. His words are a divine tirade against those who kill the spirit of the gospel.

Consider this scenario: A fellow shows up at the airport to fly as a passenger in a commercial plane. Interestingly enough, he works in the bookkeeping department of the very airline he's flying. Upon boarding the plane, he saunters into the cockpit and starts instructing the pilot and co-pilot about how to fly a plane and how to navigate to the proposed destination. The pilots ask him, "Have you ever flown a plane before?"

"No," he replies, "but I am an accountant in the business office of this airline."

They press him a bit, "So does that qualify you to fly this massive plane with its hundreds of passengers? You've never flown, never taxied an aircraft, never contacted a control tower, never navigated anything bigger than your car!"

But he persists, "You fellas don't understand. I'm an *accountant*! Let me tell you how to fly this plane!"

"Absurd!" you cry. Isn't it? Welcome to the world of ecclesiology — church life. There are just far too many desk jockeys attempting to control the people on the front lines. They have forgotten their job is to *assist* the front-line soldiers, not to thwart their efforts or tell them how to do their jobs. It's difficult and dangerous enough to be on those firing lines every day of your life, facing a brutal enemy in Satan and his cohorts, without having to cajole bureaucrats. Of course, we all need guidance and advisors. We need mid-course corrections along the way. But I tell you, it's one thing to be in the control room at NASA watching computer screens, and quite another to be in that spacecraft careening to the moon. God bless all those who counsel me with wisdom. They are great helpers, not vision-dashing hindrances. I do not write of them today. But how did the bureaucrats ever get such power in Christ's church?

Byline #62

PRAYER

O God, help me to always keep my eyes on You, as did Paul who wrote, "Looking unto Jesus. . . !" May I never allow pencil pushers or bean counters to stop the mission to which I have been called. Thank You! Amen.

HOW'S YOUR INVESTMENT PORTFOLIO?

Matthew 6:19–20: Lay not up for yourselves treasures upon earth . . . but lay up for yourselves treasures in heaven.

Consider the ramifications of this verse: "The removing of those things that are shaken, as of things that are made, that those things which cannot be shaken may remain" (Heb. 12:27). Read it again. Think it through. God is warning you and me that everything in life that can be shaken (which is most things) will be shaken so that those things that cannot be shaken (those things that smack of eternity) will remain. I woke up recently in our Florida home to learn that just north of us a few miles tornadoes had swept across the peninsula during the night. No one had any warning they were coming. Scores of homes were just obliterated. A church building was literally ripped from its foundation and scattered to the winds. An 18-wheeler was picked up and deposited on yet another truck. Several were killed. My friend, you and I should hold "things" very lightly. They can be shaken or removed in an instant!

Small wonder that Jesus encouraged you and me to invest in eternity where no deterioration or destruction is possible. Think of your health. That's a blessed commodity that can be quickly taken. A dear friend of mine sat in my office just a few days ago, the picture of health. As I write this he is in the ICU of a local hospital, breathing on a ventilator, which alone keeps him alive. Consider positions on the work force. Elected leaders hold office only on the whim of the electorate. I often remember an old gospel song with this lyric: "This world is not my home / I'm just a-passin' through / My treasures are laid up somewhere beyond the blue / The angels beckon me from heaven's open door / And I can't feel at home in this world anymore."

Perhaps we followers of Christ are much too comfortable in this temporary housing. Rather than sending treasures of our time, talents, and resources above where nothing can damage them, we just keep stockpiling on this capricious earth. That's just not a very good investment portfolio.

Prayer: O God, help me to listen to and heed Your admonition to lay up treasures in heaven, not on earth. You are the greatest investment counselor of all time. I should be listening to You all the time! Help me to be a better investor. Amen.

Infiltrating a community from a small church

Acts 5:14: And believers were the more added to the Lord, multitudes both of men and women.

I have been told on occasion that smaller churches are more pleasing to God than big ones. I don't believe that for a moment! In the Gospels of Matthew, Mark, Luke, and John, especially in the King James Version, we are informed again and again that wherever Jesus went He was surrounded by *multitudes.* And large numbers of folks continued to be reached even in Acts 5, as reported from Scripture at the top of this page.

My wife and I spent many years in northern Ohio starting churches from nothing. My very first pastorate was in Vermilion, a town of about 10,000. We began that work on Wednesday nights in the basement of our rented house. On Sunday mornings we met in a public school cafeteria. My dilemma in getting started was this: how do I get the 10,000 residents in this town to even know we exist? We had no money and precious few people in our tiny church. I began by training about a half-dozen workers, and they and I knocked on the door

of every residence in that town *twice* in the next 12 months. If you read the history of the Crystal Cathedral in Garden Grove, California, you will learn that Dr. Robert Schuller began that work in exactly the same way. Hard work? Of course, but incredibly productive. Day after day in Vermilion I walked to business places. I met the owners and the leaders of the city. I made the acquaintance of doctors, teachers, attorneys, bankers, other ministers; made friends on the golf course and tennis courts; and fished with new buddies in the Vermilion River. Point: I didn't just sit, and I did more than pray. Yes, I kept office hours, which is essential, but I knew the key of reaching Vermilion was to infiltrate, infiltrate, infiltrate in every way possible.

It doesn't matter if you have 50 people in your church or 5,000. The need will always be there to infiltrate. We are commanded by our King to take the gospel to everyone. My friend, His command is *not* an option.

Prayer: O God, let me somehow see my world as You see it, as it could be, as You want it to be. And then by Your grace, let me do something about it! I can moan and groan or I can infiltrate this mission field You have given me. Help me to be about my Father's business today and every day. **Amen.**

WHERE THERE IS NO VISION, PEOPLE DIE

Proverbs 29:18: Where there is no vision, the people perish. . . .

John Maxwell tells congregations that no church can rise for long above the level of its leadership. To those men and women whom God has placed in frontier leadership positions come eternal responsibilities for the souls of mankind. One outstanding church leader, a district superintendent in his state, told me, "Dan, when God put me in this position, only ½ of 1 percent of the people in our state attended our churches. My goal in my time of office is to increase that number to 1½ to 2 percent." Now *that's* vision! That goal involves impacting hundreds of thousands of people. With that kind of leadership, the lost are won to Christ, churches grow, and the entire state is blessed.

Such is not the case, unfortunately, with all leaders. When I was a teenager, I used to sing in a well-known church that, at that time, averaged well over a thousand in attendance. Today that church has dropped at least 40 percent. The pastor told me personally that "all is well" and that he and his board do not welcome anyone not of Anglo-Saxon background — and hopefully, those with a substantial amount of money in the bank. In other words, they have changed God's church (which is to be a hospital for the lost and hurting) into a restricted country club for the "saints." Another pastor told me that he downplays any suggestions from his youth pastors about reaching today's generation, for after all (in his words), "What do they know?"

The complacency in today's church in general has to be a stench in God's nostrils. At a recent directors' meeting of a number of churches, I asked if we could please consider starting new churches in our area. One of the leading members snorted and said, "I move the agenda." In other words, don't mess up our structured day with talk of reaching the lost. The fact is that men and women of faith, vision, and courage can reach today's world. Our nation and world appears to be going to hell in a hand basket, and yet a huge sector of Christ's body is doing a splendid impression of Rip Van Winkle.

PRAYER: O God, forgive us for our decadent complacency. You have set us as watchmen on the wall, but most of us appear to be fast asleep while the enemy is even at the gates. Spirit of God, wake up Your people! Amen.

CAN A FOLLOWER OF JESUS CHRIST BE PREJUDICED?

Romans 10:12

For there is no difference between the Jew and the Greek: for the same Lord over all is rich unto all that call upon him.

I pose a question for the day. *Prejudice* is defined by Webster's Dictionary as "preconceived judgment or opinion or an adverse opinion of someone without just grounds or before sufficient knowledge." Can a truly born-again, Holy Spirit-filled follower of Jesus be prejudiced? Especially against those of other races? Apparently many professing believers think so. There are churches that are conspicuous by their startling lack of color in the pew. This situation exists despite the fact that whites will soon be in the minority in large sections of the United States, if, indeed, they aren't already.

I have pastored a church in Florida for 22 years. When I was elected here, I observed the wall-to-wall "whiteness" of our congregation and stated publicly that I had no intention of pastoring a segregated flock. I promised that we would reach out to everyone. Quite a few folks left. But others stayed, understanding our persevering mission of reaching the whole world with the whole gospel. Today many thousands of people attend the church each week. Five of our pastors come from Hispanic or African-American backgrounds. Our church board, which we call the Church Council, also reflects the racial makeup of our community, as well as the gender makeup. It thrills me to see leaders of varied backgrounds on our platform and the overwhelming enthusiasm of the whole body of Christ, very racially mixed, which has come together to worship our Lord (who, in case you've forgotten, was a Jew).

In all of our dealings as representatives of Christ, we must understand that we are human beings, created in God's image, and now — as born-again believers — conformed to the image of Christ. As such, ill will or prejudice toward anyone has no place in the household of faith, and is a wretched witness of our professed Christian standing.

Byline #66

PRAYER

O God, today let me see my fellow human beings as You see them, not as white or black or red or brown or yellow, but rather as brothers and sisters. Let me link arms with those around me for the good of humanity and the building up of Your kingdom. Amen.

ON SANCTIFYING GOD

1 Peter 3:15

But sanctify the Lord God in your hearts.

Now how in the world am I supposed to do that? I understand that God can sanctify me, but how can such a process be reversed? Yet the verse stands: Sanctify God!

For years I have taught an adult Sunday school class in our church sanctuary every Lord's Day morning. The class members file in, supplied with coffee and donuts from our coffee shop in the lobby, and we open God's Word for study. While in the Book of Numbers, which relates much of the drama of the Israelites' journey from Egypt to the Promised Land, we came across a fascinating look into the life of Moses. Moses actually angered God. The people needed water and were complaining. God told Moses to speak to a large rock (in today's Wadi Musa in the country of Jordan) and water would flow from it. But Moses was pretty teed off at the people and snapped, "Must I, Moses, show you another miracle?" And in his pique he smacked that huge rock with his staff. Water gushed from it and the people were thrilled (see Num. 20:10–11). But God said to Moses, "You will not set foot in the Promised Land because you failed to sanctify me to these people" (see Num. 20:12).

Here's the premise: the only God most people know — or at least know about — is the One they see depicted by your life. So God commands us, "Show the people who I truly am! Don't let your life depict some false god who doesn't even exist!" Moses called the Israelites' attention to himself, not God, and totally failed in this endeavor of sanctifying Him. Think of it: Moses was very special to God. In fact, God said, "When I speak to my servant Moses, it will be face to face!" (see Exod. 33:11). My friend, if Moses could not get away with failure in this matter of sanctifying God, how in the world can I? Or you? People are watching to see "the God in you." Don't show them a false idol. Let your life reveal the true and living God. In other words, sanctify God!

PRAYER

O God, when I think of Your special relationship to Moses, and how he paid such a dear price for failure to sanctify You, I realize I have a tremendous responsibility in this matter of showing You as You truly are! By Your Spirit, enable me to sanctify You in all that I do and say this day. Amen.

The joy of asking

Matthew 7:7: Ask, and it shall be given you; seek, and ye shall find; knock, and it shall be opened unto you.

Our seven grandchildren are a source of limitless joy to my wife and me. Recently we were in a local restaurant with one of them, little Hannah Ruth — she was four at the time. She was sitting right next to me, and as always, we were having a grand lunch together.

At the end of the meal, the waiter brought me the check. Hannah touched my arm, looked up at me with those angelic brown eyes, put a radiant smile on her precious face, and asked, "Grandpa, when you get your change back, can I have it?" I laughed for a long time. Think she got the change? Ha! Of course she did. Hannah's somewhat brazen request, that perhaps would have upset anyone else, delighted me. I'm her grandfather! It reminded me of the biblical reminder that we have not because we ask not. Now I took a little time to explain to Hannah that her request was not really proper, but I can tell you my heart wasn't in it. I hope she asks again.

In our case as children of God, we may ask what we will in His name. Now does that mean I'm going to request a Rolls Royce from my Heavenly Father? Or a mansion somewhere? No, I won't ask for those things because I don't need them, don't even want them frankly, and they would comprise an improper request. But those things in life that I *do* need — health, basic provision, peace with God, a happy home — those are all things that I can confidently request according to God's will.

Someone might protest, "But God would give you those things anyway, so why pray?" We ask because it pleases God. Thinking back, I probably would have given Hannah that change without her asking. But it was the sight of that beautiful, precious little upturned face and those trusting eyes and that soft, pleading voice that made my day. I somehow reckon God must feel somewhat like that, too.

Prayer: O God, thank You for hearing me when I ask. I want to always ask for those things that are right for me, that please You and that enhance Your kingdom. Grant me this wisdom, I pray. I thank You. ***Amen.***

IS THERE A ROBBER IN THE HOUSE?

Malachi 3:8: Will a man rob God? Yet ye have robbed me. But ye say, Wherein have we robbed thee? In tithes and offerings.

For the life of me, I don't understand why Christians don't tithe. Polls indicate that only a small percentage of believers are faithful in that regard. Failure to tithe not only stops the supernatural flow of God's resource provision to the giver, but it also constitutes robbery in His sight.

In all my years of pastoring, I have never looked at the church giving records. I could not tell you if a person has given a hundred dollars or a fortune to the church ministry. There is an exception to that rule: if we are bringing on board an assistant minister, or recommending laity for the church board, I have an accountant check their giving records to see if they indicate the person is a tither. Why would I do that? Because I don't want a thief on the church board or my pastoral staff. What right do I have to call a non-tither a thief? Oh, I didn't call the person that name — God did. "Will a man rob God?" A person who buys groceries, clothes, shoes, toys, cars, house payments — you name it — with God's 10 percent is taking from the Lord for his or her own benefit.

The tragic thing is that a person who shows a lifetime of tithing to God is able to live far, far better on the 90 percent than he or she ever could have lived on the full 100 percent. I can prove that from real life over and again. Tithing indicates a lack of faith in God and His promises.

Now where does the tithe belong? In the storehouse, Malachi teaches. In 30 years of global media ministry, I never once asked a listener or viewer for tithe. We were grateful for offerings, but the tithe belonged in the local church where that person receives spiritual food. So — are you a lifelong tither? You'll be blessed if you are.

Prayer: O God, I do not want You to consider me to be a thief. And I want to keep the conduits of Your divine supply wide open. Thank You for a lifetime of proving to me that You are a rewarder for those who honor You with our giving. I thank You. Amen.

THE PRECIOUS CROSS OF CALVARY

1 Corinthians 1:17

For Christ sent me not to baptize, but to preach the gospel: not with wisdom of words, lest the cross of Christ should be made of none effect.

On a regular basis as followers of Christ when we gather around the communion table, we are reminded of the Cross. When Jesus died on Calvary, the date was April in the year A.D. 30, in all probability. We know that Tiberias was the emperor of Rome. Tiberias was 70 at the time of Jesus' death and had already ruled for 14 years, succeeding Caesar Augustus. He was a lean, assiduous, and very unhappy man, but he was a master of economics. Historians record that when Tiberias assumed control of Rome, there were 100 million sesterces (silver coins) in the national treasury; when he died, there were nearly 3 billion of them. A cold-hearted man, the emperor knew virtually nothing of mercy or compassion.

The enemies of Jesus knew all the negatives of their caesar. When it seemed for a short moment that the Roman governor of Judea, Pontius Pilate, might not condemn Jesus, they snarled at him, "If you let this man go, you are no friend of Caesar" (John 19:12; NIV). Pilate quickly relented and ordered the crucifixion of our Lord. History records that it would not have been prudent for Pilate's political life to antagonize Tiberias.

But the direction for that day had been set long before Tiberias or Augustus or Julius or Pompey or any of that crowd. God's plan for redemption was carved in eternal stone long before the creation of the worlds. Adam's sin came as no surprise to the Creator. The divine salvation plan had long since been conceived in the mind of God. By that crucial mid-afternoon so long ago, Jesus Christ, the Son of God, hung dead, suspended by nails from a brutal cross. *So I'll cherish that old rugged cross til my trophies at last I lay down.*[1] Can any place on this planet be as precious in God's sight as Calvary? Or mine?

1. George Bennard, "The Old Rugged Cross."

Byline #70

PRAYER

O God, we stand transfixed before the Cross, pondering the enormity of Your eternal plan for our personal redemption. The Cross will never be a mere trinket hanging on a necklace. No, to us, the redeemed, it will ever be the symbol of Your marvelous grace! How can we thank You? Amen.

THE THOMAS FACTOR

John 20:25: The other disciples therefore said unto him, We have seen the Lord. But he said unto them, Except I shall see in his hands the print of the nails, and put my finger into the print of the nails, and thrust my hand into his side, I will not believe.

I have recently returned once again from India where the nation is seeing a great spiritual awakening among both Hindus and Muslims. Many of the evangelical leaders there point back to July 3, A.D. 72, when an enraged Hindu Brahmin speared the apostle Thomas to death. They say it was the blood of "doubting Thomas" that fertilized the soil of India for the gospel. In one church where I spoke (Channai), the attendance that Sunday exceeded 40,000. One denomination alone plans to launch at least 25,000 new Christian churches before 2020!

To understand the greatness of the harvest in India, one has to try to comprehend the out-of-control population there. At this moment 1.2 billion people reside in the land. (In my own state of Florida we now have 18 million residents. If we had the same density of population as India, we would have over 180 million Floridians among us!) Each day there are 100,000 births in India versus 20,000 deaths. Thus the population of India increases by 80,000 each day. Eight hundred million are Hindus and 200 million are Muslims. The poverty is breathtaking: 77 percent of the population lives on less than 50 cents a day.

Into this maelstrom of humanity come Spirit-filled Christians who are fulfilling Christ's Great Commission: "And he said unto them, Go ye into all the world, and preach the gospel to every creature" (Mark 16:15). As you read this, 25,000 potential pastors are being trained in three-year Bible institutes. Each one will be *required* to start a church before being credentialed. The Thomas Factor is a reality in this strange land of strange people and even stranger gods. The Apostle's blood was not shed in vain.

PRAYER: O God, may my heart be pierced today by the need to take Your gospel to the ends of the earth. I have no right to hear the gospel over and over until everyone has heard it at least once! Make me a missionary of supply and intercession! **Amen.**

Sports fans — short for fanatics

Matthew 22:37: Jesus said unto him, Thou shalt love the Lord thy God with all thy heart, and with all thy soul, and with all thy mind.

I take second place to no one in my love for sports, especially those games I can still play in this, my eighth decade of life. (That means I'm in my 70s for those whose math skills are questionable.) I have a great love for football and baseball. I used to do chapel services for my beloved Cleveland Browns before they were unceremoniously hied away to Baltimore. To sit in old Lakefront Stadium in December with the winds howling outrageously off Lake Erie indicates that one truly is a supporter of the team.

But some fans cross the line of sanity! Take, for example, the fellow who follows a professional football team (whose name I shall not indicate here) who decided to have his bald head tattooed to match the helmets worn by the players. He had his hairless pate *pain*stakingly turned into a facsimile of his team's helmets, including the quarterback's jersey number stenciled onto the back of his neck. Little children, upon seeing this apparition, will run for their mothers! So why did he do this? In his own words, "I'm a fan!"

Not long ago, 72,000 fans sat in an outdoor, uncovered football stadium where the temperature at kickoff time was -4 degrees with winds at 20 mph! Now if people came to church in that kind of weather, critics would say, "Those people are crazy!" Depends upon where your heart is, doesn't it? Why, I know some professing believers who are ashamed to say grace before meals in restaurants.

Isn't it sad that some folks don't seem to love Jesus as much as some fans love football? I wonder if that doesn't break His heart.

Prayer: O God, may I never — never! — give any indication of being ashamed of You or the Good News bought at such dreadful price! May I ever be a true "fan" — a follower of Him who redeemed me! ***Amen.***

ECHOES FROM CALVARY

> And after that they had mocked him, they took the robe off from him, and put his own raiment on him, and led him away to crucify him.

In the past, I have led several dozen tours to Israel. Quite often on the first night in Jerusalem, after I know my guests have been fed and are sound asleep, I slip away from the hotel and walk about a half hour to the hill called Calvary. It's located on the north side of the old city of Jerusalem. There, several hundred yards away from the famed Damascus Gate, stands a diesel-smelly bus station. During the daytime it's both crowded and noisy. But at night, bathed in moonlight, it's not so bad. Just behind the bus station stands a rocky crag. Clearly etched against the facade is a skull. Golgotha! It is at the foot of this rock, I believe, that Jesus was crucified. I stand there alone, sometimes for a long time, just contemplating the enormity of the price paid for my salvation.

The Romans were experts at crucifixion. One April day, A.D. 30, three men emerged from the Antonia Prison, flanked by the death squads. Three cross-pieces had been requisitioned from the supply room. The actual uprights were always left standing at the place of execution and used frequently. Each of the three victims had his wrists bound about six inches apart, allowing his hands to curl over the timber on his shoulders. Only one of them, Jesus of Nazareth, had been beaten prior to the cruel march. His body had been bent over a whipping post in the courtyard of the fortress. The soldier who had beaten Him had used a flagellum, a whip made of strips of leather and bits of bone and chain fastened to them. Every time the whip crashed against Jesus' body, skin and flesh were torn away. Now, at Calvary, the banging of mallet against nail could be heard. Jesus' cross stood at the edge of the roadway where passers-by could revile Him and spit upon Him. But, as my friend Tony Campolo has preached so often, "That was Friday . . . Sunday was comin'!" Lest I forget God's love for me, I visit Calvary as often as possible. And I stand there — and just remember.

PRAYER

O God, what infinite love You have shown to us in the giving of Your only begotten Son that whosoever believes in Him would never die but have eternal life. Thank You! Let my life show my gratitude today. Amen.

SPEAKING IN A SECULAR COMMENCEMENT EXERCISE

James 4:14

Whereas ye know not what shall be on the morrow. For what is your life? It is even a vapour, that appeareth for a little time, and then vanisheth away.

A college student came to my study recently to talk to me about a dilemma she faced. In her speech class, she was required to give a six-minute informational talk. Her chosen subject was Jesus Christ. However, she was warned that she could not use the Bible or any church literature for support nor give any kind of evangelical nuance. Her question was, "How do I give such a speech?" I told her that I would give my proverbial right arm to substitute for her in that class.

I recalled that years earlier I received a call from the superintendent of the largest public school in a certain state. He said, "Mr. Betzer, we would like to have you give the commencement speech at this year's graduation. Last year our speaker was Bob Hope. There will be nearly 9,000 people in attendance. But you cannot mention God, Jesus, church, or the Bible." I told him I would be delighted to come. I fervently asked God for guidance on what to say. My opening line to the speech was this: "Two thousand years ago, a very smart man asked a startling question: 'What is your life?'" I kept my word to the school official and yet was able to talk about biblical values.

There is a wealth of historical, sociological, geographical, and other data in libraries and book stores that give a treasury on the life and times of Christ. My goodness, the birth of Jesus Christ split the ages! That's why we use the terms "before Christ" and "after Christ" in citing dates. Jesus and His disciples transformed the world! The "politically correct" idea to deny the life of Jesus and His impact on society shows a determination to be an intellectual know-nothing. I could talk about Jesus all day and never be required to refer to Scripture. Boy, I just wish I could have given the speech for that college gal the other day!

Byline #74

PRAYER

O God, may I never be ashamed of the gospel of Jesus Christ or deny its power to change lives. But I also ask You to make me a better student of Your Word and humanity at large so I can be a better witness for You. Amen.

PASTORING FOR DUMMIES

Ephesians 4:11–12: And he gave some, apostles; and some, prophets; and some, evangelists; and some, pastors and teachers; For the perfecting of the saints, for the work of the ministry, for the edifying of the body of Christ.

God has blessed me so much by allowing me to be a pastor for 33 years. I am still learning the impact of the Ephesians 4:11–12 passage. Along the way, God has sent some outstanding mentors to help me learn the "ropes."

One of the greatest pastors I ever knew was Wayne B. Smith, founder and senior pastor of Southland Christian Church in Lexington, Kentucky. His congregation numbered in the thousands on Sundays, and in addition, his church had mothered a number of other congregations in the city and area. Smith retired some years ago and his church has continued to expand in every area. The most amazing thing to me about this pastor was that he knew everybody's name. I often watched him in the church lobby, greeting people as they left the building, calling them by name — and never missing! He was a relational-type guy and spent most of his time visiting his people. But I have known other pastors equally successful who spent most of their time in the study.

There is no "one right way" to pastor a church, except the way God lays on that minister's heart. But all the winning pastors I have encountered have had a couple things in common: passion for the lost and a love for their people. I have kidded my staff that one day I am going to write a book called *Pastoring for Dummies*. It will have only three pages and one sentence on each page. Page 1: Love your people. Page 2: Feed your people (from God's Word). And page 3: Don't do anything stupid. It's pretty hard for any flock to love a shepherd who is uncaring, reckless, foolhardy, and selfish. Thankfully, most pastors are truly gifts of God to the church. The Bible says so.

Prayer: O God, I uphold all pastors in prayer. I know many of the challenges they face. Give them direction and encouragement this day. May they see the fruit of their labor. And may they continue to grow in grace and godly power. Amen.

Function fatigue

Psalm 119:28: . . . strengthen thou me according unto thy word.

That cell phone on your belt or in your purse will do about anything: play music, take pictures, archive information, and a whole lot more (not to mention make a slave out of you who are addicted to that infernal little machine). Sometimes the thing that cell phone doesn't do very well is give you a good phone connection. You know, audio drop-outs. It's what ABC broadcaster Paul Harvey has called "function fatigue." As a life-long participant in ministry, I suspect that those of us in church leadership roles have some "function fatigue" as well. We often forget, don't we, that our job is to win the lost at any cost. We get caught up in meetings, endless bylaws, bureaucratic committees (all too often made up of personnel who've never done much but sit on committees), church policy, and ecclesiastical small talk. And boy, if someone dares to mention that the emperor is not wearing any clothes (remember that old fable?) do we ever get defensive about our ineptitude! We're often not open to new concepts. That's one of the reasons it is so enjoyable to be on the mission field, away from the ecclesiastical "business as usual" mentality where so many of our Christian emissaries are cutting-edge in their effectiveness for the Master.

To continue doing the same old thing over and over and somehow expecting different results is truly "function fatigue." I believe God is looking for innovators. No, not someone to change the gospel message, but certainly to update the gospel delivery system. Take church planting, for example. I believe Americans are desperately hungry for the message of Christ. I see that hunger before me every day. But what is the haunting cry of defeatism we hear? "Oh, we're in the post-modern society, the post-Christian environment, and we just can't do this or that. . . ." Function fatigue! May God open our eyes to see the enormity of the spiritual harvest before us and then pray as did David, "Lord . . . strengthen thou me according unto Thy Word!"

Prayer: O God, let me never grow weary in well doing. Correct me when I hang on to old functions that no longer have relevance. Tell me the way to go and how to get there. My fervent prayer is for Your power to do Your work — today! *Amen.*

CLEOPATRA'S BEAUTY MAY HAVE BEEN EXAGGERATED

Proverbs 6:25: Lust not after her beauty in thine heart; neither let her take thee with her eyelids.

Shakespeare wrote, "Age cannot wither her, nor custom stale her infinite variety; other women cloy the appetites they feed, but she makes hungry where most she satisfies." Who was the object of this charming accolade? The bard wrote of the famed queen of Egypt, Cleopatra. The infamously awful film *Cleopatra* 40 years ago featured Elizabeth Taylor in the title role. But now archaeologists have turned up an ancient coin with Cleopatra's picture on it. Apparently Shakespeare and the casting director for that film were mistaken — or easily impressed. The coin image of Cleopatra depicts her with a sharp nose, thick lips, and a protruding chin.[1] Enough to "shiver the timbers," as Bluebeard might have observed. "Aha!" retorts the historian, "but if you were with her, her presence was irresistible and her conversation and voice were bewitching." Yes, well, they would just about have to be if the coin image is right.

Reminds me of the lyrics of a great old gospel song: "People often see you / as you are outside / Jesus really knows you / for He sees inside."[2] It's fairly easy to dress up the body or doll up the face, but it's much more difficult to transition the soul. Only Christ can do that. Paul put it this way: "Old things are passed away . . . all things are become new" (2 Cor. 5:17).

Oh, by the way, Cleopatra is still alive today. Did you know that? She is in eternity somewhere. Her body possibly lies in some musty Egyptian tomb or a museum somewhere, forgotten by most of society. But her soul is more alive now than ever before — either with God or without Him.

So her chin and nose shapes weren't really all that important, were they?

1. Original quote by William Shakespeare, *Antony and Cleopatra*, 1606; used in "Ancient Coin Undermines Legend of Cleopatra's Beauty," by Robert Barr, Associated Press, 2/15/07; displayed on USAToday.com.
2. Author unknown.

PRAYER: O God, teach me a proper perspective regarding soul and body. Yes, I want to appear the best I can to those around me, but even more do I want to appear in my best perspective inwardly to You! Help me learn the difference between things temporal and things eternal and then live accordingly. Amen.

RELEASING TALENTED PEOPLE TO CHANGE THE WORLD

Ephesians 4:7

Out of the generosity of Christ, each of us is given his own gift (MSG).

Deep-sea fishing is a great sport in my part of the world. Almost without exception, especially with game fish, we're "catch-and-release" anglers (well, with the possible exceptions of the occasional trout or red). Pastor Robert Lewis of Minnesota wrote, "Jesus was a catch-and-release fisherman. He would catch men and women with His gospel and spend time with them to develop, season, and ground them in God's ways, but then ... He'd release them!"[1] I call it the Lazarus principle: "Loose him ... and let him go!"

Unfortunately, in the church world our modus operandi is all-too-often, "Let's try to catch 'em and get 'em on the stringer, tightly attached to the boat!" I have preached over the past 50 years in about 1,600 churches in this country alone. Many times I encounter church leadership with no concept of catch-and-release. It's thumbs-on control! Micro-managing! Frankly, I've

never understood that concept. Talk about diminishing returns! The goal should be to surround yourself with brilliant people, much smarter than you are in their field, show them the basic direction you feel God wants you to go, and then set them free! Free enterprise is much more profitable than slavery.

This principle holds true for denominations and/or fellowships. We often want all the pastors and workers to go down a very narrow channel; a ditch might be a better name for the trench. Someone has ventured that a rut is just a grave with the ends knocked out. Hey, today's generation will simply walk away from such stringent direction. Today's young leaders see limitless skies and boundless opportunities. We older folks in leadership positions need to impart the wisdom of our years to these kids, train them in biblical principles and foundational theology, undergird them with prayer, and loose them and let them go! They will impact the world!

1. Alexis Wilson, "Four Models for Transforming Marketplace Leaders into Kingdom Leaders"; page 2, http://www.successtosignificance.com/Resources/FourModels.pdf.

Byline #78

PRAYER

O God, help me stop trying to defend my position or place in the Kingdom rather than building up Your name throughout the earth. Teach me to truly pray — and mean it — "Thy will be done on earth as it is in heaven." Anoint the younger generation as they take us to new dimensions in You. Amen.

FROM CHAINS OF IRON TO CHAINS OF GOLD

Genesis 37:28

> Then there passed by Midianites merchantmen; and they drew and lifted up Joseph out of the pit, and sold Joseph to the Ishmeelites for twenty pieces of silver: and they brought Joseph into Egypt.

On several occasions I have driven from Jerusalem to Cairo, Egypt. Each time, I have wondered what it must have been like for young Joseph, sold into slavery by his own brothers and arriving in the land of the Nile in chains. As the teenager looked on his surroundings, the great pyramids were already well over a thousand years old. The meandering Nile, the longest river in the world, rolled north toward its ultimate destination, leaving fertile, muddy soil in the richly productive Delta. Papyrus boats plied the waters, carrying even more wealth to the pharaoh. Joseph was only 18 years old when he entered the strange land. He left it for eternity at the age of 110. I love author John Phillips' line: "Joseph came to Egypt with an iron chain on his wrist, but he lived with a gold chain on his neck."[1]

Within a short period of time, Joseph was the overseer of a household. But that was not God's plan for his life. God meant for this young Jew to become the overseer of the world. Not even a voluptuous temptress could dissuade him from his unshakeable faith in God.

Joseph's example causes us to dwell on the reality that so many, unlike him, accept plan B (or plan X, for that matter) for their lives when God's plan was always A. Jeremiah wrote: " 'For I know the plans I have for you,' declares the Lord, 'plans to prosper you and not to harm you, plans to give you hope and a future'" (Jer. 29:11; NIV). Scriptures teach us to trust in the Lord and lean not to our own meager understanding (Prov. 3:5). Joseph trusted God and saved the world from starvation.

PRAYER

> O God, if only I would just believe what You say in Your Word! I want to learn to trust You. Joseph did and impacted the world. I don't ask to be a Joseph; I just ask to be me — but abandoned to Your will for my life. Amen.

Do you ever wonder what you could accomplish through Christ in your life if you would just commit all your ways to Him?

1. John Phillips, *Exploring Genesis: An Expository Commentary* (Grand Rapids, MI: Kregel Publ., 2001).

Passion for the lost

Proverbs 10:5: He that gathereth in summer is a wise son: but he that sleepeth in harvest is a son that causeth shame.

It is not hard for any objective observer to note what has happened to the spiritual harvest in America. So many of the workers who are supposed to be in the field are asleep in the barn and, further, don't really care much, one way or the other. The lethargy in American churches is sobering! Passion for the lost is disappearing in a personal "feel good" spiritual orgy.

I have recently returned from India. There I watched clergy and laity alike who live and breathe reaching their friends, families, and neighbors for Christ. I spoke in a church in the south of India one Sunday in a building that is about 25 years old. Now let this sink in: *In all those 25 years, there has never been one single moment that there have not been people physically in the building praying — no matter what time of day — interceding for the lost of India!* Besides the intercession, those people are infiltrating their society at every level, in every caste system. No wonder there were 40,000 present for worship that Sunday.

I related this story to some church leaders the other day, and even showed them videos of what is happening for Christ there. The response? Literally — yawns! I have been told that while the Christian church in America is growing a bit, it's due to the churches that have caught fire and are attracting thousands. On the other side of the coin, studies have shown that up to 60 percent of evangelical churches are in actual numerical decline in this country. Note again the Proverb at the top of this page: "he that sleepeth in harvest is a son that causeth shame." Causes who shame? God himself. What will it take for American churches to wake up? A war? Persecution? May we awaken from our ecclesiastical Rip Van Winkle impressions and get busy with the harvest!

Prayer: O God, more than anything, I do not want to cause You shame or embarrassment. Even in my older years, renew my passion for the lost. Renew my zeal again today, Lord! Please! ***Amen.***

A TRUTH LEARNED FROM THE CIVIL WAR

Colossians 3:11: Where there is neither Greek nor Jew, circumcision nor uncircumcision, Barbarian, Scythian, bond nor free: but Christ is all, and in all.

By 1860, the United States was a boiling caldron headed for civil war. There were two issues: slavery and secession from the union. It was not then against the law to own people as slaves. Before the war started, one American in every seven was owned by another American. Four million people were nothing more than chattel. The pro-slave states claimed that the law was on their side and demanded that owning people was their right. In Boston in 1861, William Lloyd Garrison published an anti-slavery newspaper. In an editorial championing the cause of liberty, he wrote, "That which is not just is not law!"

Americans today are losing some liberties, not just to systems opposed to our democratic way of life but to institutions within our nation. If a law is going to be proffered that in some way, shape, or form restricts the legitimate freedoms of another human being, that law must be just. Many of our social institutions are ringleaders in rights infringements. May it be so, please God, that the church is never part and parcel of this deterioration of liberty.

Read the constitution of your church. It may be ecclesiastical law, but is it just ecclesiastical law? If so, it will certainly coincide with biblical tenets. Is a person restricted in your church because of race or gender? Scripture teaches us that whom Christ sets free is free indeed. As a child of God, I live in a moral, spiritual, social liberty that I dare not violate. Nor dare anyone restrict that precious liberty that is mine by virtue of Christ's death on the cross. Remember Garrison's editorial, "That which is not just is not law!"

Prayer: O God, You sent Jesus to this sin-chained planet to set us free! Biblical liberty is a heritage of the cross. Help us to never violate Your divine plan by instituting man-made challenges You never intended to clog the flow. Use me to set spiritual captives at liberty! Amen.

THIEVES IN THE HOUSE OF GOD

Malachi 3:8

Will a man rob God? Yet ye have robbed me. But ye say, Wherein have we robbed thee? In tithes and offerings.

A buddy of mine who pastors a huge Southern Baptist church recently told his flock, "This church has never one time been broken into. Our security system is superb. Well, let me correct that: we have been robbed here. Every Sunday morning when the offering plate is passed. Some of you don't tithe!" Pretty plain talk, wouldn't you say?

But biblically right on. Each April, Americans' thoughts turn to money and the tax deadline on the 15th. I suspect that most of us still had shekels left in our pockets. The average American lives better than 99.4 percent of all the human beings who have ever lived, observes Gregg Easterbrook, author of *The Progress Paradox*.[1] So ... are *you* a tither?

The first question I ask, as a pastor, of any prospective employee in our church is exactly that: are you a tither? I would never knowingly hire someone who would rob God. My goodness, if they would rob God, think what they would do to our church. David Barrett, author of World Christian Trends, reports that while Christians (including nominal, or name-only ones) comprise one-third of the world's population, they receive 53 percent of the entire world's income. Sadly, they spend 98 percent of their after-tax money on themselves. Only 3 to 5 percent of Christian adults tithe to their church, although most would tell you a different story. The typical alleged tither gives about $1,200 annually to the church, which means the giver is testifying to an annual income of $12,000, far below poverty wages.

What if everyone gave in your church the way you do? What kind of church would you have? Are you "the weakest link" in your congregation? Tithe belongs to God. And, Malachi adds, it belongs in your local church, the storehouse where you receive spiritual food. So — are *you* a tither?

Byline #82

1. Gregg Easterbrook, *The Progress Paradox* (New York: Random House, 2005).

PRAYER

O God, I thank You for Your sustaining hand to my wife and me for well over a half century. What a privilege it is to present to You the first fruit of our income! And how You have blessed us! Thank You. Amen.

HEY, DON'T FORGET THOSE OF US OVER 60!

2 Timothy 1:5: I call to remembrance the unfeigned faith that is in thee, which dwelt first in thy grandmother Lois, and thy mother Eunice; and I am persuaded that in thee also.

It is often said that many churches today are directing their ministries primarily to the youth. God forbid that we fail to reach today's young generation. But . . . God forbid also that we fail to present a balanced ministry that reaches everyone. Are you aware that there are more Americans *over* the age 65 than *under* the age of 18? That's easy to comprehend when you realize that in 1900 the average life expectancy in America was 47 while today it is 77.

The Church must come up with new and highly creative ways to reach these older Americans, especially since only about four in ten have any religious affiliation, let alone a personal experience with Christ. Yes, we must certainly reach the youth, without question! But we must also impact the older folks as well, not to mention the "sandwich generation" somewhere in the middle. In this day of "specialized" everything, does the Church have the prerogative of leaving out some age categories? As a pastor, I would think not.

The word "balance" comes into play here. In reaching the older generation, are we providing meaningful experiences, helpful, spiritually uplifting times together? Or are we just eating cake and ice cream and playing Rook or Scrabble? Someone has termed what I'm talking about here as "intergenerational ministry." I tell you, if we could truly mobilize those in churches over the age of 60 or so, we could shake the entire nation. These folks have time and resources. They have friends that only they could reach for Christ. They all have eternal souls and destinies. They deserve our attention. They deserve effective ministry!

PRAYER: O God, I thank You for long life. I am blessed! But I intercede for millions of others who have also been blessed with physical life, but not with spiritual life. In my zeal to reach the youth, may I not set aside those whose hair has grayed and will soon be in eternity. Anoint me to touch their lives, too. Amen.

Too little, too late in Tuzla!

1 Thessalonians 4:10: And indeed ye do it toward all the brethren which are in all Macedonia: but we beseech you, brethren, that ye increase more and more.

Some time ago, an 18-year-old kid went on a shooting rampage in a mall in Salt Lake City. In six minutes, he shot nine customers, killing five and seriously wounding the others. When he would not surrender his shotgun, police shot and killed him. The boy, a Muslim and a native of Bosnia, was buried in Tuzla, a city north of Sarajevo.

I know the city of Tuzla fairly well, having spent time there shortly after the genocidal war between the Serbs and Muslims ended some years ago. Some churches in our part of Florida raised several hundred thousand dollars to build a church and feeding center in Tuzla. (We also worked in Sarajevo and Mostar.) You cannot imagine the devastation in Bosnia after that massive killing spree. The most noticeable horrors to me were makeshift cemeteries everywhere and the almost unbelievable lack of young men. Why the lack? They had been slaughtered wholesale in the battle. The kid who did the shooting in Salt Lake City was from that area. His family reported he had deep emotional scar tissue because of the things he had seen and experienced in Bosnia.

Here's my very sobering thought: What if we could have started a church in Tuzla earlier? What if more churches in our state had given? What if we had been able to impact that boy for Christ before he ever left Tuzla? What if he had met Christ instead of Allah? (No, they are not the same!) What if . . . what if . . . what if . . . ! Oh, my friend, every time we have the opportunity to give in a missions' offering we must do it, and with joyful generosity. Christ put us on this earth to be His emissaries, His witnesses. What we do makes a difference. But what if we do . . . nothing? Or give nothing? How in the world will we ever face God?

Prayer: O God, a dead boy from near Macedonia sobers our minds today. He was lost to humanity and eternity because we didn't get to him in time. Impress upon our hearts today the urgency of missions, of outreach, of evangelism. May situations such as this Bosnia boy be the unfortunate exception and not the rule. *Amen.*

WELL, DON'T BLAME ME!

> **Genesis 3:12**
>
> And the man said, The woman whom thou gavest to be with me, she gave me of the tree, and I did eat.

The United States Supreme Court recently threw out a nearly $80 million judgment against the Philip Morris tobacco company. A lower court had awarded that amount in damages to the widow of a long-time smoker. In fact, it is reported that he smoked two packs of cigarettes a day for 45 years before dying of lung cancer a decade ago. The widow had won the preliminary judgment after contending in court the major judgment was appropriate, as it punished the tobacco company for decades-long "massive market-directed fraud" that misled people into thinking cigarettes were not dangerous or addictive. The victim allegedly never gave any credence to the surgeon general's health warnings.

While I would have wept no tears had the Court ruled the other way, I have to wonder: at what point do people take responsibility for their own lives? For example, most coffee drinkers, such as myself, want their coffee extremely hot. So if I then spill that steaming brew on myself, is it not my fault? If I die of cirrhosis of the liver after a lifetime of boozing, is it my fault or the whisky-maker's? If I commit a crime and now face the penalty, is it my fault or did my mother or father do something wrong in my upbringing?

How wonderful it would be if we could live up to our own responsibilities and say, "My fault!" How hard is that? According to Genesis 3, that admission was too tough for Adam. He blamed his wife, Eve, for his downfall. His weakness set the tone for the human race, didn't it? Yes, Eve enticed Adam, but he acquiesced to it. No one twisted his arm.

> **PRAYER**
>
> O God, give me the courage, the backbone, to stand behind my own decisions and not attempt to blame someone else. And may I listen to the teaching voice of Your Holy Spirit so I don't make bad choices. Lead me today, I ask! Amen.

We want to blame parents, government, teachers, judges, TV shows, popular music, and other forces for our problems. True, they can all influence our decisions, but after all, we do make our own choices, don't we?

EXCELLENCE IN THE HOUSE OF GOD

Exodus 25:3–4

And this is the offering which ye shall take of them; gold, and silver, and brass, And blue, and purple, and scarlet, and fine linen, and goats' hair.

When 80-year-old Moses ascended Mount Sinai, God gave him the Ten Commandments and the plans for the tabernacle in the wilderness. Moses was to challenge the people of Israel to bring supplies for the construction of the tabernacle. Those supplies included "fine linen."

As a pastor of nearly four decades, I am extremely concerned about Christians doing their best for the Church. I am not addressing "style" of worship here because that is open to all kinds of likes, backgrounds, and needs. But I certainly am addressing quality in God's house. God requested "fine linen" for the tabernacle, not throwaway junk. The very least we can offer God is our best. All too often, I have personally witnessed far, far less than fine linen offered in church. For example: church services that have not been prayed through and thought out. Just kind of "winging it," you know? I speak in scores of churches every year, primarily in missions' conventions. Many of those churches are dirty or unkempt. The bathrooms would not pass any health code requirements. The lobbies are less than clean and pleasant and the church grounds are untended. The church neighbors must find it embarrassing to have the building there, as it downgrades everyone's property values. What kind of testimony is this?

The way we keep God's house is a reflection of our deepest inner thoughts of Him. If our concepts of God are noble, lofty, and majestic, as they well should be, then His house will reflect those values. No, the church does not have to be some multi-million-dollar facility. The singers do not have to be from the Metropolitan Opera House. But our offerings to God should be fine linen, that is, the very best we can offer our precious Lord.

Byline #86

PRAYER

O God, forgive me if I ever think less-than-noble thoughts about You or Your house of worship. As David and Solomon, let my first thoughts be about Your temple and thoughts about my dwelling place be subsequent to that. May I want and pursue the acquisition of fine linen in all my dealings with Your church. Amen.

WHAT IN THE WORLD ARE YOU TRYING TO DO?

2 Timothy 4:2: Preach the word; be instant in season, out of season; reprove, rebuke, exhort with all longsuffering and doctrine.

These words from Paul, scratched on parchment by the light of a flickering candle, deep within Nero's death dungeon, remain vital to everyone in Christian leadership today. There are many accolades you can ascribe to the Apostle's ministry, and one of those is relevance. Relevancy doesn't have as much to do with methods as it does with principles. Methods can be like Saul's armor; the suit may fit the king, but it's excess baggage on the shepherd boy. Principles are transferable. Such as this one: What is the stated, printed, well-known philosophy of your ministry? Is it clearly understood by one and all what you are trying to do?

When I was a young pastor, decades ago, this concept of fully understanding what I was trying to do was drilled into my mind by a highly successful and caring pastor. I learned quickly that if I did not have a God-given plan for almost anything in my life, my activities for the Lord quickly meandered into meaninglessness. A well-known pastor helped me the most when he said, "Dan you have to be able to answer three basic questions about your work for God: (1) What are you trying to do? (2) How do you plan to go about it? (3) What motivates you to stay on course?"

The first of those questions (the "what") is your philosophy of service to God. The second question (the "how") is your vision. The Bible warns flatly that without vision people die. Most Christians will tell you most sincerely that they are trying to reach their area for Christ. Fine. But how do they plan to do that? Such success in evangelism doesn't just "happen." And the third question puts in place very firmly your reason for ministry unto God (and yes, we are all ministers unto God!). If our motivation is not to exalt Christ and give Him the glory, then we are wasting our time as far as the Judgment Seat of Christ is concerned. Read very carefully 1 Corinthians 3.

Prayer: O God, help me to understand my mission in life. Teach me how to accomplish it. And help me examine my motivation for everything I do. If it's for my own pride, forgive me. If what I do is truly for You, help me! Amen.

The house of the hopeless

Matthew 25:43: I was a stranger, and ye took me not in: naked, and ye clothed me not: sick, and in prison, and ye visited me not.

From my driveway to the Florida Death Row is 284 miles. Every other month, I make the trip on a Friday night, staying in a tiny hotel in Starke. By 7:30 Saturday morning, I am at the prison gate going through the prescribed rigmarole that finally gets me past six sliding, locked doors into the death house an hour later. I never get used to it — the electrified fences that will kill you instantly should you touch one and the coiled razor wire atop them, the sliding locked doors behind me, the vacant stares of the guys who have been on the row for as many as 30 years, and the fear in the faces of the new inmates. Across the roadway is the small building where inmates spend their last nights before being strapped to a gurney and having the lethal needle inserted into a waiting arm.

There are nearly 350 guys currently on Florida's death row. The justice system is so convoluted that some of them have languished there for 30 years. The average time between pronouncement of the death sentence to the actual execution is usually about 11 to 12 years. Yet some men have died after as few as 5 years. Makes no sense, does it? The wait depends upon the attorneys, the judges, the prosecutors . . . the money.

For Christmas last year, our church wanted to do something special for all the inmates. The warden said no. All we were allowed to do was put a dozen cookies and a can of coke in each cell. But you would have thought we gave them something of terrific value. Such mundane offers are treasures in this house of extinguished dreams and hopeless days.

So why do I make that long and truly harrowing trip? Simple. It's a task put upon me by the Holy Spirit himself. Jesus said, "Inasmuch as ye did it not to one of the least of these, ye did it not to me" (Matt. 25:45). That's really all I need to know.

Prayer: O God, don't let my heart ever become so hardened that I forget those behind bars. Some deserve to be there, I know; others do not. All of them deserve to know the love of Christ. Let the beauty of Jesus be seen in me to these men waiting to die. May I make at least some kind of hopeful difference in their lives. ***Amen.***

THE STORED FILES ON GOD'S COMPUTER

1 John 1:7: But if we walk in the light, as he is in the light, we have fellowship one with another, and the blood of Jesus Christ his Son cleanseth us from all sin.

One night recently, sleep would not come, so I made my way into my study. I turned on a computer that I had not used for a year. When it finally came on, I started searching the files. I was pleasantly surprised to find pictures of our family there that I had forgotten were ever taken — or still existed. Some of those shots were okay, but others were rejects best forgotten. I thought about deleting them but changed my mind. After all, they are good records of the past, warts and all.

It made me remember that God has on His eternal computer the lives of us all. Some of those memories are quite grim. I think, for example, about the apostle Paul. He had the death of the martyr Stephen on his files. But after his encounter with Christ on the road to Damascus, those files were permanently deleted. God's record of the Apostle begins not at Jerusalem but Damascus! Small wonder that Paul testified that all the old things of life pass away when we come to Christ and all things become new. The powerful and cleansing blood of Jesus not only blots out the old records of our lives but also totally eradicates them — to the point where God says that by an act of His sovereign will He cannot remember those stains on our record at all. I tell you, that's a marvel of the new birth!

Recently I heard someone on TV say, "I'm a Christian, but not one of the born-again ones." Well, thank God I *am* one of them! Truth is, I don't know of any other kind of Christian. So — that old computer the other night made me very thankful for my memories of the new birth experience. Now I think I'll just go ahead and delete those awful pictures. I think all my family members will feel better about it.

PRAYER: O God, I am so thankful that the blood of Jesus covers my past! What a relief to know that there is nothing in our lives that cannot be eradicated because of His death on the cross. What can wash away my sins? Nothing but the blood of our Savior! To Him be all glory for such victory over sin! Amen.

FISHING WITHOUT BAIT

Matthew 4:19

And he saith unto them, Follow me, and I will make you fishers of men.

Do you like to fish? Me, too! Especially when I'm actually catching them. Near my home on the Gulf of Mexico, the fishing can be sensational. I watched my wife hook, play, and land a five-foot tarpon not long ago. Wow, was she impressive! (My wife, not the fish!) The baits we use run the gamut from small fish to squid to worms. Now, believe it or not, I have never eaten a worm, although I have consumed a squid. Just one. There won't be a second one. But the fish we try to catch like those awful creatures. See, the bait is for the fish, not the fisherman. Oh, another thing intrinsic to angling: I've never had a fish come to me and ask to be hooked; I have always had to go to the water and search for them.

An unhappy person reminded me the other day of the philosophical mandate of our church: Reach/Teach/Send. She explained that she rather liked the Teach/Send part, but not the reaching aspect. She said we were catching fish she didn't really like on our "stringer." And she vociferously objected to our bait.

Here's what bothered her: We recently dedicated a small part of our church lobby to a sitting area where people can congregate, sit around, talk — and (dare I say it?) even drink coffee. Now I'm the last pastor who wants the church lobby to look like McDonald's; however, with the proper care, that small spot in the foyer can serve as a grand fishing dock for souls. That's what it's for. But the lady objected because . . . well, primarily because it was just different! She said to me, "Pastor, the church lobby ought to be sacred." I asked her, "Is there anything more sacred than obeying Christ's command to be fishermen?" She replied, "Yes, keep coffee out of the church lobby!" In other words, catch fish without any bait.

Byline #90

PRAYER

O God, we take extremely seriously Your mandate to evangelize Jerusalem, Judea, Samaria, and the uttermost parts of the world. May our motives always be proper and our fishing gear in good order. May our stringer be full of precious souls to present to You on that eternal day when we dock our boat for the final time. Amen.

THE JOY OF GIVING

> The liberal soul shall be made fat: and he that watereth shall be watered also himself.
>
> Proverbs 11:25

USA Today reporter Martha Moore reported recently that during the year there were 21 charitable gifts, each in excess of $100 million. The biggest was Warren Buffet's commitment of over $43 billion to universities and hospitals. Moore's summary was this: "The reason for the increase in mega-gifts is simple: There are more people with deep pockets."[1] Another source, Stacy Palmer, editor of the *Chronicle of Philanthropy,* reported, "It's a sign that wealth is growing and people are just raising their sights in terms of giving."[2] Stanley Katz, Princeton University professor, said, "It's sort of gotten out there that it's the right thing to do to be generous."[3]

Now most Christians could not dream of giving such lavish amounts (and if they could, I wish they were members of the church I pastor). But they can certainly start by giving God what He absolutely requires, His tenth — or 10 percent — of their income. But note this: tithing is not giving. That 10 percent is God's in the first place. Our giving comes after that.

I often hear it said, "I cannot afford to give." The Bible teaches that God blesses givers. But hear this: we don't give to get! As a pastor, I never teach that kind of motivation. We give simply because we love God. It has been rightly said that God blesses us not so we can increase the level of our living, but so that we can increase the level of our giving. Do you know that expert church pollsters believe that fewer than 3 percent of all Christians actually tithe of their income? How sad!

Now here's a question for you to ponder today: What if every follower of Christ in your church were as faithful in giving to Him as He is in giving to us?

> **PRAYER**
>
> O God, I want to be a liberal soul, one made fat by Your goodness and faithfulness. Let any vestige of a carnal "Scrooge" mentality be stricken from my soul. May I be a giver for the sole joy of just being . . . a giver! Amen.

1. Martha Moore, "Philanthropy Hits Record as Number of $100 Million Donations Increase," *USA Today* (Feb. 26, 2007).
2. Ibid.
3. Ibid.

Entrepreneurial ministry in Barbados

Acts 9:15 But the Lord said unto him, Go thy way: for he is a chosen vessel unto me, to bear my name before the Gentiles, and kings, and the children of Israel.

Make no mistake about it: Paul was an entrepreneur in the ministry! He dared to go where few even dreamed of entering. That is one of the reasons God used him so powerfully. Entrepreneurial leadership in expanding God's kingdom around the world usually yields an overflowing harvest (and not only around the world but in our own home towns as well). Here is an example of what I am proclaiming: Nearly 50 years ago, Holmes Williams was an up-and-coming businessman in the West Indies and Canadian banking. He and his wife, Rosie, found Christ as their Savior and were soon called into ministry in their home of Bridgetown, Barbados. They took a tiny church and began to pour their lives into it.

Recently, it was my joy to return to that island after a 20-year hiatus and preach at the Peoples' Cathedral once again. The Sunday morning crowd was over 5,000, the usual complement of attendees. And on Sunday night the cathedral was packed with people — even sitting outside on the church lawn to enjoy the service. When God called Holmes to that work, He told him what to do and how to do it. It is to that preacher's credit that he never swerved from the divine call. Holmes had more than his share of critics in the beginning days who complained, "Holmes, this is not the way missions should work!" And, "We've never done it that way before!" But the One who called my friend to Bridgetown had nail prints in His hands, not a pencil. Holmes listened to that One, believed, and obeyed.

A committee will never save the world, but brave soldiers of the Cross who march to divine rhythm, who hear the voice of God and respond strongly and affirmatively, can reach it effectively. Read some good church history books for more validation to this truth.

Prayer: O God, I do want to do my work for You effectively and thoroughly. I understand You may call me to methods that fall "out of the box." Don't let me fear that, but to trust always in Your guidance. You never fail, and You're never wrong. *Amen.*

MOM

Proverbs 31:10: Who can find a virtuous woman? for her price is far above rubies.

My childhood was decades ago, but I think about it often and with great delight. I cannot remember any bleakness about it at all. I was blessed with a great mother and father. Both have long since departed into glory. My mother was not the typical, tied-apron, apple-pie-cooking, rosy-cheeked matron of *Saturday Evening Post* cover fame. She was quite a tough woman, actually. Tough enough to keep living plus running her nursing home ten years after doctors wrote her off with cancer. The ladies in her care loved her, including the aunt of Bob Barker (of *The Price Is Right* fame). Bob once wrote me a handwritten note expressing his gratitude for Mom's care of his loved one. And Mom was determined enough to dissuade the Missouri State Legislature from closing nursing homes operated in facilities not built for that purpose.

Mom was also tough enough to me and my brother, who had a very successful career in banking. It can truthfully be said that Mother never took any nonsense from anyone. The discipline she ingrained in us two boys has stood us in good stead. Neither he nor I could ever disqualify ourselves from any challenge with puny protests of incapability. "Nonsense!" she would cry, "my boys can face every challenge of life — and I'll see to it that they do!" Frankly, I'm grateful for that stability in upbringing. Life is not easy. No one owes us a living. Mom saw to it that we could care for ourselves. And both she and Dad were in church faithfully, like every Sunday (twice) and every Wednesday. She taught us God's Word. She sang gospel songs to us, although her voice was, uh, was atrocious.

My brother and I can celebrate Mother's Day every weekend, I suspect. We were blessed. We could not have asked for better.

Prayer: O God, I thank You for such a spiritual and social heritage. We never had much money, but I was an adult before I knew that fact. Let me be a link in a continuing chain of faithful parenthood (and grand-parenthood). Amen.

GOD'S GPS

Psalm 139:9–10

If I take the wings of the morning, and dwell in the uttermost parts of the sea; Even there shall thy hand lead me, and thy right hand shall hold me.

Recently I had to buy a car. Because I go to quite a few places to speak, I decided to spring for a GPS, a global positioning system. I don't understand much about the system yet (on one occasion the thing took me to a wrong town — my fault!) but when it works, it's pretty smooth. The first time I actually got the GPS to function properly it just blew me away. There I was, out in the toolies somewhere, and the screen in front of me lit up, showing me exactly where I was. Every place that car moved, so did the arrow on the screen, guiding me exactly to the place I wanted to go. I was also receiving audible instructions from the voice of a very soft-spoken lady. Somewhere in space, a satellite was keeping tabs on me and where I was. It didn't matter how many times I changed directions, that GPS knew exactly where I was. And when I listened to that marvelously soft voice, the lady told me exactly where I needed to turn.

It makes me think: if a man-made hunk of metal, careening somewhere in space, knows my exact whereabouts at any given time, then why in the world wouldn't *God* know where I was? David made his thoughts on that query pretty obvious in the text I used at the top of the page. On a negative side, God knows what I'm doing all the time, so I'd better watch it! But on the positive side, it doesn't matter what I may be doing or going through, God is there and knows everything about the situation. Further, He is ready to guide me through my "lostness." I may not be consciously aware that God is there, but He is there nonetheless.

I don't really have to have much faith to conceive this reality. All I have to do is climb into my little car and turn on that GPS. It's only a tiny microcosm of the omniscience of Almighty God.

Byline #94

PRAYER

O God, how thankful I am that even the darkness will be light about me! It is such a relief to know by faith that You are understanding of every nuance of my life at this very moment. Not only that, if I will just listen, Your voice will guide me to the right destiny! How reassuring! Thank You! Amen.

TRANSFORMATION

Romans 12:2: And be not conformed to this world: but be ye transformed by the renewing of your mind, that ye may prove what is that good, and acceptable, and perfect, will of God.

I used to drive by an old rickety commercial store in a nearby town. Talk about an eyesore! A hurricane would have done about a thousand dollars' worth of improvements! The place spread out for almost a city block. Finally, the owners decided to abandon doing business there and put the whole thing up for sale. Oh, it sat vacant for a long time. Then a church purchased it. Everyone wondered, "Have those people lost their minds?" Last week I had occasion to drive by it again. I was shocked. What had happened to that old facility? Oh, it was still there, but what a transformation! The congregation, now numbering in the thousands, put their hearts and minds (and pocketbooks) to work and turned that hideous monstrosity into one of the most beautiful church venues I have ever seen. And what a parking lot!

It nudged my mind to think a bit about people whose lives have been transformed by the redeeming power of Christ. I thought about Jim LaMarr, whom I had the joy of leading to Christ 35 years ago. He had been a hard-living film producer in Hollywood. Then he met Christ and became a film producer for Bill Bright and Campus Crusade until the day he died. I thought about one of the leading clergymen in our city who motorcycled into our town from New York about 35 years ago, a drugged-up hippie. Then he gave his life to Christ and now pastors one of the truly great churches in all our part of the state.

What a difference Christ makes in a life! He transforms it!

PRAYER: O God, I thank You that I'm not that "old man" I used to be. I'm not what I'm going to be, at least not yet, but thank You for the terrific progress Your Spirit is making within me. Day by day, I am being transformed. As John put it, I am becoming a child of God! I am thrilled by the very thought of it. Amen.

Suspicious Minds

1 Corinthians 13:7: [Love] beareth all things, believeth all things, hopeth all things, endureth all things.

There appears to be something deep within a lot of folks that makes them want to believe the worst in people. Newspaper publishers know that bad news certainly sells better than good news! Remember the 12 spies from the Children of Israel whom Moses sent into the Promised Land to "spy it out"? Ten brought back horror stories while only two returned with a positive report.

I sit on several committees in which potential church leaders are evaluated. Several on those committees can see a bogeyman behind every bush. They could find something negative to say about Mother Teresa. Maybe they've been stung by people in the past so they now protect themselves with a veneer of skepticism. They often eschew reality for what they call "gut" reactions, or "I think," or "I have suspicions." It's almost as if they hope there truly is something wrong with the candidate so they can say, "See, I told you so." These sad people look through coke bottle bottoms rather than through clear lenses. Often, when even confronted by positive truth, they respond with, "Yes . . . but. . . ."

The Bible critiques these attitudes. First Corinthians 13, the famed "love chapter" of the New Testament, teaches that real love believes all things, does not ponder the wrong in review, and refuses to harbor dark thoughts that are rooted in nothing more than suspicion. Yes, I grant you, dear friend, that we can sometimes get hurt by unscrupulous people who take advantage of us. But that should not change our focus. Christ takes us at our word. He believes in us. He doesn't forsake us, even when we stumble. You and I are to be Christ-like. So how can we accept a lesser standard of evaluation than our Lord? All of us should read 1 Corinthians 13 before uttering any criticism. We would be better examples of our Master if we did. And the world would be much quieter.

Prayer: O God, forgive me for having a suspicious mind. Let me see the best in everyone. I will leave the judging to You. ***Amen.***

MISPLACED JUDGMENT

1 Samuel 16:7
But the LORD said unto Samuel, Look not on his countenance, or on the height of his stature; because I have refused him: for the LORD seeth not as man seeth; for man looketh on the outward appearance, but the LORD looketh on the heart.

It's very easy to make snap judgments based on initial appearances, that can be very mistaken. Someone recently gave me a copy of author Russell Schneider's enormous book, *The Cleveland Indians Encyclopedia,*[1] which tells Cleveland fans, such as myself, everything you could ever want to know about that American League baseball team. For instance: In 1949, a former great ballplayer, Hank Greenberg, became the farm director for the team (meaning he carefully perused the talent coming up in the minor leagues). This was a classic case of "the Peter principle" — that is, being elevated to a position for which one has no competence. Greenberg was told to scout three players and send back a report on each of them. Greenberg's response was that one of the guys had a hitch in his swing and would never hit major league pitching; another of the three, Greenberg said, was too slow and could not play big-league shortstop; and the third player, he reported, just couldn't hit a curve ball. He refused to sign them. Those three players, in order, were Hank Aaron, Ernie Banks, and (ready for this?) Willie Mays, three of the all-time greats in baseball history. How different would the prowess of my beloved Indians have been if Greenberg had been a better judge of ability?

I remember the number of people who told me 55 years ago that I had no future in the ministry and should try some other "line of work." The problem was this: the One who called me had nail prints in His hands. My critics didn't. God looks on the heart of a person. Remember, He designed and created you; He ought to know your capabilities better than anyone. Those critical outsiders usually don't know you. So don't be disheartened when you are rejected early in life.

PRAYER
O God, don't let me be discouraged when there are those who would disparage my call, my talent, and my determination. You are my Master Designer. Your approval is all I need to continue on in my "pilgrim's progress." By Your grace, I will continue on, in Your strength and love! Amen!

(Willie Mays could have been a Cleveland Indian player? I need to go lie down!)

1. Russell Schneider, *The Cleveland Indians Encyclopedia* (Philadelphia, PA: Temple University Press, 1996).

GOD MAY CHANGE THE DIRECTION OF YOUR LIFE ... TODAY!

Jeremiah 29:11

For I know the thoughts that I think toward you, saith the LORD, thoughts of peace, and not of evil, to give you an expected end.

You never know how quickly your life can be changed. In 1967, my wife and I walked into an arena in Pittsburgh, Pennsylvania. We had come to hear the well-known evangelist Dr. Ford Philpot for an evening service of the Christian and Missionary Alliance General Conference. I found myself captivated by the gravel-voiced preacher, his clear-cut message, and his Kentucky twang. Also, his sense of humor was refreshing. I never heard any preacher ever give stronger altar calls — especially for men to receive Christ.

A couple of years later, while pastoring in Sandusky, Ohio, the evangelical churches had an area-wide crusade for Christ, the first in their history. Dr. Philpot and his team were invited to lead us in the eight-day effort. The Lord had been dealing with me that a change was coming in my ministry, but I had no idea what it would be. When the crusade was over, Dr. Philpot asked me to spend a few days with him. During that time he said, "Dan, I want you to pray about coming to our home city of Lexington, Kentucky, and serving as my associate evangelist. I want you to write and produce our syndicated television show, *The Story*, edit our magazine, *The Storyteller*, and preach in crusades that I cannot get to." Three months later my family and I found ourselves moving to the Bluegrass State. For the next three years, I was with that wonderful minister in crusades all over the world. One night in Kinshasa, Zaire, over 100,000 attended a night meeting and thousands came to Christ.

My friend, if you are feeling in your heart that God is about to do something with you, be open to His leading. He knows what is best for your life and His kingdom. It could be this very day that the new path is opened to you.

Byline
#98

PRAYER

O God, may my heart and mind always be tuned in to hear Your voice. I don't want to miss any door that You have opened. You have created me for a special reason, and I pray that my life will truly and accurately reflect that reason. Amen.

WHAT MAKES THE BIBLE DIFFERENT FROM OTHER ALLEGED "HOLY BOOKS"?

2 Peter 1:19: We have also a more sure word of prophecy; whereunto ye do well that ye take heed, as unto a light that shineth in a dark place, until the day dawn, and the day star arise in your hearts.

It is often suggested by media gurus today, in this time of non-absolutes, that all "holy books" are pretty much the same. Nothing could be further from the truth. Only the Bible contains masses of prophetic truth. I have recently been studying once again Daniel's encounter with the angel Gabriel in which was given the 70 weeks prophecy. You can read it for yourself in Daniel 9. The narrative occurred during the Jewish exile in Babylon (current-day Iraq). In that stunningly remarkable prophecy, it was revealed by God that from the date of Persian King Artaxerxes' decree to his Jewish cupbearer Nehemiah to rebuild the temple in Jerusalem to the date when Jesus would enter Jerusalem in triumph, 483 years, each year containing 360 days, would pass exactly. From history (for the facts) with concurrence from the Royal Observatory in Greenwich, England (for the timing), we know that Daniel was accurate to the very day.

In the Old Testament alone there are several hundred detailed prophecies of Jesus' coming birth in Bethlehem, all of which happened precisely as Scripture stated. Someone fed all this information into a computer to find out the odds of each facet of prophecy actually occurring. The odds were 1 in 93, comma, followed by 87 zeroes. With due respect to all other belief systems, none of their holy books has that supernatural aspect. They are simply — books. The Bible, on the other hand, is the total revealed mind of God to mankind. It is supernatural! The more you study the Bible, the stronger your faith will be. Faith comes by hearing. Hearing what? The Word of God! Spend some time studying your Bible today. Your faith will be elevated to new heights as you ask God to make very clear His message for you.

Prayer: O God, I thank You for the written Word. It truly is a lamp unto my feet and a light unto my path (Ps. 119:105). As I read Scriptures today, may their divine and eternal meaning become very clear to me and then by Your life within me, let me so live today that I truly please You. Amen.

The cost of leadership

2 Corinthians 11:6: . . . we have been throughly made manifest among you in all things.

There is more to being a leader than simply election to a position. Any corporation, whether secular, educational, or ecclesiastical, will suffer if personnel are elected to leadership roles simply because of popularity or charisma. Churches face this each year in their business meetings. One of my mentors, the late Leonard Ravenhill, used to say that oftentimes people are elected to a church board simply because they own a gas station and a hot dog stand. Unfortunately, Ravenhill's observations have merit.

There is a cost to leadership. There is the cost of possession of certain giftings, such as instinct. I suspect that leaders are born and not made. How can you teach something like instinct? There is a blessing from the Lord in the mind of a true leader that clearly and almost instinctively guides that leader in the proper direction. That leader somehow just "knows" the right way and the wrong way. No, that instinct does not alleviate in any way the need for study and prayer, but "knowing" is truly a blessing for someone in authority. There is also the cost of a thick skin. You are going to get wounded while exercising leadership efforts. Sometimes those wounds can seem fatal. Small wonder that Scripture admonishes us to put on the whole armor of God. Leaders make decisions sometimes that are right but not popular. Oh, the slings and arrows of outrageous comments that come winging their way to that person. Paul himself said he bore the marks of his calling. But the great leaders just shake off the wounds and keep going.

Great leaders seek the good or benefit of those they represent, not their own well-being. They are glad to sacrifice personal benefits for the overall good of those they represent. So — still want to be a leader? Why? What's your motive for being one? Proper motivation is still another attribute of great leadership.

Prayer: O God, in the role You have placed me, I seek Your strength, Your counsel, and Your guidance. I have no real leadership outside of Your anointing. Help me understand the cost of leadership and never shrug from paying my dues. May I care more about those I represent than myself. *Amen.*

ON BEING STEADFAST
AND UNMOVEABLE

1 Corinthians 15:58 Therefore, my beloved brethren, be ye steadfast, unmovable, always abounding in the work of the Lord, forasmuch as ye know that your labour is not in vain in the Lord.

Webster's Dictionary defines *steadfast* as "firm in purpose, steadily directed, unwavering." Paul's words to us then are, "Christian, be sure of what you're doing and why you're doing it, stay at it no matter what, and don't waffle about!" Yes, I like that!

Paul was not speaking about methodology. Methods change all the time, although we all know some folks whose song is, "Come weal or come woe, my status is quo!" No, the word *steadfast* here has to do with our personal commitment to Christ and our absolutely unshakeable love and faith in Him.

I recall a Youth For Christ rally I attended as a kid. The speaker-singer that night was Phil Kerr, a giant for God back in those long-ago days. He sang a song with this lyrical promise to God: "I'll be true to Jesus / though a thousand voices from the world may call / 'twas He who died to save me / He demands my life, my love, my loyalty, my all."

Let it be understood that circumstances of life can shake you to your very toes. I, too, know what it's like to go through protracted times of real struggle. Yes, there are victories, but let's face it — there are also wounds with resulting scars. So what? As the legendary NFL coach Vince Lombardi used to tell his injured Green Bay Packer players, "Shake it off and get back in the game."

Are we so easily swerved in our direction by any wind of misfortune? Are our eyes taken off our blessed Lord just because someone says something or looks at us crossways? Oh, my discouraged friend, be ye steadfast today, unmovable, always abounding in Christ's work 'til He comes!

PRAYER: O God, how it must break Your heart when You see Your followers become so disoriented by life that they lose their way. Let us be like Paul who looked unto Jesus, the author and finisher of his faith. As we keep our eyes on the Son, the shadows will always remain behind us. Amen.

MY NUTRITIONIST AND ME

Proverbs 13:17

A faithful ambassador is health.

Recently I hired a nutritionist. I must say that, at my age, beginning to eat properly is not unlike putting a new paint job on a '37 Packard. I have always had an aversion to eating anything green except peas. No, I've never been addicted to sweets. Pies, cakes, and even ice cream are not a temptation to me. But starches — like bread, now we're talking! And Kellogg's Raisin Bran — with a couple bananas in it? Heavenly! The nutritionist shivers when she hears my testimony. But patiently, gently (not really), she is teaching me that there are foods that are good for me and foods that are not. Unfortunately, some of those foods I love are not in my best interest. (I heard one comedian say he was eating only healthy foods now, like cheesecake salad.)

I need to understand that to a far greater extent than my nutritionist, God wants me healthy. He wants the best (His best!) for me. The concept of God as the "Ogre of the Skies" is just not scriptural. As reported to us by the Holy Spirit through the prophet Jeremiah, God's thoughts for us are good, healthy, and life giving. When we adhere to His ingredients, our lives are meaningful and fulfilling. It's when we start adding that strawberry shortcake of our own desires that we hit the wall, so to speak.

Well, my nutritionist encourages me. I told her that one day I'd like to be able to shoot my age on the golf course. She assured me that I should be able to as soon as I have my 138th birthday. At any rate, I hope to be healthier than ever as I continue to work for the Lord. Yes, I'll keep going back to my nutritionist, despite her sarcasm. She's helping me help myself to better health. I believe God likes that.

Byline #102

PRAYER

O God, You have challenged us to holiness that is moral, mental, and social health. Our world is so sick that many who are very ill actually think they're normal. In this life I'm never going to have another body, so help me keep this one as physically fit as possible. But even more so, let my soul be healthy. Amen.

IF I FORGET THEE, O JERUSALEM

Byline #103

Each year for several decades, my wife and I have hosted tour groups to our beloved Israel. There are so many joys of journeying there. Even before arriving at the gorgeous new airport in Tel Aviv (Lod), I love to watch peoples' faces as they strain against their seat belts to look out the windows of the plane for their first glimpse of the Promised Land. The first time Darlene and I ever visited Israel was March of 1971. Oh, I remember our excitement. But you know what? Even now, dozens of trips later, the excitement of walking in the footsteps of Jesus remains as strong as ever.

It has been said there are ten measures of beauty in the universe and nine of them belong to Jerusalem. Yes, I know, that's stretching it quite a bit, but Jerusalem does truly get a grip on you such as no other city in the world. Another person observed, "Whoever has not seen Jerusalem in her glory has never seen such a beautiful city in his or her life." King David bought the land for the temple in Jerusalem and, beginning in the south part (the Ophel), began building his capital. Jerusalem was — and remains — the spiritual and cultural lifeblood of the Jewish people. It is a thrill just to walk the streets, hearing the sounds, smelling the aromas, seeing people from all over the planet, and realizing where you are. Well, I cannot even begin to describe that inner sensation. You must see it for yourself.

Tell you what: at least in our imagination, let's go walk around the walls tonight. Let's look to the east across the Kidron Valley toward the Mount of Olives and remember that our Lord Jesus ascended from somewhere on that ridge. Oh my . . . who could ask for anything more?

PRAYER

O God, of all the cities in the world, I wonder if you don't love Jerusalem the most. That's where You gave heaven's most precious gift, the Prince of Glory, to die for the sins of the world. At this moment, on the screen of my imagination, let me walk those stone streets again and remember the price paid for my redemption. Amen.

Good old Luke!

2 Timothy 4:10: For Demas hath forsaken me, having loved this present world, and is departed unto Thessalonica; Crescens to Galatia, Titus unto Dalmatia.

According to a report from *USA Today* (July 31, 2007), the church faithful are growing restless. Writer Cathy Lynn Grossman informs us: "A new study of Protestant churchgoers suggests they're switching from church to church." Nothing new there. We used to call such folks "church hoppers." Bear in mind here that we are discussing people who are not moving to other cities but from one church to another within the city where they live.

Grossman listed some of the reasons the church hoppers gave for transitioning: (1) Their former church failed to engage their faith; (2) The church did not utilize their talents; (3) Another church offered a more appealing doctrine; (4) They liked another preacher better. And so it goes. Interesting to note that it's not just church hopping any longer either; it's denomination hopping.

Church loyalty is becoming a rare virtue. As a pastor for the past four decades, I have seen people who jump from "one spout where the glory comes out" to yet another spout. Let's agree that sometimes churches are less than they should be and families move to another congregation to maintain spiritual food and energy among the members. Other times, people want to be entertained, so they go to this church and then another one because of the "newness" of the experience. Some go to escape responsibility in tithing or volunteering. They want to be inconspicuous spectators in a "strange land." The fact is that great churches are built upon men and women who believe the church is the body of Christ and they serve it faithfully, year in and year out, through good times and bad. Their support is given to the Lord through that church. Pastors come and go, but they stay put. God bless these pillars of the church! By the way, to that Scripture at the top of the page, Paul added, ". . . Luke is with me!" I just want to be a "Luke."

Prayer: O God, if everyone in the church I attend were just like me, what kind of church would it be? I want to be a strong support, one the church leaders can depend upon, a "Luke." You have always been faithful to me; now I commit my faithfulness to Your body on earth, the Church. *Amen.*

THE HARVESTING CAN RUIN THE CROP

Mark 4:29: But when the fruit is brought forth, immediately he putteth in the sickle, because the harvest is come.

It was a sad day in a Midwestern town recently. After nearly 140 years of ministry, one of the mainline churches closed for good. Once a thriving and expanding ministry, the church had only 12 members left. The pastor reported, "Oddly enough, it's not money. It's the lack of woman and manpower. There are just too few of us left to do anything."

Now here's where this story gets our attention. The remnant of the congregation was asked for favorite memories. Note these tell-tale responses: One lady answered, "The communion set is quite special. It's the original one." Another member said, "Oh, I loved the pipe organ. What wonderful music it provided." One fellow responded, "I love the stained-glassed windows. As the light changes, the people depicted look different." Well, you don't have to be Columbo to figure out the problem. Nobody mentioned people! Or evangelism, or outreach, or altars, or the baptistry. They all highlighted "stuff," trappings, symbols. There's no energy in those things! Jesus didn't suffer and die on the cross so the church could have new carpet.

The life of the Church is in the divine impartation of redemption by Christ himself through the Holy Spirit to people. Now think about your church for a moment. What's the first thought that comes to you? Pews? Pulpit? Windows? Hymnals? Carpet? Steeple? Parking lot? If so, your church could be in jeopardy. All these "things" are merely tools. We are not in the tool business; we are in the redemption business. The tools are to help us harvest the lost. A church is in grave peril when it thinks more about its tools than its mission. The harvest is not inside the Church; it's outside. One has to go into the field in order to reap the crop. Let's get our priorities straight in the Church. The harvest will be lost if we don't.

Prayer: O God, all around me today are people who are so terribly lost. Get my mind and heart directed toward them, not the tools needed to reach them. Forgive me for giving more of my attention to stuff instead of souls. Amen.

THE DEATH OF "MR. EXCITEMENT"

Daniel 1:12

Prove thy servants, I beseech thee, ten days; and let them give us pulse to eat, and water to drink.

That was Daniel's diet. It's called: beans and water. How exciting! But it surely worked on the prophet, didn't it? Look at his productivity!

In mid-2007, Tommy Newsom died of cancer. He was 78. Who was he? Those long-time watchers of the old *Tonight Show* starring Johnny Carson remember him well. He was the great saxophone player and arranger in the show's band, headlined by Doc Severinson. He also arranged for many pop singers. The thing that made him so special to millions was his deadpan humor and his image as "Mr. Excitement" — a title he got because of his laid-back style and his ultra-conservative brown suits. But under his mortician's demeanor Newsom was a world-class musician. I used to laugh out loud at his image but delight to his arrangements.

Byline #106

It is a lesson perhaps many of us in God's work need to learn, and I am most certainly including myself. We are so drawn to the splashy, the pizzazz. But it is those workers who stay on the front line, year in and year out, giving substantive work to the Kingdom, day after day, unknown and unsung, who make the difference in most lives. These good folks seldom get the headlines. Most don't have the incredible opportunities on media that have been afforded some of us all these years. They don't receive the letters and calls and cards and e-mails. If they would walk into a church convention, hardly anyone would even know who they are. But God knows them! And they know Him! Their work for eternity will bear gold and silver and precious stones — rewards far more precious than those who sought the applause on earth.

Tommy Newsom was a superb pop musician who never meant to be a ministerial example, I'm sure. But I surely have learned a lot from old "Mr. Excitement."

PRAYER

O God, help me to be much more enamored by faithfulness than fame, more concerned about the Holy Spirit's searchlight than humanity's spotlight. Let me be a loyal "plugger" for the Kingdom all the days of my life. Amen.

HOW LONG CAN A BUILDING STAND WITH CRUMBLING FOUNDATIONS?

2 Timothy 1:5 I know that you sincerely trust the Lord, for you have the faith of your mother, Eunice, and your grandmother, Lois (NLT).

The other night, about ten o'clock, my wife Darlene and I sat on our screened-in back patio, sipping diet cokes and chatting. We did so for a long time. It's a strange thing, but we grew up about 50 miles apart (she in South Dakota and I in Iowa), and yet we never met. Neither knew the other even existed. Her father was a pastor and mine was a barber. It would seem that the two of us didn't have much in common in our growing-up days. Yet over the years, we have realized the enormous bond we enjoyed, and it was Christ's Church.

We both grew up in Sunday schools. We never failed to attend. We both loved summer vacation Bible schools. Both of us knew the Bible very well by the time we were in junior high school. We had both gone to lengthy revival meetings in our respective churches, some of them lasting months, and we were there each night. No, not always willingly. We had both heard the finest evangelists our fellowship could provide. We both attended summer Bible camps and loved them. We each had great pastors; Darlene had her father C.T. Beem and I had Pastor A.M. Alber. Over the past half century or longer, those spiritual foundations have provided the footing we needed in ministry and raising our own four kids. We would have doubtless failed in our life without them.

But what about today's generation? Many churches don't have Sunday schools any longer. Many don't have protracted revival efforts. Some churches don't even have altars. How can any building, and I speak of society here, stand very long without solid foundations? Think about it. Where can the Bible knowledge, the church loyalty, the basics of Christian discipleship originate if churches continue to shrug off their responsibilities? Oh, my friend, let's consider once again foundational Christianity!

PRAYER: O God, this devotional makes me consider my own tie to the Church. Let me see my "discipleship" as You see it. Am I faithful? Or faithless? Is Your Word, the Bible, the lamp of my life? Am I bringing up my progeny in the faith of our fathers? Convict me in this matter, O God, and don't let me fail! Amen.

Don't let catcalls deter your calling

2 Timothy 4:2: . . . be instant in season, out of season . . . with all long suffering. . . .

For many years I pastored in the greater Cleveland, Ohio, area. I became, and remain, a huge fan of the local teams, college and professional. Even now, decades later, I am a passionate fan of the NFL Browns (for whom I did a number of chapel services) and the American League Indians. At that time, the Cleveland Lakefront Stadium was home to both teams, but no longer. Now both have gorgeous new stadiums.

Norm Schachter was a top National Football League referee, certainly one of the most thankless jobs in the country. It is said of these guys that they have to be perfect in the first game they call, and then get better! Schachter was working one of the games at old Lakefront and not having one of his best days. Several of his calls had elicited storms of boos and catcalls. Schachter wore glasses — or contacts, I forget which.

At halftime, he received a telegram. It read, "Saw the first half. Time for a new prescription for your glasses." It was signed by his optometrist!

Leadership is tough, in case you've never tried it, no matter what the arena of endeavor might be. Sometimes you have to make calls that turn out to be brilliant. People say, "Wow, he's good!" At other times both your sanity and your ancestry will be questioned. Uncle Buddy Robinson, the great Nazarene preacher, was told by a parishioner that he was the best preacher in the world. Before he left the church building, another parishioner told him he was the worst preacher on earth. Robinson prayed, "Lord, I didn't let the first person puff me up; don't let that second one puff me down!" Great prayer! Stay by the stuff, friend. Forget the catcalls.

Prayer: O God, there will be days when people say nice things about me. I really like those days. But . . . there will come times when the words hurled my way are not so pleasant. Don't let me be swayed by the good or the bad. Really, the only words I am desperately eager to hear are those that could come from You, "Well done, thou good and faithful servant" (Matt. 25:21). Don't let me forget that today. *Amen.*

THOUGHTS ON LIFE'S "MORNING VAPOR"

> For what is your life? It is even a vapour, that appeareth for a little time, and then vanisheth away.

Did you ever ask yourself, "Does what I do in life make much difference? Do I just push pencils around? Shuffle papers? Or is my activity producing life-giving change to at least one other person?" My friend, church statesman Bob Rhoden, asks, "Is what you do transformational?" Great question.

I had a full annual physical the other day. The doctor said I was fine and should live a number of years yet (he didn't say how many). Okay, so good report! Now what do I do with those potential years left? Of course, just because the doctor said I should live longer, his words don't guarantee that fact. It is still "one day at a time."

So what about those potential days and (hopefully) years? Am I going to just hit golf balls (a most pleasurable pursuit, to be sure)? How many fish do I really want to catch? Lots of them, frankly. Do I really need to jump onto another plane and go somewhere? I ask the Lord, "Dear God, what can I do that will be transformational to somebody? Is there a load I can lift somewhere? Can I do something to change directions of something or someone going nowhere?"

The apostle James shakes us with his warning that our lives are just a vapor that appears for a short time until the rising sun burns it off. I used to do a lot of trout fishing in the Ozarks. I would arrive at an old mill just as the sun was coming up and the vapor would rise off the water so thick you couldn't see across the river. But then the sun would make its appearance and the vapor was gone. Just like that! That's how short our lives are. So what are we going to do with this precious day? I mean right now, today?

O God, this very breath that now fills my lungs is a precious treasure. I have no guarantee of another. Help me not to waste my life doing anything that is not productive somehow for the Kingdom. Your gift of life cannot be wasted. Thank You for enabling me to understand the importance of each day. May I make this one count for You. Amen.

RODNEY, THE DILLARDS, AND ANDY GRIFFITH

1 Kings 19:10

And he said, I have been very jealous for the LORD God of hosts: for the children of Israel have forsaken thy covenant, thrown down thine altars, and slain thy prophets with the sword; and I, even I only, am left; and they seek my life, to take it away.

When confronted by Queen Jezebel's threats on his life, Elijah disintegrated into a pity party. "I'm the only one left serving You, God!" he moaned. Which, of course, was not the case, and God made sure the prophet understood that.

Over the years, I've been privileged to have friends from all walks of life, from politics to ministry to show business to sports. I still see one of those buddies quite often on the reruns of the Andy Griffith Show. I'm speaking of that funny face of the TV Darling family, Rodney Dillard. One of Rodney's brothers once said of him, "It's possible to observe him and understand why some animals eat their young." Another brother observed (with admiration), "Nobody has ever looked as stupid as Rodney and still been able to walk and chew gum."

There are four brothers in the Dillard family: Douglas, Dean, Rodney, and Mitch. (Remember on the Griffith show they were always known as the Darling family.) I have known Rodney for quite a few years. We've done some television together, and Rodney and his wife Beverly have been guests in our church. I can tell you they truly love Jesus Christ!

I was a guest on a Christian TV talk show years ago when I met Rodney. He walked up to me and I did a double take. I said, "Hey, I know you!" He just grinned and gave me that blank "Darling" look, and I laughed out loud. It is such a delight to find brothers and sisters in Christ in so many areas of life. We followers of the Lord often do the Elijah bit, feeling sorry for ourselves, and mumbling, "We're the only ones left serving God." Nonsense. There are believed to be at least 1.5 billion followers of our Lord, and that number is growing every day! Hallelujah!

Byline #110

PRAYER

O God, open my spiritual eyes to see the multitudes of people who love You. Keep my attitude toward Your kingdom positive and helpful. May I never allow depression to rule my life. And don't let me be a negative thinker either. You already have enough of those to go around! Thank You! Amen.

IF GOD SAYS IT'S OKAY, IT'S OKAY

Acts 10:15: And the voice spake unto him again the second time, What God hath cleansed, that call not thou common.

The ancient Old Testament community of Joppa lies just south of Tel Aviv and is nestled along the shore of the Mediterranean Sea. It provides one of the most stunning views in all the Middle East. It was here that the apostle Peter was staying with a friend of his, a fellow named Simon who was a tanner of hides. Sidebar here: it's interesting that when the black plague scourged England several hundred years ago, rats carried the disease. However, many people living in or near tanneries were spared the plague because the places smelled so bad that rats wouldn't bother them.

Peter was on the roof of Simon's house praying when God gave him a vision. A sheet was lowered on which were animals and reptiles. God told Peter to eat them. Well, no self-respecting Jew would touch them. But God said, in effect, "If I say it's okay, it's okay." The Lord was preparing Peter's heart for a visit from Gentiles coming from Caesarea, about 50 miles north of there, where lived a Roman centurion named Cornelius. Up to this point, only Jews followed Jesus. As far as we know, Cornelius was the first Gentile convert.

This story touches my heart because, when the Lord began dealing with me about ministry, I drew back. It seemed as if folks (who should know about such things) discouraged me from this pursuit. One Bible college official even told me, "You have no business even thinking about ministry." His quip cut quite deeply into my heart, I will tell you. But, see, that official didn't call me. God did. If God says it's okay, then it's okay. Perhaps you are called of God to frontline ministry. You have shrunk back from the challenge because you've been told you're not eligible. Listen, if God is in it, do it! It's okay.

Prayer: O God, thank You for Your divine call on our lives. After all, You designed and created us in the first place. You are much more capable of knowing our destiny than anyone else. So we will listen to You and follow Your directives. Oh, and thanks for telling me it was okay. Amen.

Transformational leadership

Acts 9:15: But the Lord said unto him . . . he is a chosen vessel unto me, to bear my name before the Gentiles, and kings, and the children of Israel. . . .

Those lines characterized the ministry of Paul. A friend of mine occasionally uses the phrase "transformational leadership." Pretty noble phrase, if you ask me. Webster defines *transformational* as "a system of grammatical analysis that posits the existence of deep structure and surface structure and uses a set of rules to derive surface structure forms from deep structure." You say, "What?!" Coach Vince Lombardi of the NFL Green Bay Packers had a simpler definition: "Keep it simple, stupid!" As a pastor, I define "transformational leadership" in this way: "The system by which one takes the great theological truths of Christ to make them work in a relevant and productive way in our secular society." While leadership is not always necessarily rocket science, it is indeed visionary — or it's not leadership. It might be managerial, but it definitely is not leadership.

Let me put this in tangible form: How do we tap into the enormous treasure lode of young church leadership among us and still maintain our core value system? Many of today's young spiritual leaders abdicate what they term "the system" to go into independent ministries, free of what they think are restrictions. Ah, but there is a steep price to be paid for that sojourn. Loneliness is part of the price. Lack of accountability is yet another. We must incorporate the vision and energy of today's youth into the Church and yet maintain those biblical, eternal values that keep us holy and acceptable unto God. That, my friend, is a tall order. And that's where this "transformational leadership" must come into existence. Maintaining status quo is not acceptable.

Jesus was a progressive leader even while He maintained conservative values. That's transformational!

Prayer: O God, I never want to be status quo in what You have ordained me to do. But I also do not want to renege on those truths of the gospel that have maintained Your kingdom on earth. Guide me by Your Spirit, I pray, to always be transformational. Oh, how I thank You for such anointing! *Amen.*

THE MISSIONS CALL: WE MUST GO OURSELVES OR SEND A SUBSTITUTE

Mark 16:15: And he said unto them, Go ye into all the world, and preach the gospel to every creature.

In 1986, Billy Graham preached the funeral for my friend, mentor, and missions legend Dr. Oswald J. Smith. Few men have ever influenced missions as did Smith. Yet when he was in his 20s, his denomination turned him down for missionary status. The issue apparently was his health. Smith would live to be in his late 80s, yet he was somewhat frail most of his life. After attempting independent missions work overseas and contracting a number of sicknesses, Smith concluded that the missions board had been right in its assessment of him as a potential candidate.

But he still felt responsibility for the lost of the world. In his own words, "Realizing I could not go (to the mission field myself), I turned to substitutes." Though he built a strong church in Toronto, Smith never lost his passion for missions. He wrote, "I am a pastor second. I am a missionary first. I tried to go myself, but each time it seemed that I had to come back. I knew then there was only one thing left to do: namely, to send others."[1] And send them he did — by the hundreds!

In the late '60s, Smith invested a precious week of his life in me. He revolutionized my life, and I felt the mantle of his missions' passion descend upon me. Is the call of God any less on us than it was on Smith? I think not. In India some years ago, God impressed upon me that I, too, was a missionary: a missionary of supply. I never had the call or the privilege of going to some foreign field as a commissioned missionary. But our church has now sent out hundreds of such messengers all over the world. And how greatly God has blessed us for the effort! You see, God is in the redemption business; and so are we. If we want His blessing and anointing, we must be in the same pursuit as the Creator. As Smith said so many times, "Why should any of us have the right to hear the gospel twice until everyone has heard it once?"[2]

1. Lois Neely, *Fire in His Bones* (Wheaton, IL: Tyndale House Publishers, 1982).
2. Ibid.

PRAYER: O God, I can sing from my soul, "I'll go where You want me to go." I am so grateful for the legacy Dr. Smith left with me decades ago. Let the missions fervor he left upon me never diminish, even as the years pass. I thank You for sending him to me and for the missions impression he forever left in my soul. Amen.

THE BLESSINGS OF HERITAGE

Genesis 12:2

And I will make of thee a great nation, and I will bless thee, and make thy name great; and thou shalt be a blessing.

In our church denomination, we publish a magazine called *Heritage*. It features pictures and articles about the history of our fellowship. I love it! To us nostalgic types, the magazine is a blessing and comfort. We read those stories and gaze at the pictures of the great men and women who shaped who we are — heroes in the truest sense of the word. I believe I have every issue of that magazine ever printed, bound in huge volumes so they're easy to pick up and read.

Church members need to understand where they came from and who made them what they are. They need to know basic dates or time periods when these historic activities took place. Now you should probably be aware that I have actually lived through 75 percent of the entire history of our denomination, the Assemblies of God, so many of those heroes were good friends of mine, or at least I knew who they were at the time of their impact. They certainly made that proverbial indelible impression upon me. *Heritage* is certainly an appropriate name for the magazine because the lives of those men and women were exactly that — a heritage to each of us.

Now you may not belong to our fellowship, but I ask you, how well do you know the history of your group or denomination? Today's youth — and God bless 'em every one! — want to be a part of the changing landscape of ecclesiastical movements, and well they should! But they also need to know where their roots are. They need to be aware of sacrifices made by their elders without which they would not even have a fellowship or denomination. God bless every man and woman who has contributed to who we are, to those who have successfully walked this way before us. Let us never forget them! Or our heritage!

Byline #114

PRAYER

O God, just as millions look back to Abraham as their heritage, their roots, so many others of us look back to the men and women who paid so sacrificially of their time, resources, and very lives to give us what we enjoy today. In pursuing the future, may we never forget the past and our foundations. Amen.

BOOZE — THE UNDERMINING OF AMERICA

Byline #115

Esther 1:7–8

And they gave them drink in vessels of gold . . . and royal wine in abundance, according to the state of the king. And the drinking was according to the law. . . .

Those verses tell of a horrible night in the history of the Persian Empire that resulted in the banishment of a beloved queen and the first concepts of genocidal holocaust. But then that's pretty much the universal history of booze.

For 50 years I have spoken out against the booze trade. I do again on this page. And why not? There are so many demerits on alcohol's report card that there is no room to sketch in a kudo, even if there were one. Note these black marks against the purveyors of the bottle: Booze is responsible for 50 percent of all auto fatalities. It is behind 80 percent of all home violence. It is believed that 30 percent of all suicides have some roots in alcohol. Domestic authorities report 60 percent of all child abuse comes from a drunken parent. Here's a shocker (at least to me): 60 percent of all drownings can be attributed to the bottle or flask. Now here's a fascinating stat: It is estimated by syndicated columnist Kathleen FitzGerald that when a woman becomes an alcoholic, her husband leaves her in nine out of ten cases. But when a man succumbs to the bottle, his wife leaves in only one of ten cases.[1]

The Old Testament prophet Isaiah wrote, "Woe unto them that . . . follow strong drink" (Isa. 5:11). Shakespeare warned, "That men should put any enemy in their mouths to steal away their brains."[2] Today we read about university and college frat houses having booze orgies, the students passing out everywhere. Advertisers make tens of millions of dollars coming up with clever ads to get people to drink. I have said it often and say so again: "The proper label for any kind of alcoholic beverage should be a skull and crossbones."

PRAYER

O God, forgive us in this "home of the brave and land of the free" for drinking ourselves into possible oblivion. I pray for the addicted one reading this column: Let these chains be loosed and set this person free! Amen.

Someone once asked me, "Well, don't you have anything at all good to say about drinking — like, even social drinking?" Read my lips: "No!"

1. Kathleen W. FitzGerald, *Alcoholism: The Genetic Inheritance* (New York: Doubleday, 1988), p. xii.
2. William Shakespeare, *Othello*, act 2, scene 3.

An incredible leap of faith

Matthew 1:1: The book of the generation of Jesus Christ, the son of David, the son of Abraham.

Most people quickly pass over the first chapter of Matthew. "How dull," they groan. "It's just a genealogy." Well, that's true in that this chapter contains 42 generations that led to the birth of Jesus Christ. But look at the people in that listing! A lot of those folks had very shaky backgrounds. Judah, one of Joseph's brothers, was a louse before an encounter with God changed his life. Rahab was a woman of ill repute in ancient Jericho. Manasseh was arguably the most despicable king to ever sit on the throne in Jerusalem. But look how God ultimately used all of these people!

In 2007, the legendary motorcycle daredevil Evel Knieval passed away. But several months before his death, he appeared on a well-known national television program to tell millions of viewers of his commitment to Jesus Christ. In years gone by, I watched Knieval climb aboard his motorcycle and jump as many as 52 cars at one time. I saw his near-fatal fall in Las Vegas after missing the ramp. I saw him climb into his rocket-bike in a failed attempt to jump the Snake River Canyon. His lifestyle was as far away from a follower of Christ as you can imagine. Then Knieval met Jesus! His testimony was incredible; his every thought centered around Jesus. All he would talk about in his last months of life was Jesus. What an amazing turnaround!

Why are we so surprised when these conversions take place? Have we forgotten the woman at the well in Samaria? Have we overlooked Zacchaeus? Have we dropped from memory the thief on the cross? Let's never give up on that friend for whom we earnestly pray. Our Lord has proved far too many times that He is not willing that anybody perish and that all people can be reached with the gospel. But how can they believe in Him of whom they have never heard? It's our job as witnesses to make absolutely sure that they do hear!

Prayer: O God, I do thank You that I will meet that incredible daredevil in heaven one day! I am grateful that somebody reached him with the gospel. His story proves once again the majesty of Your redemption and that down in the human heart there is a longing for God. Help me to remember that today when my path crosses that of someone very reachable with Jesus' love. *Amen.*

BODILY EXERCISE PROFITS LITTLE. BUT THEN AGAIN . . .

1 Timothy 4:8: For bodily exercise profiteth little: but godliness is profitable unto all things, having promise of the life that now is, and of that which is to come.

So wrote the apostle Paul to his protégé in the ministry, young Timothy. "Bodily exercise profits little!" Humorist Robert Orben apparently agreed with Paul. Orben wrote, "To exercise is human; not to is divine."[1] But we should remember that the apostle Paul walked all over any number of countries, so he should have been in good shape without any other exercise. Paul Dudley White gives us this perspective: "A vigorous five-mile walk will do more good for an unhappy but otherwise healthy adult than all the medicine and psychology in the world."[2] My own personal doctor agrees with that analysis.

As a type-2 diabetic, if I walk three to four miles vigorously every day, I don't need the pills. If I don't do the walking, I do need the meds. Yes, of course, diet enters into that picture, without question. So there is much to be said about getting off our couches and hitting the treadmill, gym, or walking trail. Does such exercise make a person more spiritual? No, but it gives you more years in which you can be spiritual. Think ye on that!

I mentally fight bodily exercise tooth and nail. I am quite weary after a long day — usually a 12-hour workday. I want to sit back on that soft leather recliner, turn on the plasma screen idiot tube, and just laze. But, you know, it's a funny thing: after I've made myself get up, put on some jogging (translate: walking!) outfit, get out the door, and actually start the workout, it is very pleasurable. I suspect it's like prayer. More people talk about praying than actually pray. And more people probably think about exercise than those who actually . . . exercise. How about changing your routine today? Get up and get out of the house. Put on those walking shoes. Give a good workout a try. It will profit you . . . at least a little!

Prayer: O God, I thank You for the degree of health that I have at this moment. I want to be a good steward of it. I won't take it for granted, but I will actually do something to care for this body You have given me, instead of just asking You to heal it after I've broken it through carelessness. Amen.

1. Bob Phillips, *Phillips' Book of Great Thoughts & Funny Sayings* (Wheaton, IL: Tyndale House Publ., 1993), p. 116.
2. Ashton Applewhite, Tripp Evans, and Andrew Frothingham, *And I Quote: The Definitive Collection of Quotes, Sayings, and Jokes for the Contemporary Speechmaker* (New York, St. Martin's Press, 1992), p. 232.

AT WHAT POINT IN CHURCH HISTORY DID THE PULPIT TAKE A BACK SEAT TO THE SINGERS?

1 Corinthians 1:21

For after that in the wisdom of God the world by wisdom knew not God, it pleased God by the foolishness of preaching to save them that believe.

I love Gospel singers, but I wonder about them oftentimes. Some of them truly do very strange things. A few Sundays ago, we had a singing group in all services of the day in our church. In both morning worship services, they sang their songs and, as a group, walked out of the sanctuary, never staying for the sermon. Fortunately (for them), I was not speaking that morning or I promise you, I would have publicly "invited" them back into the sanctuary. (And with some "anointing," I might add.)

After the service, I asked the singers, "Did you hear what the preacher spoke about this morning?" "Oh, yes," they lied. "Hmmm," I responded, "what was his message about?" They blushed and hemmed and hawed around. I kept at them. "Why did you leave the service before the preaching?" I insisted. "Well," one of them said, "we had done our part." I pushed the matter a bit further and asked, "How would you have felt if, after I introduced you, the entire preaching staff had just got up and walked out?" "Well," one sniffed, "we wouldn't have appreciated that." I don't think my point ever got through to them because they were so wrapped up in their own little musical world.

(And selling CDs in the church lobby after service.)

At what point did singers, whether worship bands or guest artists, decide the preached word was secondary to their performances? And I hasten to say, if they walk out on the preaching, then their music was just that, a performance, not ministry. I usually quite frankly enjoy all kinds of music for the Lord. But musical prima donnas have no place in the house of God. Preaching prima donnas don't either. I have been asked when our church is having that particular aforementioned musical group back to our church. Oh, surely you must know the answer to that.

Byline #118

PRAYER

O God, help us all remember that the one thing You have absolutely committed yourself to honor is Your Word. "My word shall not return to the heavens void." Let us always keep preaching front and center! Amen.

JERUSALEM, BELOVED CITY OF GOD

Psalm 122:6: Pray for the peace of Jerusalem: they shall prosper that love thee.

I am often asked, "Dan, in your half-century of travel around the world, what is your favorite city?" Not even a close contest. Jerusalem! Some years ago, my wife and I were invited guests at the 25th anniversary celebration of the reunification of Jerusalem. The gala evening was held in the Citadel of David near the Joppa Gate of the old city. The Israeli Symphony Orchestra, a marvelous choir, special artists, and a fabulous laser show added to the deep feelings and festivity of the nation. Surprisingly to me, both Jews and Arabs took part. The master of ceremonies was a dear friend of mine, an Israeli newscaster and journalist.

The highlight of the entire evening to me was the singing of Naomi Shemer's classic song *Jerusalem of Gold* by the talented Shuli Natan. I thought that David had the same emotion of heart when he penned in Psalms, "O Jerusalem, Jerusalem!" Did not our Lord Jesus utter the same words from the Mount of Olives, overlooking the city? "Jerusalem, Jerusalem . . . how often would I have gathered thy children. . . !" (Matt. 23:37 and Luke 13:34). Both the city and the song moved my soul to its very depth that night. A rough translation of that Shemer Hebrew lyric is this: "Your name (Jerusalem), so dear, so old / If I forget Jerusalem of bronze and light and gold / Jerusalem all of gold and bronze and light / within my heart I shall treasure your song and sight." What a song of hope and yearning. Naomi Shemer passed away at age 74 and was laid to rest at the Kinneret Cemetery on the western shore of the Sea of Galilee. The world can never forget her immortal song, or the city of gold about which it is written and sung.

And remember: we are commanded in Scripture to pray for the peace of that city of gold, Jerusalem!

PRAYER: O God, whenever I think of that beloved walled city, my heart leaps within my chest. Is there any city on earth so dear to Your great heart? Here the Prince of Glory, Your own beloved Son, willingly laid down His life for my sins. No, I will never forget Jerusalem. And I will faithfully pray for peace within her walls. Amen.

Forgetting the important things in life

Psalm 59:11: Lest my people forget. . . .

Eager patrons surrounded the music hall as the hour for the concert arrived. A married couple was observed coming through the lobby.

The husband turned to his wife and said, "Oh, darling, I do wish our piano were here!"

She looked at him nonplused and asked, "Why would you want our piano here?"

He replied, "Because our tickets are on it." That would be an embarrassing situation, would it not?

But the Psalmist reminds us of an even greater mental faux pas: "Bless the LORD, O my soul, and forget not all his benefits" (Ps. 103:2). We are so blessed by our precious Lord in so many ways, the chief of which is our eternal salvation. Most of us have reasonable health, jobs that provide needed income, a house or apartment of some sort, friends, adequate food, vehicles to take us here and there, a great nation with all its liberties — all benefits that millions of people have never had.

And yet we so often complain. Or we envy our neighbors who appear to have even more. Envy, spurred by present-day advertising in various media, often causes us to want more and more, such as a bigger house (or a second one), a fancier car, custom clothes, or whatever. For the most part, we have everything we want for a happy and productive life. We should get down on our knees before God every time we utter a complaint and beg His forgiveness. The Psalmist called upon us to bless the Lord, not forgetting all the good things He has done in our lives.

I suppose forgetting concert tickets left home on the piano would be an embarrassment or inconvenience. But nagging God because we want more is a sin. The apostle Paul wrote about being content. May we all be so savvy.

Prayer: O God, forgive me when I complain. Or when these eyes of mine see something I think I just must have when I don't really need it at all. I am not going to forget all Your benefits; and further, I am going to be extremely grateful both in my spirit and my words. Thank You! Thank You! *Amen.*

SECOND THOUGHTS ABOUT ISRAEL'S KING SAUL

Byline #121

1 Samuel 18:12

And Saul was afraid of David, because the LORD was with him, and was departed from Saul.

It is a thought-provoking concept that Samuel (believed by most to be the author of 1 Samuel in the Old Testament) definitely did not like Saul. Scarcely a good word could drip from his pen quill onto parchment about the king. But David, on the other hand, despite Saul's very clear opposition to him, had different thoughts when he learned of the king's death: "How art the mighty fallen!" he lamented. Don't you find that dichotomy of impressions rather strange?

Most Bible commentators I read seem to share Samuel's distaste for Saul. They recall Saul's indifference to the prophet Samuel's dictates or the king's consorting with the Witch of Endor the night before he died in battle on Mount Gilboa. Or they comment on Saul's disobedience to God that caused Samuel's disapproving words, "To obey is better than sacrifice" (1 Sam. 15:22). Okay, all you critics, I grant you the points you've just made. However, are you overlooking the fact that Saul was the first man to unite the tribes of Israel since Joshua's death some four centuries earlier? What about Saul's courage in battle? What do you think about the fact that Saul was not a womanizer as were David and Solomon? Have you considered that Saul was apparently a marvelous father as witnessed by his outstanding sons Jonathan, Malchishua, and Abinadab? These brave young men died in battle at their father's side while some of David's sons killed, raped, and attempted an overthrow of their own father from the throne. The Bible even admits that David was a sorry disciplinarian. So it's small wonder then that David called Saul "mighty" in his grief over his monarch's death. One Israeli scholar told me recently that he would list Saul in the top three of all Israel's kings.

PRAYER

O God, let me not be judgmental today. I will leave that up to You. Instead, I will do what I can to lift some person's load this day. I am needy of Your grace and mercy, not Your justice. So I will extend that grace and justice to others. Amen.

Well, it's not really a matter of how we consider others, is it? It's how God sees us. He is the final judge and jury. As John reminds us in the Revelation, God has a full set of books. He will judge us, too, out of those books.

DOES THE CHURCH STILL HAVE APOSTLES?

Ephesians 4:11

And he gave some, apostles; and some, prophets; and some, evangelists; and some, pastors and teachers.

Evangelists we know, and certainly pastors and teachers. Perhaps even prophets. But apostles? In his letter to the Christian church in Ephesus, Paul wrote clearly that God gave the gift of apostles to the church. The answer to this question of whether apostles exist today or not is a definite yes! They were essential to our Lord's mission 2,000 years ago and remain so today. Apostles in the New Testament often referred to the original 12 disciples; however, there were others such as Paul who were definitely commissioned representatives of Christ's body on earth, which is the Church. It is my strong conviction that effective missionaries are apostles. Our fellowship strongly endorses the ministry of such men and women.

So who is an apostle? My late (and so truly great) mentor

Leonard Ravenhill used to tell me, "Dan, you can always tell an apostle; he does apostolic ministry."

Missionaries confront the powers of darkness and confirm the gospel with supernatural signs following, as Jesus promised in Mark 16. Now it's true that in a narrower sense of the word apostles were those who saw Jesus after His resurrection and were personally commissioned by the Lord. But since the outpouring of the Holy Spirit on the Day of Pentecost, according to the second chapter of Acts, there have been hundreds of thousands of apostles who have evangelized great parts of the world. I know of one such apostle and his wife, still in their 40s, who have personally opened nearly 500 churches in the frozen climes of Siberia. Today, apostles continue to proclaim the New Testament gospel "with signs following," sometimes even at the risk or loss of their own lives. Where would Christ's church be today without the ministry of these apostles of faith?

Byline #122

PRAYER

O God, we truly need the same power among the reapers in Your eternal harvest as the original apostles had. I thank You for those men and women who stand on the front lines of the world, establishing beachheads for the gospel that previously were not there. Protect them today, I ask fervently. And would You bless their ministries once again "with signs following"? Amen.

WORN OUT AFTER SIX INNINGS

Galatians 6:9: And let us not be weary in well doing: for in due season we shall reap, if we faint not.

The great, now-retired sports columnist Hal Lebovitz of the *Cleveland Plain Dealer* wrote a column in 1986 titled, "Why Must Pitchers Be Babied?" We're talking about baseball's major league hurlers. The columnist claims they're bigger, stronger, better-conditioned than ever, yet the theme of most managers is, "Just give me six good innings." Lebovitz observed, "Once a pitcher has thrown 100 times, look out! The poor fellow's arm may fall off." A sarcastic, but true, report, I'm afraid.

Listen, there was a day when big-league pitchers hurled both ends of a double-header. Yes, of course, in the same day! There was once a big league pitcher named Iron Man McGinnity who pitched two-thirds of the entire season's games for his team. Today? Why, my goodness, if the guy is still upright after six innings, he's patted on the back and he goes back to the dugout to think on the quarter-million bucks he just made that afternoon or evening. Well, the last I heard, a baseball game lasts nine innings, not six.

So why am I on this soapbox? Because some of the folks I hear in frontline ministry moan about "burnout." John Wesley, who preached three to five times daily, going from village to village on horseback, might have had reason to complain about burnout, but not us today. We have everything from laptops to iPods to air-conditioned cars to cushy offices and custom-made pulpits. I have a good friend who just started a new church and he's 82 years old! My kind of guy! The famed evangelist Billy Sunday once said that when he could no longer have enough teeth to bite Satan, he'd gum him to death.

Six-inning pitchers, indeed! Humbug!

Prayer: O God, help me to still be in the race to the finish line! Thank You for the health You have granted me. Now let me use it to its maximum utility as long as breath courses through my body. There is just too much to do, and too little time to do it, to go back to the spiritual dugout after a mere six innings. Amen.

Promiser of much, deliverer of little

Matthew 4:8–9: Again, the devil taketh him up into an exceeding high mountain, and sheweth him all the kingdoms of the world, and the glory of them; And saith unto him, All these things will I give thee, if thou wilt fall down and worship me.

What a liar Satan is! The kingdoms of the world were not his to give away in the first place. They already belonged to Jesus, the One he was tempting. How sad that so many learn too late there isn't a trace of truth in what the enemy promises.

Every other month or so I spend a day on Death Row in Florida. I have been ministering to some of the guys there for several years. In the summertime, it gets so hot down on the Row, with all the suffocating humidity, that you almost have to have fish-gills just to breathe. The inmates there spend 23 hours a day in tiny cells, seven by nine feet in dimension. They have absolutely no air conditioning in the summer and precious little heat in the winter. So many of them are there because they believed Satan's lies and lived out his directives. Now they are paying the price of learning that Satan promises so much and delivers absolutely nothing! I met one fellow on Death Row who has languished there for over 34 years, waiting for the lethal needle.

The other day I passed a wreck on an interstate highway. A car and its trailer were upside-down. A body lay by the wreckage. The cause? Booze! I occasionally get a call to a local hospice where a man or woman awaits, breathing laboriously through an oxygen mask, valiantly attempting to get enough air in the lungs to last one more hour. Emphysema. Tobacco. Wow, is that ever a long way from that cool, sophisticated doll in the moving picture, waving her cigarette around! The film producers never quite get the gal to "wheeze," do they?

No wonder Jesus referred to Satan as "the father of all lies." How does the devil stay in business? Because he gets people to believe him! If you're being tempted by Satan today, run like the wind. You are dealing with a liar.

Prayer: O God, protect the one who reads this page today. May these few words somehow be a bulwark against the enemy. Put a hedge of protection around my friend's heart and watch over him or her for Jesus' sake. *Amen.*

BELIEF IN MIRACLES

Acts 4:16: What shall we do to these men? for that indeed a notable miracle hath been done by them is manifest to all them that dwell in Jerusalem; and we cannot deny it.

The apostles Peter and John had been used of God in the healing of a lifelong crippled fellow beneath the Gate Beautiful at the Great Temple in Jerusalem. The miracle caused a stir in the city, one not appreciated by some of the religious leaders. While they were not happy about the miracle, they could not deny that one had occurred.

Do you believe in miracles? The dictionary defines a miracle as an extraordinary occurrence that surpasses all known human powers or natural forces and is ascribed to a divine or supernatural cause. With all my heart, I believe in miracles. I've seen so many of them. My cousin Faye was the first one. In 1936, she lay in a hospital ward, dying of cancer. In fact, she was in the "terminal coma," as her physician explained. He told Faye's husband, Cecil, that she would be gone in three days. He was right. She was gone. Home! A pastor had anointed her with oil and prayed a prayer of faith over her. She lived nearly a half century more of good health in which she faithfully served her Lord. I told the story to a fellow once who responded, "Well, Dan, I just don't believe that." I replied, "That doesn't change it."

I have seen miracles of God's provision. One day I would like to write a book about those things that I have actually experienced for which there is no normal rationale. If a person believes in God, he or she must believe that He works within human lives. And, further, what He does far transcends all human capability — or perhaps even understanding. If you're facing an obstacle currently through which there is no transport, may I encourage you to look unto Jesus? There is no shadow of turning with Him. What He has always been, He will always be. The One who transformed water into wine in Cana can transform your seeming disaster into stunning victory.

PRAYER: O God, the greatest of all miracles is the way You redeem broken wrecks of lives and create whole new life within them. I thank You for the miracle of redemption. I pray each day, "Lord, increase my faith." I pray that again today, for without faith, I cannot please You. Thank You! Amen.

THE MEDIA —
OPEN WINDOW
TO THE WORLD

Exodus 33:19

I will proclaim the name of the LORD before thee.

When I was just three years old, I stood on a chair before an open microphone on WNAX, a powerful AM radio station in the Midwest, and did my first broadcast. The year was 1940. By the time I was a teenager, I had my first full-time job at a commercial radio station. The salary was minimal, but the perks were terrific. I had the privilege of meeting people I would probably have never met, interviewing celebrities from so many walks of life. I was still in high school when I spent a day interviewing R.G. LeTourneau, the brilliant industrialist of Caterpillar fame from Peoria, Illinois. He was absolutely sold-out to God. If you've never read his story, look it up on the Internet. I met and interviewed other well-knowns, including having a one-on-one session with President Harry S. Truman. I posed questions for ball players, motion picture stars, musicians, and figures on the grand stage of history such as Menachem Begin and Abba Eban of Israel. I missed by a hair's breadth an opening to interview PLO chief Yassir Arafat. Now that would have been some interview, I'll tell you! The great Israeli General Moshe Dayan told me I could have 30 minutes with him for $2,500. I had never paid anyone to interview them, and I wasn't about to start with him, as much as I respected him.

Media has opened the windows of the world to me. There is no way I could have crossed paths with all those people unless I had been on the speaking end of a microphone. But even more, I'm thankful for the 30 years I spent as the radio and television voice of the Assemblies of God on such programs as *Revivaltime, Every Day With Jesus,* and *Byline.*

At one time, we had literally hundreds of radio and TV programs for our Lord being aired around the world five days a week! What a privilege! By mail alone, I have heard from well over a million listeners and viewers. By phone and e-mail, thousands and thousands more! It will be a joy to see so many we reached in heaven one day. God bless sanctified media! Let's continue to use it for His glory.

Byline #126

PRAYER

O God, I never would have dreamed as a grade school kid the doors You would open for me, just a wet-behind-the-ears kid from Climbing Hill, Iowa. But when You call someone to do Your work, You open the doors. And even now, in these later years, doors are still opening to the world. Thank You! Amen.

GETTING
MIXED REVIEWS

> Blessed are ye, when men shall revile you, and persecute you, and shall say all manner of evil against you falsely, for my sake. Rejoice, and be exceeding glad: for great is your reward in heaven.

My line of work requires that I frequent restaurants. The other day, I pulled up reviews on the Internet for some of our leading local eateries. I was shocked! Restaurants that I think are just fine got some awful reviews, and some of the places where I would not even darken the door, because of previous experiences, got sheer raves. I had to laugh out loud.

If you are in public work very long, you realize you cannot make everybody happy. It dawns on you one day: Hey, that person really likes what I do. Or: Hey, that person really doesn't! Over the years, primarily because of international media, I have received literally hundreds of thousands of letters, e-mails, and phone calls. Some of my respondents have fitted me with a halo; others have suggested with some passion that I need to be saved. I have been studying the life of Nehemiah lately. His critics could not get him to come down from the wall to even discuss his activity for God. He had been given a divine command and no one could distract him from that noble purpose. Listen, you're going to have critics. You might as well face that fact now. It's hard to believe, I know, but not everyone is going to really appreciate you. (Are you over the shock yet?) Remember, in the United States you could have tens of millions of people vote against you and STILL be the president of the United States. So settle your thoughts and heart on the One who called you.

There is really only one person you need to make happy all the time. That person is Jesus Christ. His is the last and binding review. If at the close of a day Jesus says, "You did well today, my child," sleep well. If He does not give you that accolade, you might want to rethink your activities of tomorrow. Rex Humbard helped me when I was a kid preacher. He said, "Danny, the only One who really matters has nail prints in His hands." I've never forgotten that. Be grateful for those who love and appreciate you. Pray for those who speak disparagingly of you. My goodness, our Lord Jesus himself certainly got mixed reviews, now didn't He?

O God, if someone recently has praised something I've done, let me graciously be thankful and move on. If someone has criticized me, let me also be gracious and move on. As Paul said: "None of these things move me" (Acts 20:24). He never said they didn't "hurt" him. Today, I will not be moved! Amen.

Majestic song lyrics

Exodus 15:1: Then sang Moses and the children of Israel . . . unto the LORD. . . .

On a brutally hot July night in 1951, I gave my life to Christ in the civic auditorium of Sioux City, Iowa. At the close of the message by Evangelist Jack Shuler, the great massed choir sang the invitation song, "Come, Ye Disconsolate." Thomas Moore wrote the lyrics in the early 1800s. And what lyrics! "Come, ye disconsolate / where'er ye languish / come to the mercy seat / fervently kneel / Here bring your wounded hearts / here tell all your anguish / earth hath no sorrow / that heaven cannot heal."

My wife and I were talking about those words as we drove somewhere the other day. We love that song, but many in today's generation probably would just stare numbly if we sang it now. "Come, ye *disconsolate*?" What in the world does that mean? "Where'er ye languish?" And languish means what? "Come to the mercy seat?" Exactly what is a mercy seat? I find it rather sad, quite honestly, not that we have changed musicality so much, but that we have lost the majesty of words. Such as another verse of that same great hymn: "Joy of the desolate / light of the straying / hope of the penitent / fadeless and pure / Here speaks the Comforter / tenderly saying / earth hath no sorrow / that heaven cannot cure."

When a person has been through the foxholes of life, and witnessed firsthand again and again the joy that emerges on the desolate and the liberty that can come to the disconsolate, all of it through the graciousness of our Lord Jesus, well, some of those old songs speak intensely to us. We want to treat those truths with some verbal dignity. We may not be able to jump to the beat of those anthems, but our hearts certainly leap! I can tell you that for sure!

Prayer: O God, we never want to speak in a vocabulary not understood by most people most of the time. But on the other hand we don't want to dumb down the majesty of who You are and what You have done among us. Teach us balance in our musical worship. May we never bring reproach to Your holiness and name. ***Amen.***

THE GANGSTER AT THE ALTAR

Luke 19:5: And when Jesus came to the place, he looked up, and saw him, and said unto him, Zacchaeus, make haste, and come down; for to day I must abide at thy house.

Was Zacchaeus a gangster? Some of the people in Jericho apparently thought so, although the Bible doesn't verify that. But we know he came to Jesus.

For years, it was my joy to be the speaker on the Assemblies of God international radio weekly broadcast *Revivaltime*, heard in 80 nations on over 600 radio stations. One Sunday morning, here in the church I pastor in Florida, I gave an invitation for those who wanted to give their lives to Christ. Suddenly one of our altar workers motioned frantically for me to help him. I knelt beside a tough-looking guy who stared intensely at me and asked, "You the guy I hear on *Revivaltime*?" I told him that I was. He said, "I'm an enforcer for a gang in New York City. Last Sunday I was driving through Manhattan and I heard you say that God would forgive anybody of anything. Is that true?" I assured him that I, indeed, said that and it was true. The fellow slowly reached inside his coat and pulled out a pistol and a good supply of bullets and laid them on the altar. He told me, "I have hurt a lot of people — and more than hurt — with this gun. I've driven clear down here from New York to ask you, do you think God would forgive me and let me have a second chance at life?" I put my arm over his shoulder and responded, "Of course He will. No question!" The man began to sob and confess his sins to God. He became a strong believer in the months that he remained with us. I still have three of those bullets just in front of me on my bookcase, a great reminder of the compassion and love of God.

Isaiah wrote that though our sins be as scarlet, they shall be as white as snow (Isa. 1:18). Paul wrote that all things pass away and under God's mercy, all things become new when we come to Jesus (2 Cor. 5:17). Perhaps this is where you are today, even as you read these lines. You need forgiveness. Let's pray about it together:

Prayer: O God, You see all things and so You are very aware of this dear reader who calls out to You now for love, forgiveness, mercy, and understanding. What Jesus did for us on the cross provides atonement for these sins. We ask You to wash away all this sin from this precious life today and let a new life begin. Thank You. Amen.

REPORTING THE TRIVIAL
WHILE OVERLOOKING
THE MAJOR

Philippians 4:8

Finally, brethren, whatsoever things are true, whatsoever things are honest, whatsoever things are just, whatsoever things are pure, whatsoever things are lovely, whatsoever things are of good report; if there be any virtue, and if there be any praise, think on these things.

Local television news can be amusing. I know because I was a TV news anchor myself once upon a time. We have seven TV stations in our area and they fight it out for ratings for the five, six, and now even seven p.m. local news reports, trying to outdo themselves in what they call "breaking news." When I was on the tube, breaking news meant something major. Now local newscasters try to make something big out of rather trivial stories. For example: "Tonight . . . Channel X has this exclusive story . . . at four o'clock today a local resident ran into a tree." Or: "Stay tuned to Channel Y for our exclusive story on Bill Smith's cat that just gave birth to a litter of kittens." (This is only somewhat exaggerated.) Local newscasts are "cash cows" for television stations. Whichever station gets the highest news ratings can charge the highest rate for commercials.

The late, legendary Jack Paar once worked as a newscaster on a Cleveland station. The fellow who preceded him on the air, *The Town Crier*, constantly ran overtime, cutting the news coverage time down, as he described trivial information. Paar finally had just had all he could take and one evening in 1935 he said on the air: "The Town Crier has taken so much time with his items about Mrs. Howell spraining her ankle, the Reillys' missing fox terrier, and next Tuesday's strawberry social at the Methodist Church, that I don't have time for the news today concerning Mussolini's and Italy's attack on Ethiopia. Good night." True story!

Which brings me to the Church. We must never major on minor things to the exclusion of solid preaching and altar calls. Nothing, absolutely nothing, is as important as preaching the Word of God and bringing people to Christ. Do we take up so much service time with trivial things that the Word of God gets diminished? Well . . . do we?

Byline #130

PRAYER

O God, we repent of majoring on minors in so many areas of our lives. Help us to see things in the same priority You do and then live and act accordingly. May we never substitute the "good" for the "best." Amen.

BAD INVESTMENTS

Matthew 19:21: Jesus said unto him, If thou wilt be perfect, go and sell that thou hast, and give to the poor, and thou shalt have treasure in heaven: and come and follow me.

The Dallas-based Institute for Luxury Home Marketing estimates that home sales at the $5 million-plus range seem to rise substantially year-by-year. This happens even when overall housing market sales decline. I write here of homes listing in excess of $100 million. While I was in India recently, I learned of a *billion-dollar* home being constructed in Mumbai (formerly known as Bombay). An Indian billionaire is building a 60-story, vertical palace that will include three floors of Babylon-inspired hanging gardens and three rooftop helipads. He will reportedly spend a billion bucks on the project. The fellow, whom I am leaving nameless, is constructing this monstrosity in the midst of Mumbai's have-nots. Well over a million people in that city live in poverty that is impossible to describe, many of them in dwellings where the flooring is raw sewage. I have seen personally many of these impoverished areas of India, and I can report to you that the sight of such subsistence will pierce your very conscience and tend to keep you up at night.

It is no secret that many of today's *nouveau riche* like to flaunt the fruits of their labor in the form of sumptuous residences that encompass tens of thousands of square feet. They build virtual estates. They remind me of Jesus' story of the rich man who decided to build even bigger barns to house his "stuff." God said to him, "Thou fool, this night thy soul shall be required of thee: then whose shall those things be. . . ?" (Luke 12:20).

Of course, it is not a sin to have nice things. But it is a sin to know the price of everything and the value of nothing. When we stand before God, those luxurious excesses we made on ourselves will prove to be the worst investments we ever made.

PRAYER: O God, sanctify my eyes. Somehow make it possible for me to see and evaluate what I behold with eternal scales. You'll never ask me about my earthly house or what kind of car I drove. You will ask me if I fulfilled my part in Your great commission and if I somehow lifted the load from someone who needed me. O God, may I ever keep these values in mind. Amen.

Faith to reach the whole world for Christ

Matthew 28:17: And when they saw him, they worshipped him: but some doubted.

How it must grieve the great heart of God when He sees us, His children, doubting Him, His power, and His Word!

Today a veteran frontline missionary soldier of the Cross was in my study. He ministers in Western Europe, particularly in France. He reported some breakthrough victories there. Many, myself included, would rank Western Europe high on the list of the unreached with the gospel. Yes, it is true there are many churches in Europe, but so many of them are museums of art and architecture. My guest today reminded me of the need that escalates for prayerful intercession, missions giving, and "going" if we are truly to reach that continent for Christ. I spoke recently at a convention in Copenhagen, Denmark, and the spiritual need of Europe hit me once again.

There is literally not a day that goes by that I don't get a phone call, e-mail, or letter from a missionary needing material help in his or her field of endeavor. In our congregation, we do everything we can to fulfill those responsibilities and do so with great joy and vigor. We frankly put the needs of missionaries ahead of our own church necessities and even staff salaries. God has been so faithful to us in these decades of ministry to help our congregation financially so that we have never missed a payment or a payroll. How can any Spirit-led person, pastor, or layman say no to a missionary? How can that possibly be reconciled to Christ's command to take the gospel to the whole world? We are under a divine mandate. It is not a *suggestion* from some mere good friend; it is rather an *order* from our sovereign Lord! Further, Jesus promised that upon our obedience to His directive He would make sure our needs were met.

You may be thinking, *Well, that requires a lot of faith from pastors and laity.* Precisely! Hebrews 11:6 teaches us that we cannot possibly please God without faith. Good friend, ask God to elevate your believing today. A lost world requires it!

Prayer: O God, please increase my faith today — substantially! More than anything on earth I want to please You and bring honor to Your kingdom. Please make me better at these pursuits than I've ever been, for Your glory.

Amen.

DEVELOPING SPIRITUAL ROOTS IN THE CHURCH

The New Testament Book of Ephesians teaches there are five ministry gifts from God to His Church: apostles, prophets, evangelists, pastors, and teachers. Many scholars link those last two, pastors and teachers, together. I would tend to agree with them. Far and away the most satisfying part of pastoring to me is the teaching aspect of it. Even after all these decades, I still teach Sunday school every Sunday morning. On Wednesday nights, I watch between 1,000 and 1,200 adults fill the sanctuary for my weekly Bible study. I provide each one a syllabus of 10 or 12 pages covering the material for that particular study. It's so fulfilling to me to do this.

As each student enters the sanctuary, he or she is given the syllabus with each page and each line on each page numbered. I encourage them to bring Bibles, but if they happen not to, there's a full Bible in the hymnal rack in front of them. I am absolutely determined that on my watch as their pastor they will not be biblically illiterate. When I was a little boy, my church drilled us kids in Bible knowledge. At the age of 12, I knew the Scriptures very well. It was that background that undergirded me all these decades since.

Here is the challenge: the Bible makes it clear that the study of God's Word is what spawns faith in the human heart and mind. Not clever outlines. Not fascinating illustrations. No, not even the worship singing. It is that expository study of God's Word that brings about the stability God wants in each of us. Yet we hear of churches abandoning Sunday school (or its equivalent). We hear "sermonettes for Christianettes." This kind of irresponsible leadership will create a generation of professing believers who have neither faith nor spiritual roots. As a pastor, I write this with passion: The buck stops at the pastor's desk!

GOLF...AND PRIORITIES IN LIFE

Matthew 6:33

But seek ye first the kingdom of God, and his righteousness; and all these things shall be added unto you.

On literally dozens of occasions, I have stood on the summit of the Mount of Beatitudes, overlooking the north end of the Sea of Galilee, with my Bible in my hand. I invariably turn to Matthew, chapters 5 through 7, and read our Lord's verbal giving of the Constitution of His kingdom. There I read: "Seek ye first the kingdom of God!"

I truly love to play golf. I started pursuing the little white sphere over meadows, forests, and into lakes when I was 18. After a half century one would think I could play well. One would be wrong! But my lack of skill does not detract from the sheer joy of smacking that Titleist in the general direction of the fairway. I love the friendly competition from lifelong friends and the good-natured kidding.

(I think it's good-natured.) But I don't get to play as much as I would enjoy, perhaps once or twice a month. That's a real shame because there are 180 fabulous golf courses within 45 minutes of my house.

It would be so easy to get consumed with golf, or any other hobby, to live and breathe the nuances of that given pursuit. I am not at that point, thank God. I still derive much greater satisfaction from my family and ministry. I cannot imagine, in the last hour of my life, looking back and thinking, *Wow, that was a great putt on the 14th green!* But achievements for God, relationships, providing for my wife and children, and now the grandchildren, reaching people for Christ, building churches around the world — yes, those are the things that will fill my mind in that last hour.

Now it's a pretty day in Florida and I'm about finished with my appointments, so I think I'll grab my clubs and — and — no, wait a minute, I have church tonight. See what I mean about priorities?

Byline #134

PRAYER

O God, don't let me get so mesmerized by the things of this world, good and pleasurable though they may be, that I forget my primary purpose for life. I want to seek You with all my strength and soul. Your smile of approval is my reward. Amen.

DEADLINES

Hebrews 9:27: And as it is appointed unto men once to die, but after this the judgment.

For over 40 years, I have lived with daily writing deadlines. As news director and anchor in radio and television years ago, I had four such deadlines every day. It didn't matter how I felt physically, or if it was snowing (it was in Ohio) or raining, those deadlines had to be met. I went on the air for the major TV newscast at 6:00 p.m. Not 6:01. If I failed to make the deadline, if I wasn't at the news desk at the appointed time, someone else would be there the next day.

During that Ohio sojourn, my wife and I were pioneering a church in our town. Obviously, there was not enough funding through church offerings to put food on our table, so I did what Paul did in Corinth: worked on the side. Paul made tents; I wrote and read newscasts. I made the daily news beat, interviewed potential sources of news stories, covered court trials, raced to the scene of wrecks, homicides, suicides, and city council meetings — you name it, I was there. I loved the job! Not only did it pay fairly well, but it also gave me the opportunity to meet everybody in town, which was an enormous help to me since my main interest was to start a church. Then, from 1979, in Christian radio and television I continued with daily deadlines, broadcasting, and telecasting for the Assemblies of God fellowship around the world. With the help of the Lord, I never missed a single broadcast. Not one deadline was ever missed, even during a week when I had spinal surgery. I kid you not!

But there is coming a far more urgent deadline than any I've ever faced before. As I grow older, I am confronted by my mortality. Should the Lord delay His return, the reality of the above verse from Hebrews 9:27 will be my portion as it is with all mankind. I am going to face God, not a news desk or pulpit. My homework will have to be finished when that last breath escapes my body. It will be my final deadline. Yours, too.

Prayer: O God, You have enabled me to meet thousands of deadlines throughout my lifetime. I have one major one yet to go. Let the thoughts I think, the words I say, and the way I live through faith in Your Son Jesus make me totally prepared for that last deadline. I am confident that You will. Amen.

An unforgettable character

2 Corinthians 5:17: Therefore if any man be in Christ, he is a new creature: old things are passed away; behold, all things are become new.

I met Gary Sanford Paxton in the old PTL television studios in the mid-80s. This is the man who gave the world such songs as "Alley Oop" and "Monster Mash." But then — that was *before Christ.* After he met the Savior, Gary gave us songs such as "He Was There All the Time."

When my wife, Darlene, and I lived in Missouri, on occasion I'd get a phone call from this performer and raconteur. He'd say, "I'll get up there in a day or two." Knowing Gary would not fly unless it was the Rapture, and then he'd complain about it, I understood he'd drive from Nashville to our house. So I'd just leave the front door to our house unlocked. On several occasions I'd hear our "wonder dog" (a weird poodle named Muffy) bark and hear Gary's distinctive voice bark back, "It's just me, Muff. Back off!" I'd laugh, turn over, and go back to sleep, knowing Gary would sack out on the front room sofa by the fireplace or go into the kitchen and cook himself an early breakfast. We always loved having "Pax" in the house.

On the Internet's Louie Report, the writer reported, "Gary Paxton has no idea of his remarkable position within the pantheon of 1960s Hollywood record men. He either wrote, arranged, performed upon, sang upon, engineered, A & R'd, or published any item that has his name on it. There is absolutely no one else in the American record industry like him." After years of living in the drug and booze culture, Gary surrendered his life to Christ several decades ago and has since written some of the true classic songs about Jesus. I still see him occasionally. And he still makes me laugh. I mean this is the guy who wrote a pop song with this title: "She Asked for Very Little; That's What I Gave Her; Now She's Gone!" How can you not love a guy like that? And I still appreciate his music.

Prayer: O God, I thank You for reaching Your saving hand into the life of my buddy Pax. The apostle Paul was so right when he wrote that when we come to Jesus we are made into new and different creations. Thank You for new life in Christ. Bless all those who are coming to the Master today. Keep them in Your great care. *Amen.*

WORDS

Proverbs 6:2: Thou art snared with the words of thy mouth, thou art taken with the words of thy mouth.

Have you ever inadvertently said something so dumb you just wanted to kick yourself? My goodness, if I actually did the self-kicking, I'd be black and blue. There is an old proverb, "There's many a slip 'twixt the cup and the lip." It can also be observed that there's many a slip 'twixt the brain and the mouth. Some examples:

A college basketball player was interviewed on TV concerning his knee surgery. He said, "I've never had a major knee surgery on any other part of my body." An actress, leading an anti-smoking drive, informed us, "Smoking kills; if you're killed, you've lost a very important part of your life." A former U.S. vice president, speaking out West, told his crowd, "I love California; I practically grew up in Phoenix." But here's my favorite from a pro football player: "The word 'genius' isn't applicable in football. A genius is a guy like Norman Einstein." But, look who's talking, me — the guy who said on a television newscast concerning a drug bust, "In his possession, police found a hypodeemic nerdle." And then I proceeded to repeat those words two more times.

Well, all those things are amusing. But the Bible teaches that some day we will give an account to God for every idle word we've spoken. The angels might even smile at the aforementioned goofs, and other similar gaffes. But what about other things we have said in anger, in a fit, uninformed, judgmental, and so forth. Small wonder David prayed, "Let the words of my mouth and the meditations of my heart [those things I even think!] be acceptable in thy sight, O Lord . . ." (Ps. 19:14).

Today let's think before we talk, and may our words exalt Christ.

PRAYER:
Prayer: Holy Spirit, may I bring each thought into captivity this day. And then may the words that I speak be honorable and uplifting. Guard my mind and my mouth today, I humbly pray. Amen.

THE EMPEROR'S LAST FUTILE EFFORT TO ESCAPE GOD

Psalm 139:7–8

Whither shall I go from thy spirit? or whither shall I flee from thy presence? If I ascend up into heaven, thou art there: if I make my bed in hell, behold, thou art there.

Recently it was my privilege to visit Xian, China, and the exhibition *in situ* of the thousands of terra cotta soldiers put there over 2,000 years ago. I purchased a museum full-sized replica of one of them and had it shipped home. It stands not more than 20 feet from the very spot I write this article, all 6'6" and 350 pounds of him. Those strange soldiers were put there by the first emperor of China, Qin Shihuang, hopefully to protect him from the spirits of the thousands of soldiers he had murdered or had someone else kill during his regime.

Now Chinese researchers report they have found a pyramid-shaped chamber in the emperor's underground tomb. The tomb has never been opened for fear that onrushing air would corrode or destroy the treasures believed to be housed inside. The chamber was located by the use of remote sensing equipment. The 100-foot-high chamber is believed to have been intended as a path for the emperor's ascending spirit, complete with ladder-like steps leading to the outlet above. I suspect that old Qin was disappointed in every aspect of his efforts. The thousands of terra cotta (which means dried mud) soldiers could not have stopped a mouse. And the moment he breathed his last, the emperor now stood before the Creator of the universe, God himself. The Chinese ruler was outranked and outflanked at every point!

Isn't it strange how various people attempt all sorts of things to prepare themselves for death — except the most vital effort of all, and that is reconciliation to God through Jesus Christ? All the king's horses and all the king's men could never put Qin back together again. His chance came in life and he blew it. But that was Qin. Now what about you, good friend? Are you prepared for eternity or are you, like the emperor, attempting to outwit God? You won't be any more successful than he was.

Byline #138

PRAYER

O God, through mankind's history we have tried to out-think You. No one has ever been successful. Yet we still try. We remember our Lord's words that He is the way, the truth, and the life and that no man can come to You except by Him (John 14:6). You prepared the only way to eternal life! That's the way we will accept. Amen.

THE POSITIVE INFLUENCE OF THE YOUNG SHORTSTOP

Byline #139

Matthew 5:16

Let your light so shine before men, that they may see your good works, and glorify your Father which is in heaven.

It is interesting how people influence your life. Recently somebody asked me why I'm such a die-hard fan of baseball's Cleveland Indians. Why indeed? Makes little sense, really. I grew up a thousand miles away from Cleveland and live even farther away now. If I am ever in northern Ohio in the summer, I do attempt to make it to at least one game in the "Jake" — that's Jacobs Field. I have been a fan since 1948. The reason is one man: Lou Boudreau.

Boudreau was an incredible shortstop, an exceptional hitter, and — get this! — in 1942, at the age of only 24, was made manager of the team. Who ever heard of such a thing? He was clean-cut, personable, and more handsome than most movie stars. But it was that 1948 season, the last World Series Championship year for the Tribe, that Boudreau had the fairytale year. Besides successfully managing the Indians, he had a torrid .355 batting average, an on-base percentage of .453, smacked 18 home runs, and drove in 106 runs. And remember, please, that was back in the days of the 154 games season (compared to the current 162 games season). There were many notable players on the Indians' roster that year: Joe Gordon, Ken Keltner, Larry Doby, Al Rosen, Bob Lemon, Bob Feller, and the legendary, ancient Satchel Paige. But it was Boudreau who captured my heart and attention.

Young people need heroes. And that is certainly true in today's church. They need men and women who are leaders in character, in strength, in values, in productivity in God's work to the extent that youth say, "I'd like to know God like that guy or gal!" Or, "I want my life to be like that person's." A young world is watching you, church leader. Don't fail them! Be the "Lou Boudreau of the church world."

PRAYER

O God, I want my life for You to be like that 1948 baseball season was for Boudreau — a major success. Help me to keep my eye on the ball. I want to win "the game" for You. Give me the incentive to stay in good shape, and to keep my eye on the prize that awaits me. I want to be spiritually victorious! Amen.

What if every church gave its members a test on the Bible?

2 Timothy 3:16: All scripture is given by inspiration of God, and is profitable for doctrine, for reproof, for correction, for instruction in righteousness.

Prolific author and thinker Leonard Sweet recently posted an article on his website about the Bible. He noted that 125 of the world's greatest writers listed their top ten books. Only six of those famed scribes mentioned the holy Scriptures of the Bible. Sweet asked, "What is happening to us? When your mind is not marinated and your spirit is not saturated on a daily basis in the Word, what is the potential of living out a faith-based life? How can we live without the Word?" And Sweet concluded, "Every home and heart needs to be pressed between the pages of the Bible. When you die, will they find your heart pressed between the pages of this book?"[1] Good question.

What do you suppose would happen in your church next Sunday morning if your pastor handed out tests? Let's say, oh, maybe 100 multiple choice questions on Bible basics. Nothing complicated, just questions that most kids in Sunday school should know. How do you think your congregation would do? I am afraid to even guess what the average scores would be. As a pastor, I feel it is incumbent to work on the Christian education emphasis just as much as other often-more-attractive ministries. I remember that Paul admonished young Timothy to "preach the Word," not preach *about* the Word. In today's prosperity-obsessed, feel-good religiosity, a return to the basics of the Bible is mandatory, as is our corporate and individual knowledge of it.

The cry of Israel's great king and psalmist, David, "Thy word have I hid in my heart that I might not sin against Thee" (Ps. 119:11), is still the remedy for most of the ecclesiastical and personal ills that confront us today.

1. www.leonardsweet.com.

Prayer: O God, I want to love Your Word, so much so that each time I open it, I feel as if I am sitting down to a multi-course meal prepared by the world's finest chefs. I want to feast on the eternal food I find therein. I pray that Your Holy Spirit will anoint the Word to my heart so that I might not sin against You or fall short of the work to which You have called me. *Amen.*

THOUGHTS ON DIVINE HEALING

Isaiah 53:5: But he was wounded for our transgressions, he was bruised for our iniquities: the chastisement of our peace was upon him; and with his stripes we are healed.

Is there a more soul-stirring verse to be found? Divine healing is an integral part of the gospel. Scriptures teach that divine healing is provided for in the atonement and is the privilege of all believers. One of the cardinal tenets of evangelical faith is that Jesus Christ is still the Great Physician.

As a boy, I can remember healing lines in our church services. We still have them in our church today. This practice is based on James 5:14–15: "Is any sick among you? Let him call for the elders of the church; and let them pray over him, anointing him with oil in the name of the Lord: And the prayer of faith shall save the sick, and the Lord shall raise him up; and if he have committed sins, they shall be forgiven him." In our church, we gently touch the foreheads with oil of those requesting prayer and ask God to heal them. No theatrics, no playing to the crowd. Only simple prayers to God for deliverance for those sick bodies. Is everyone healed? No. But many are.

The question must be considered, "Why isn't everyone healed?" The two main answers usually given, with too little thought or scriptural backing, are: not enough faith or sin in that life. Could be, but it's not necessarily so. Not being blessed with omniscience, I have no idea why God doesn't heal everyone. But the reality that He does not do so does not change the fact that Christ is still the Healer and many do receive physical release. One thing I have observed, though, is this: Decades ago, we relied a whole lot more on God for health than we do today. Thank God for doctors and the medical profession! They are true gifts to humanity. But perhaps if we looked to God more than we do, we would see more divine healings. When we're sick today, it's easy to take out our cell phone and call the medic. It is quite another thing to have developed faith, based on God's Word, that makes looking to Jesus the first priority.

Prayer: O God, I do believe, yes, even after all these scores of years, that You are truly the deliverer of both soul and body. I know You still heal for I have seen such healings with my own eyes — marvelous, miraculous deliverances. Our faith still "looks up to Thee, Thou Lamb of Calvary, Savior divine." Amen.

THE DANGER OF MISSING THE SIGNAL

Nehemiah 4:9

Nevertheless we made our prayer unto our God, and set a watch against them day and night.

The first church I pastored was in Vermilion, Ohio, a quaint and quite lovely village tucked against the southern shore of Lake Erie. My wife and I started that church in the first week of January 1963. We pulled into town in our tiny car with our (then) two children and dragging behind us a 5 x 8 U-Haul trailer containing everything in the world we owned. The weather was horrible, a blizzard, in fact. With our extremely limited resources, we rented an old house about 300 yards off the frozen lake, just 50 feet from railroad tracks. The first night we were there, we were awakened about two a.m. with the blast of a train whistle and the rushing iron beast shaking the whole house. I thought perhaps the Lord was coming!

Just west of town, one of the worst rail disasters in northern Ohio took place in August of 1906. The locals knew it as the Wreck of the Niles #152. It was an electric train that could move about 70 miles an hour. The engineer allegedly missed a signal to stop on a siding and careened head-on with an approaching train. Somewhere in my files I still have pictures of that colossal wreck, a grim reminder of what happens when a person neglects warning signs.

The Bible asks, "How shall we escape, if we neglect so great salvation?" (Heb. 2:3). Friend, that is the most vital question of life. The Wreck of the Niles #152 is small potatoes compared to missing God's redemption, an omission that costs an eternity of regret, sorrow, and torment away from the Father. How many times have you heard the gospel story and turned aside from it? How many altar calls? How many personal witnesses have been directed your way? Better be alert, good friend. Eternity's train is headed down your track. Don't miss the signals.

Byline #142

PRAYER

O God, may I ever be spiritually alert. As Paul wrote, "Be vigilant." There are always signs of impending danger, and Your blessed Word gives us a true map toward our eternal destination. Today, yes, this very day, may I be on my toes, always looking unto Jesus! May my life never become just human another wreck. Amen.

EFFECTIVE MINISTRY, EVEN UNDER SEVERE HANDICAPS

Acts 20:24: But none of these things move me, neither count I my life dear unto myself, so that I might finish my course with joy, and the ministry, which I have received of the Lord Jesus, to testify the gospel of the grace of God.

Victor and Rose Mars were heroes to me. For years, Victor had suffered the disease that slowly but surely turns the body into a stiffness resembling stone. But even confined to a wheelchair, unable to turn his head or raise his hands, Victor continued his weekly radio broadcasts. The time was in the early 1940s. His broadcast was known as the *Gospel Fellowship Hour* and was heard every Sunday morning at seven o'clock for a full hour on a powerhouse station, WNAX, that blanketed five states. Interestingly enough, the first half was in English and the second half was in Swedish. In that same studio, a polka-playing accordionist named Lawrence Welk had a regular show in the evenings. Some years later, a young newscaster named Tom Brokaw would learn his trade there. For Mars' program, I was the kid singer. I recall that the microphones in that day were huge, looking like soccer balls with wires hanging out of them. Recording tape had not been invented and all recordings were made on huge discs.

But it was Victor who commanded my attention and admiration. Attended to faithfully and skillfully by his wife Rose, Victor had a fresh and worthwhile message every Sunday morning. I never heard him complain, not even several years later when he had to do the broadcast from his living room, unable to leave his house. Victor proved to me that a person is pretty much limited only by his courage, vision, and faith, and not by his body. Victor had all those positive virtues and was faithful to his calling until the last day of his life. In that lifetime, hundreds of thousands of people were touched by his radio messages all over the Midwest. Eternity's morning will reveal how effective that dear man was.

PRAYER O God, I remember Victor so often and marvel at his faithfulness to You and his divine call, despite the pain and stony flesh. Like Paul, he could say, "None of these things move me. . . ." I regret and repent for my moaning and groaning over things of no consequence. Let my life today reflect Your purpose and heart — and that of Victor's. Amen.

Giving to God is a privilege and an honor

Matthew 10:8: . . . freely ye have received, freely give.

A pastor told me recently that no offerings are ever taken in the church he leads. He informed me that there is a wooden box in the lobby where any and all offerings can be placed. He said, "We never call attention to money in our church." I didn't say it, but I thought, "This guy hasn't ever read the New Testament apparently." Jesus talked about money — a lot!

And I had to chuckle because our church folks know we always take an offering and on some Sunday mornings we receive *two* of them. The first and regular offering is God's tithes, our actual offerings above and beyond the tithes, our missions giving, and our building fund contributions. The second offering, when needed, is for special projects such as a visiting missionary, a need in the church, or some unusual project not included in the budget.

Someone has observed that there are three books that highlight a person's spiritual life: the Bible, the hymnal (which is packed with solid theology), and the checkbook. Folks who are truly committed to God love to give! They are faithful tithers, that 10 percent right off the top that belongs to God. On top of that they give offerings because of their love for Him. They support missions with their faith promises, which brings another supernatural element of resource supply into their lives. And, in our case, the folks feel responsibility for capital improvements that are always necessary in a growing church. So, no, we don't have that wooden box in the lobby of this church. We love to give. And God blesses us over and again. Jesus said, "Seek ye first the kingdom of God, and his righteousness; and all these things shall be added unto you" (Matt. 6:33).

Have you ever noticed that people who love to give never seem bothered by references to money in church?

Prayer: O God, You loved us so much that You gave. We who love You also thrill in the privilege of giving to You and Your kingdom. Thank You for making it possible for us to tithe and then to give above and beyond that. It is not out of necessity that we do this, but out of our passion for You. *Amen.*

JESUS PAID IT ALL

John 17:4

> I have glorified thee on the earth: I have finished the work which thou gavest me to do.

Every year our Jewish friends celebrate a time called Yom Kippur. It is an extremely important time in their calendar. Many Jews who do not observe any other Jewish custom will refrain from work, fast, and attend synagogue. This holiday was instituted long ago in the Bible, and you can read the basis for it in Leviticus 23:26–30: "And the Lord spake unto Moses, saying, Also on the tenth day of this seventh month there shall be a day of atonement: it shall be an holy convocation unto you; and ye shall afflict your souls, and offer an offering made by fire unto the Lord. And ye shall do no work in that same day: for it is a day of atonement, to make an atonement for you before the Lord your God. For whatsoever soul it be that shall not be afflicted in that same day, he shall be cut off from among his people. And whatsoever soul it be that doeth any work in that same day, the same soul will I destroy from among his people."

This is a day in which Jews atone for the sins of the past year, sins between God and the supplicant alone, not sins against another person. No work can be done on this day; even restraint from drinking water must be observed.

We who are Christians believe that Jesus did all the atoning, the paying for our sins, on His cross. We understand that we cannot work for our salvation. That truth, however, does not eliminate the need for self-examination, as Paul commanded the church in Corinth. While I have the greatest respect for Yom Kippur and appreciate the Jewish people and their holidays, I am even more grateful for the fact that on Calvary's cross Jesus paid the entire cost for my atonement. The debt has been paid fully and completely and my trust is in Jesus alone.

PRAYER

O God, what a cost it was! Darkness covered Jerusalem even though it was only afternoon. The rocks were split by an earthquake. The charred corridors of hell were shaken when our Lord cried, "It is finished!" Even the Roman centurion declared, "Truly, this was the Son of God!" I thank You today for my salvation and I thank You that You paid it all. Amen.

SEVEN MILES IN THE AIR IN A PLASTIC TUBE

Hebrews 11:1

Now faith is the substance of things hoped for, the evidence of things not seen.

Scriptures make it clear that we cannot make God happy unless we have faith. We do not mean salvation faith here, but the gift of faith that ushers us into the world of the supernatural. For years, my daily prayer for myself has been a simple one: "Lord, please increase my faith." I suspect that the Holy Spirit reveals to each of us that we actually have more faith than we suppose.

Let me give you an example: Many of us fly commercially as a routine thing. Multitudes of Americans fly daily. If I had a dollar for every mile I've ever flown, I quite honestly would have over $3 million from that enterprise. Now, my friend, it takes a measure of faith to climb into a metal tube and be launched seven miles into the sky. Believe me! But now we learn that this act will require even more faith. Why? Because the Boeing Corporation recently unveiled its newest aircraft, the Boeing 787. Already well over 600 orders have been placed for this magnificent $162 million airplane. But here's the thing about it that stretches my faith: This new plane is made of (and I hesitate to even break this to you) *plastic*! I kid you not. And even scarier to me was when I watched the video report of the manufacturing of these planes that I learned the fuselage is made up of 19-foot sections of this plastic *popped* together. Now the fact is this new composite material is stronger than anything ever before used in aircraft construction. So a flier should think he or she is safer than ever. And probably is. But the thought of being with several hundred fellow passengers 39,000 feet above the ground in a plastic tube is hardly reassuring.

Now let's reason this out: if we can have a measure of faith in an aeronautics concept of flying miles high in a plastic container, we can certainly have faith in the Divine Creator who made all things and who watches over us all. Now see — you *do* have faith, a whole lot more of it than you thought.

Byline
#146

PRAYER

O God, I do believe! Honestly I do, but please help my unbelief. My old human nature all too often rises to the surface to sputter, "But . . . but . . . but. . . ." Help me to fully understand that if You declare something to be, it is! Amen.

DON'T LET THAT BABY DIE!

1 Corinthians 4:15: For though ye have ten thousand instructors in Christ, yet have ye not many fathers: for in Christ Jesus I have begotten you through the gospel.

It has often been observed that most men can sire a child, but as Paul put it, there sometimes aren't "many fathers" to raise them. That line jolts the mind and brings to us the thought that it's one thing to give birth to a church, but it's quite another thing to raise it. In our own fellowship, for every 100 churches birthed, over half of them die before reaching maturity. If parents bring a baby home from the hospital and neglect feeding it, changing it, cleaning it, nourishing it, and certainly loving it, that child will doubtless die. If somehow it survives, it may not be normal.

This is just another reason why, as a pastor, I have always been so sold on "satelliting" new churches. We have four of them, in addition to the "mother church." They are each healthy, growing congregations because they are given constant supervision, direction, feeding, and when needed, changing and cleaning. With all the heresies infiltrating churches today, from the extreme prosperity teaching to inclusion (which is rank heresy), a congregation must have biblically knowledgeable direction. It is unrealistic to think that new converts, hungry to grow spiritually, can always tell good food from bad. Or to know when they are being exploited for whatever reason. Our mother church, the central campus, gives diligent watch over the other four campuses, working with its leaders, teaching the Word in every way possible, supervising, giving direction and vision, and maintaining the finances when necessary. Nothing is more offensive than a deadbeat dad, unless it's a church that spawns another congregation and allows it to die.

There comes great responsibility with church planting. It isn't easy or inexpensive. It is very hard work. But it is just incredibly worth it! I encourage your church to plant another one. But when you do, nourish it.

Prayer: O God, as a pastor and a church leader, I want to be a good parent to those congregations that have come from us. I gladly accept the responsibility for fulfillment of the vision you have laid upon my heart. Thank You for Your Holy Spirit power to spread the Word to our region. Amen.

What might have been

James 4:14: For what is your life?

Many years ago I pastored a church located 50 miles west of Cleveland, Ohio. Being a baseball fan, I often made my way to old, creaky, cold Lakefront Stadium to watch the Cleveland Indians. The team was truly awful back in those days, the doormat of the American League, and so the crowds were sparse. Facetiously I tell people that I'd call the stadium box office and ask, "What time is tonight's game?" And they would reply, "What time can you get here?" It wasn't really that bad, but almost. The park would hold over 80,000 fans; but I can remember one night against Baltimore the announced crowd was under 1,500 fans. No, not 15,000 — 1,500! It was a good place to spend an evening if you wanted to be alone.

The Indians had a pitcher, Sudden Sam McDowell. He actually won 20 games in 1970, and for his career in the majors won 143 games. The lefty had a blazing fastball and a curve that would make hitters look foolish. I watched him play a lot of times, always enjoying the sound of his pitches smacking into the catcher's glove. What an explosive fastball! But in his ten-year hitch in the majors, Sam really had only two good years. Why? Booze. He was arrested eight times for driving while intoxicated and was also picked up on assault charges. In his own words (as reported by the *Cleveland Plain Dealer* sports editor Hal Lebovitz), "Only by the grace of God I didn't kill my wife — or get killed. There is no way I should be alive today." It's been some years now since Sudden Sam drank. He summarized his life by saying, "I now live alone in an apartment. My marriage ended in divorce. I can't deal with might have been if I weren't an alcoholic. But I am one and I'm trying to deal with it if I can."[1]

Every teenager should have to listen to Sam's witness. Maybe then they would never take that first drink to appease their peers. Maybe they'd never live with a lifetime of regrets. McDowell can only wonder . . . what might have been.

1. Hal Lebovitz, *The Best of Hal Lebovitz* (Cleveland, OH: Gray and Co., 2004), p. 243).

Prayer: O God, may we, as parents and grandparents, not only encourage our progeny in right living, but may we also show them how to do it by the lives we ourselves live before them. I bless the memory of parents who taught me right from wrong. Now that I am old, I will not depart from it, as Your Word promises. ***Amen.***

THOSE WHO HAVE GONE BEFORE US

Deuteronomy 32:7: Remember the days of old, consider the years of many generations: ask thy father, and he will shew thee; thy elders, and they will tell thee.

There is a recurring triad of names we encounter in the Old Testament narrative: the God of Abraham, Isaac, and Jacob. Over and over again we read those three names. It was a bonding of what was taking place at the moment with the historic foundations of "what had been." That's an important lesson for us to remember today. We are what we are now because someone went before us, expanding his or her reality into an unknown possibility that we enjoy today.

This is true in so many arenas of life. Think of the tens of thousands of unknown U.S. colonies soldiers who lost their lives fighting the British in the Revolutionary War so we could be free from King George III's outrageous taxation tyranny. Go down the history of American wars and consider the hundreds of thousands of casualties. Democracy is not free, friend. On the spiritual side, think of those men and women who founded the church you attend, who gave of themselves sacrificially, who went without necessities so one day you could have a strong and effective congregation.

Today, there are those who apparently think churches just "happen" and so they can take just 'em or leave 'em. They forget the human lives involved in the formation of those Christian institutions. And they forget, apparently, the ultimate price that was paid for them on a rugged cross near the hills of Jerusalem 2,000 years ago. To thumb one's nose at the Church is to tell God His Son Jesus wasted His time and life on Calvary. This page is a call to remembrance! Remember all that long historic line of heroes who preceded you. And be thankful!

PRAYER: O God, when I think of all the extraordinary men and women who have paved the path for our ministry here, I am very moved. Some of those heroes of the faith poured out their health on this church, both clergy and laity. I thank You for them. I have tried to contact these folks personally to express my appreciation. I will not forget those who have gone before us. Amen.

G.A. COMSTOCK, GOD'S PIONEER

1 Corinthians 3:13

Every man's work shall be made manifest: for the day shall declare it, because it shall be revealed by fire; and the fire shall try every man's work of what sort it is.

As a little kid, I used to see a quaint, older gentleman in our church in Iowa. He had a bushy mustache and sparkling eyes behind rather thick glasses. Sometimes he even sat on the platform, and I often wondered why. Then my father told me his remarkable story.

In the 1920s, there were very few Assemblies of God churches in the Missouri-Iowa-Nebraska area. The superintendent of that district made a call for pastors to establish a home base in each county and then proceed to evangelize the balance of the county. No one did it better than the old gentleman in question. His name was George Comstock. He was amazing. Within a few years' time, he had started thriving and solid churches in such towns as Homer, Dailey, Pender, Macy, Walthill, Thurston, Emerson, Allen, New Castle, and Rosalie. Among his converts was a young man whose name was Willis Smith, who sometime later built the great congregation in Sioux City, Iowa, then the largest church in our fellowship in about five states. Smith was also the man who brought all my family to Christ, about 75 of them in all. This is all back in WWII days. "Daddy Comstock," as he was known, set up teams all over the region, including to the Winnebago Native Americans in Nebraska. More times than I can remember, as a little boy, I was placed on a chair to sing to those precious people on the reservation.

Someday at the Judgment Seat of Christ (you watch carefully for this!), the name G.A. Comstock will be called out by an angel. That quaint little man will walk to the throne to receive his eternal rewards. I suspect he'll have an avalanche of them. May God give us 21st-century "Daddy Comstocks," men and women who will go anywhere to establish strong works for the Lord.

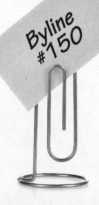

Byline #150

PRAYER

O God, how many times, as a boy, I watched that old man, wondering about him. Little did I know at first the greatness of his stature in eternity. Had it not been for his devotion to do the impossible, there is a chance that my family never would have been reached for You. Help me, Lord, to ever be faithful to You, yes, even in the smallest of tasks, and of course, the big jobs, too. Amen.

PREACHING IN DENMARK

Byline #151

John 20:31
... that ye might believe that Jesus is the Christ, the Son of God; and that believing ye might have life through his name.

Several months ago, our missions' outreach took my wife and me to Denmark and Russia. Denmark is a truly lovely country with about eight million residents. Only about 15,000 of them are known evangelicals. You would find most of those 15,000 in church on any given Sunday morning; however, on any given Friday, you would find 150,000 Muslims in their mosques. That's almost a ten-to-one ratio! How about the rest of the Danes? It is observed by some that they worship the God of materialism.

I was invited to address a Lutheran convocation in the charming seaside town of Arhus. There were 2,000 there that night, most of them charismatics. There was a powerful move of God in the service. An hour after the message, there were still hundreds of those Lutherans at the altar and in group prayers throughout the auditorium — and even scattered around the campus. My friends and I had to leave because we still had a two-hour drive to Miriager, in north Denmark, Jutland, where I was to speak early the next morning. As we drove off the grounds in Arhus, we could still hear the people calling out to God.

Materialism is a huge issue in Denmark. Despite heavy income taxation, the people live on a very high standard, with cradle-to-grave care from their government. Like the Laodicean church of Revelation, they feel they are in need of nothing. Much of Western Europe is like that. Yet God says, "You do not realize that you are wretched, pitiful, poor, blind and naked" (Rev. 3:17; NIV). Good friend, support your effective missionaries in Western Europe. Don't assume that Europe is Christian. It isn't, any more than America is. Both continents desperately need God, but in all-too-many instances, the churches are sound asleep, doing business as usual.

PRAYER

O God, You have called us to be watchmen on the tower. If we were awake and really watching, we would see the encroachment of the silent enemy, materialism and laissez faire attitudes toward the issues of eternity. Forgive us, O God, and restore to us a sense of urgency of the moment! Amen.

How to spend $30,000

Matthew 16:26: For what is a man profited, if he shall gain the whole world, and lose his own soul? or what shall a man give in exchange for his soul?

What would you do with $30,000? Any idea how many hungry people you could feed in Sudan or some other deprived region of the world? You could build five full church buildings in rural China, each one seating over 500 persons, with that amount of money. Thirty thousand dollars would train several hundred ministerial students in Bangalore, India. Oh, the magnificent work for God that could be done with that money.

You know what else you could do with $30,000? You could rent the new penthouse in a New York City hotel — for *one night!* I kid you not! This suite contains 4,300 square feet and cost over $50 million to build. It rests on the 52nd floor of the Manhattan hotel with views in all four directions. This penthouse is just the latest in an explosion of $15,000-a-night-and-up crash pads at top city hotels around the world. For example, I recently drove by a hotel in Moscow — *Moscow*! — where the penthouse rents for just under 20 grand a night. (Notice, I just "drove by it.") The aforementioned New York City facility features cantilevered outdoor glass balconies that cost $2 million apiece. Gold-threaded curtains from Morocco surround the bed. The bathroom shimmers with a rare translucent onyx. On and on this opulence goes.

It is said of many Americans that we know the price of everything and the value of nothing. We preachers like to lament various sins of mankind. In fact, we can wax positively eloquently about them. But I wonder sometimes if America's and (Europe's) worship at the shrine of materialism isn't perhaps the greatest sin of all. It is kin to idolatry. And God has never in history tolerated that affront from anyone. It's that "thou shalt have no other gods before me" edict (Exod. 20:3).

Prayer: O God, how bitterly sad when we opt for that which so soon tarnishes or tears over those things of life that are truly eternal. We settle for earth's cheapjack wares when You offer treasure that will last when a star's last ember has flickered into darkness. Teach us to know that which is Your value and that which is not. *Amen.*

THE GAMBLING RACKET

Acts 24:25: And as he reasoned of righteousness, temperance, and judgment to come, Felix trembled, and answered, Go thy way for this time; when I have a convenient season, I will call for thee.

Those were the words of Roman Governor Felix to the apostle Paul. He took a gamble with his eternal soul. He lost. What else do you expect when you gamble?

There are some who claim gambling is merely an innocent pastime. Try telling that to a National Basketball Association referee who lost his job, his reputation, and his freedom. What would cause a person making a quarter-million-dollar annual salary, doing something he truly enjoyed, to violate his job to the extent it could cost him 25 years in the slammer? What, indeed! Gambling! This referee shook up the sports world after his admission of betting on games, some of which he allegedly refereed. The felony charges against him include conspiracy to engage in wire fraud and transmitting betting information through interstate commerce. It brings to mind the tragic case of Pete Rose, who had more hits in major league baseball than any other player. Yet he was barred from Baseball's Hall of Fame because of — you got it! — gambling on games. Who knows how many professional boxing matches are on the up-and-up anymore? One of the indictments against gambling is this: if you do somehow win, it will be at the expense of somebody else. You win? Then someone else loses. It is the nature of this epidemic that someone inevitably will get the "short end of the stick." The Bible teaches that material gain without commensurate work or investment is immoral.

But the greatest gamble of all is playing with one's immortal soul, such as the Roman governor, the aforementioned Felix. Every breath one takes without committing to Jesus Christ is a gamble of unprecedented potential disaster. No wonder the Bible declares, "Now is the day of salvation" (2 Cor. 6:2).

Prayer: O God, I am so grateful for the "blessed assurance" of knowing that all is well with my soul. Every hour spent with You is a pleasure, a delight, a blessing. I will not gamble with that which is so precious to me, and that is my relationship to You. Amen.

GOD'S CREATIVE GENIUS THROUGH THE INDIVIDUAL

Genesis 1:1

God created. . . .

Those two words speak volumes. God was creative. James writes that there is no shadow of turning, or change, with God, so He is still creative. Since He dwells within His children, there must be creative instincts within us as followers of Christ. Sadly, the status of far too many believers is "quo."

For 17 years, it was my privilege to be the speaker on the internationally syndicated radio program *Revivaltime*. We were heard on about 700 stations in over 80 nations. One of our outlets was a powerful network of stations with towers in such major cities as New York, Chicago, Denver, San Francisco, and Dallas. It was our delight to be on that marvelous network each week. At that time, all of us who were broadcast producers, including Billy Graham's *Hour of Decision*, produced 29-minute broadcasts. That was the standard. But this great network I have just described wanted more time for commercials and required a 27-minute format instead. That was

Byline #154

a major problem for us all, for no producers in Christian media could afford to produce both a 29- and a 27-minute format. Almost all of us adopted the 27-minute program, which caused concerns to those hundreds of other stations who still needed 29 minutes of programming. Where would hundreds of religious stations get a 2-minute broadcast?

Our agent at the time, David Clark, suggested we produce a 2-minute release that these other hundreds of stations could use as a public service, a broadcast that would give commentary on the day with a spiritual "spin." Clark said, "Dan, you're an old radio/TV newsman; use the 'byline' concept." And that's how it started. Before long, radio stations across the country had scheduled *Byline,* and the television off-shoot started shortly thereafter. We were soon released hundreds of times daily, Monday through Friday, on radio and several thousand times around the world through Christian television networks. Then came the Internet, which wrapped itself around the world, and once again, *Byline* was there. The last year we produced these programs, we were given literally millions of dollars in free airtime! And, you know, we would have missed it all had it not been for the creative hand of God in our agent.

PRAYER

O God, I do truly thank You for Your continued creativity in Your children. Make me aware of my opportunities to serve You today. Amen.

EXACTLY WHEN WAS THE CUT-OFF DATE FOR THE SUPERNATURAL?

Acts 5:12: And by the hands of the apostles were many signs and wonders wrought among the people.

What place do supernatural signs and wonders have in today's Church? The head of the Church, Jesus Christ himself, promised that signs and wonders would follow in the wake of a missions-minded church or individual. He gave no cut-off date on that commitment. We should still be seeing God's sovereign hand at work in our congregations, not to mention our private lives, considering, of course, that we are personally obedient to Christ's Great Commission (if not by actually going to the missions field, then certainly by supporting those who do).

Yes, there is danger in pursuing signs and wonders rather than pursuing Christ himself. Paul made it clear in 1 Corinthians 3 that Jesus alone is the foundation of His church, not personal anecdotal experiences. But even while acknowledging the misdirection our emotions can take, should we still not see the miraculous in our midst? Perhaps we disregard divine intervention because we have gotten so good at taking care of ourselves, thank you very much.

I often read in commentaries and religious journals that the day of miracles ceased with the original Apostles. I don't believe that for a moment. There is not a word in Scripture to indicate the cessation of the supernatural. I have seen too many miracles, such as healing and resource provision, to ever doubt their existence. Many of us grew up seeing God's hand at work in our families. My wife often tells me similar stories about her preacher father and his terrific faith and the resulting signs and wonders that occurred in their household. Yes, we believe in modern medicine and are thankful for every break-through in discovery to alleviate suffering. But we believe even more that God is still the Great Miracle Worker. No, my friend, there was never a cut-off date for the supernatural. Never!

PRAYER: O God, I rejoice today that You hear us when we pray. I exalt Your name when I think of all the times You have answered those prayers "with signs following" our faith. I am grateful to understand that You are the same, yesterday, today, and forever. My faith increases even as I pray this prayer. Thank You. Amen.

On meeting Betty Baxter

Acts 3:6: Then Peter said, Silver and gold have I none; but such as I have give I thee: In the name of Jesus Christ of Nazareth rise up and walk.

The other day, while online, I read once again one of the most marvelous stories of divine healing I've ever seen. As I read it, my mind raced back to the late 1940s. My parents and I drove across Sioux City, Iowa, to a tiny church (I can still recall the address, 9th and Court). The meager sanctuary was standing room only. Everyone had come to hear a young woman tell her amazing story of divine healing. Her name was Betty Baxter, the same woman and story I read online this morning.

As a child, Betty's spinal cord looked like a train wreck. Every bone, every muscle, every nerve was out of place, twisted, and deformed. Her head rested against her knees. Her pain was beyond bearing, and she would often lapse into multi-day unconsciousness. Physicians told her folks there was simply nothing that could be done for her but to make her as comfortable as possible until she died. Betty loved Jesus passionately, and she prayed constantly. One day she heard the Lord speak to her, "Betty, in ten days, at three o'clock in the afternoon, I am going to heal you." Amazingly, her mother received the same word from the Lord.

Ten days later, precisely at 3:00, with family and friends around her bedside, Betty reports literally seeing Jesus walk into her room. He greeted her in love and compassion and then placed His hands upon her body. In ten seconds, she was completely healed. Betty devoted her life to lifting Jesus in testimony around the world. As far as I know, she is still telling the story. What an impact she played on me and so many others in our family 60 years ago when we first heard the story. My friend Jesus remains as He always was, the Great Physician. If your body is broken or failing today, ask the Lord to heal you. Give Him your life and your praise.

Prayer: O God, I never cease to be amazed at Betty's incredible miracle. How good You have been to her and millions of others. May someone reading this page today feel his or her faith elevated to a new level and then sense Your healing presence in the room. I bless You, faithful Master-Healer, that You still feel compassion toward us. *Amen.*

A TREASURE FOUND IN A STACK OF OLD RECORDS

2 Timothy 1:5

When I call to remembrance the unfeigned faith that is in thee. . . .

The other day, a fellow came by my office and said he wanted to give me something. His gift was a couple hundred old LP records. (Remember them?) He said, "Keep what you want or just throw 'em all away." I just went through that stack. Oh, my goodness, there are treasures in that pile of "wax." Among them the Longines Symphonette Society's "The Years To Remember." These records featured the most dramatic and vital newscasts in radio history, exactly as we heard them when they changed the course of human events. Such as: The funeral of Britain's King George V, the Munich Conference with British Prime Minister Chamberlain and Germany's then-Fuhrer Adolf Hitler, the first Pearl Harbor news flash in 1941, President Franklin Roosevelt's "Day of Infamy" speech, President Truman's announcement of an A-bomb attack on Hiroshima, Japan, and General Douglas MacArthur's signing the peace treaty ending World War II.

Radio, as we knew it then, made history burst to life for us. I believe it deepened our love for America and gave us a keener insight into our heritage of liberty. I wonder sometimes if today's generation has even a clue of what forces formed this nation: of the fountains of blood spilled at Corregidor, in Germany's dark forests, at Pearl Harbor, of the courageous heroes who kept us on course and out of harm's way. America did not just emerge from some vacuum.

Listening to those precious LP album treasures has caused me to remember once again. It is possible that remembrance is one of God's greatest gifts to us. That gift keeps us from having to relive all our mistakes over and over again. Memory gives us a moral compass. But our memories have to be used, to be referred to, over and again.

PRAYER

O God, You programmed memory into our brains for a reason. I thank You that we can look back and see life's treasurers re-unfolded before our eyes. May we learn from the past and enjoy the precious things that we recall. And may we never forget Calvary and all that was done there for our redemption. Amen.

OBSERVATIONS ABOUT THE APOSTLE PAUL

2 Corinthians 2:4

For out of much affliction and anguish of heart I wrote unto you with many tears; not that ye should be grieved, but that ye might know the love which I have more abundantly unto you.

Taylor Caldwell wrote a novel about the apostle Paul, titled *Great Lion of God.* It was based on Scripture and remained amenable to the Word. About the same time, John Pollack, who wrote the famous biography of Billy Graham, wrote *The Man Who Shook the World,* also about Paul, but this book was a bio, not a novel. I have many other books in my library about the apostle Paul, one more fascinating than the previous one.

Few men in human history have evoked more debate than Paul. Few have ever been more misquoted or misunderstood. Critics have labeled him anti-woman; but the reality was that he elevated their status to new heights in his highly sexist society. Some have charged that he was a cantankerous old man; but the reality was that he gave love its ultimate definition in 1 Corinthians 13. This man poured out the sacrificial offering of his very life in taking the good news of God's redemption all around the northern Mediterranean Sea. His last will and testament, scratched by quill from Emperor Nero's death cell in Rome, is classic literature of tender and gentle concern for his peers. Pollack was pinpoint accurate with his description of Paul: the man who shook the world! Yet who would have ever guessed such an accolade when Paul was known as Saul and was ravaging the early church like a man possessed?

We all too often underestimate the power of the Cross in a person's life. Didn't Paul himself write that when we come to Jesus all the old garbage of our lives is eradicated and we become totally new in Christ? If you have never studied the life of Paul, don't just accept the word of his critics. Find out for yourself what the man was truly like. I suspect that Paul will ultimately become one of your champions.

Byline #158

PRAYER

O God, thank You for giving us heroes such as Paul. When we see where he came from, by the grace of God, to the heights of victory he achieved in Your name, we are encouraged to believe that You can use us, too. We also look unto Jesus, the author and finisher of our faith as we labor for You. Amen.

MAKING SOMEONE LOOK GOOD

JOHN 16:13: Howbeit when he, the Spirit of truth, is come, he will guide you into all truth: for he shall not speak of himself. . . .

Richard Champion slipped away from us to be with the Lord quite a few years ago. In his very successful career, he was the editor of the famed *Pentecostal Evangel* and was listed in Who's Who in America and Who's Who in Religion. He was also a very proficient writer and authored several books. But it was as an editor that he made his mark. He was so good at it, in fact, that he could even make my copy look reasonably good when it appeared in his magazine. I used to tease him about it. "Dick," I'd grumble, "I don't even recognize my stuff when it appears in your magazine." He'd just grin and retort, "For that you should be eternally grateful."

Writers often lambaste editors, but the whole point of their work is to make the scribe look good. In that regard, the Holy Spirit is an editor. His work, first of all, is to call humanity's attention to Christ Jesus. But in the process, He also cleans up our humanness and sophisticates it for the Master, or as Paul put it, He "conforms us to the image of Christ" (see Rom. 8:29). Some of the fruit of the Holy Spirit's abiding includes longsuffering, gentleness, goodness, and temperance. None of us have all those qualities in very great abundance, and the "copy" we turn in can look pretty messy, especially when illuminated by the holiness of our Heavenly Father. Oh, we think we come out looking pretty fine, but we're not objective about ourselves, are we? But when the Holy Spirit is in control, He takes all those split infinitives and dangling participles of our "copy" and makes our work actually look presentable.

Still, we fight Him. We want to be left alone and then wonder why the Eternal Publisher, who is God, rejects our offerings. The fact is, we attempted to bypass the Editor. That's always a no-no.

Prayer: O God, I want Your precious Holy Spirit to edit from my life anything that is offensive to You. I pray with David, in effect, "Search me, O God, and know my heart." I present my life to You for a full edit. Thank You! Amen.

Byline #160

No, never alone!

Deuteronomy 4:31: . . . he will not forsake thee . . . nor forget the covenant of thy fathers which he sware unto them.

David assured us in the 139th Psalm that God is always near us. He penned, "If I ascend up into heaven, thou art there. If I make my bed in hell, behold, thou art there. If I take the wings of the morning, and dwell in the uttermost part of the sea; even there shall thy hand lead me and thy right hand shall hold me" (Ps. 139:8–10). That verse, by the way, is the Scripture Colonel Charles Lindbergh had inscribed on his Maui tombstone at Hana.

Has God deserted you? Absolutely not. But are you consciously aware of His presence? Perhaps not. We walk by faith and not by feeling. There are those times of barren desert in our pilgrimage when there is absolutely no conscious awareness that God is near. We sometimes feel deserted and forsaken. However, we accept, by faith, that God is there because His Word declares that He

is. God is omnipresent, that is; He is everywhere at one and the same time. It would be impossible to find any nook or cranny in this universe where we would be exempt from His presence. Yes, we have that head knowledge, but not always that heart feeling. Circumstances often pile high on us, making us feel that we are flying solo. But we are not by ourselves. My friend, we have heard it so many times, but it's true: we live by faith, not feeling. God is there! Sometimes it's hard for us to rationalize that heavenly principle, isn't it? We must believe what the Word says. Our human emotions are roller coasters, while our faith in God is life's one constant.

No, you are not alone today. God is with you. He will always be with you. Practice your faith even now and begin to reach for Him. You won't have to reach very far.

Prayer: O God, with great relief we stand upon the foundation of Your written promise to us that You will never forsake us. When we come to You, through Jesus, You never reject us, never turn us away. Even in the most remote corners of our life's experiences, You are there. Always and ever! I am so grateful. ***Amen.***

PRAYING TO WHOM? OR WHAT?

Matthew 24:24: For there shall arise false Christs, and false prophets, and shall shew great signs and wonders; insomuch that, if it were possible, they shall deceive the very elect.

In His Mount Olivet prophetic discourse, Jesus listed signs of the end time. The sign He mentioned multiple times was deception, especially of believers. We are living in that time of a proliferation of false Christs and re-definitions of the real Christ (which makes Him become something other than who He truly is, which is rank idolatry).

Just when you think you've heard everything, something comes along that just about paralyzes your mind. Case in point: Recently, a supposed Christian cleric in Europe proposed an idea he believes could heal Christian/Muslim tensions. His idea is for Christians to begin praying to Allah instead of God. He opined, "After all, God and Allah are the same being." What?! Did we hear this fellow right? God and Allah are synonymous? Not unless daffodils grow daily in Antarctica. Not until the same day a blueberry is the same thing as a watermelon. God and Allah become the same thing in the theological world on the same day a Yugo becomes the same as a Maybach in the world of automobiles.

To this cleric, whom I leave unnamed, I have a better suggestion: how about from this day on, in the name of international good will, every Muslim prays to God and Jesus? What is this insanity among us that drives otherwise thinking people to capitulation to the world of Islam? Are we so bent on accommodation, so determined to pound nails in our own coffin of liberty, that we would yield all thinking processes to such nonbiblical suppositions? Christians and Muslims do *not* worship the same God. Christianity does not exist without the Christ of God, the person in whom we have personal access to the Creator. To Muslims, Jesus is a mere prophet, nothing more. Most Muslim fundamentalists will tell you that Jesus did not even die on the cross. To us who follow Jesus, He is the way, the truth, and the life, and no one comes to the Father other than through Him. Allah came from the mind of a sixth-century camel driver. God was in the very beginning. No, I just believe I'll keep praying to God.

PRAYER: O God, forgive us for such blasphemy against Your name that we would even consider You to be anyone other than who You truly are, or that we would even consider praying to any other entity. Amen.

PORN AND PANCAKES

Romans 1:26

For this cause God gave them up unto vile affections. . . .

Our telephones at the church rang off the hook. One right after another. All because of a giant billboard in town. It read: "Porn and Pancakes Breakfast/ First Assembly Ministries." Wow, did that jolt a lot of people! The questions flew at me: "What in the world is a porn and pancakes breakfast?" News crews from two of the local television stations showed up, wondering the same thing. The answer is simple. Many churches, including ours, have decided to become aggressive in an antipornography campaign.

A talented and enterprising young fellow in California, Craig Gross, founded the XXX (pronounced Triple-X) Ministry. Using God's Word, brilliant presentations, and a heart hungry to see people set free from this addiction, Gross comes to churches on weekends, kicked off with the "porn and pancakes" breakfast. Men and boys signed up for our event by the hundreds. Yes, we have some naysayers who question our tactics. One said to me, "Pastor, I find this offensive." Well, let me tell you what I find offensive: knowing that even in Christ's church there are many who have become addicted to this devastating behavior, and pastors and church boards still do little or nothing about it. That, to me, is incredibly offensive. Hey, it's not just men, either. It is believed that 30 percent of all those addicted to pornography are women. As a pastor, when I hear parents tell me their ten-year-old kids purposely or inadvertently download porn sites on their computers, it makes my blood chill. They are heading for lives pockmarked by tragedy, loss, and a perverted value system.

The church of Jesus Christ must become more clever and more powerful than the enemy who would destroy us. Through Christ and the power of His Holy Spirit, we can be victorious in this absolutely vital effort against pornography.

PRAYER

O God, forgive us not only for a national bent to this kind of destructive viewing, but also forgive us just as much for our shocking lack of concern for those who are addicted. Your Word teaches us that to know to do something right yet refrain from actually doing so is a sin. And so, we put on the whole armor of God and march into the fray, even while knowing some of our fellow believers may not understand. Help us be steadfast in Your work. Amen.

THE GREATEST CHURCH GROWTH BOOK EVER WRITTEN

Byline #163

There are literally thousands of books in my library. And, yes, I have read them all (with very few exceptions). Some of those volumes, quite honestly, are church growth books. Some of them have been helpful; others are a waste of reading time. But I have come across one book that transcends them all. It is quite simply the most powerful church growth book I own. It is called the Book of the Acts, the fifth book in the New Testament. It is the story of ordinary people just like you and me, people in whom the Holy Spirit began to dwell and move. It is the story of good people and bad, of saints and sinners, of kings and paupers, of emperors and tent makers. It is a drama recounting how the Jews of Israel who accepted Christ as Messiah were dispersed over much of the known world after bitter persecution for their faith. It is the story of missions and evangelism, a pattern for the same kind of activity in our generation. Most of all, it is the continuing story of the Christ of God and of the rise of His church all over the earth. The author was Luke, a physician from Macedonia, northern Greece. God used this anointed man to stretch our minds and hearts toward new horizons for our Master.

But here is the mystery: the book ends suddenly in chapter 28, verse 32. No ending. No goodbye. No see-you-later. No finale. It just . . . stops! Why is that? Because the Book of Acts is an ongoing drama. You and I are living in the unfinished, still unwritten 29th chapter. Those early believers ran with passion to reach the lost. Their theme might have been, "Whatever it takes!" We must have an infusion of that same vigor in our congregations today. We must have the same drive, the same creativity. There is nothing about the Book of Acts that is passive. Those people were "driven." May we be so today, driven by the passion of the Holy Spirit to complete the global mission of redemption in our generation.

The Book of Acts is the pattern book for the New Testament church. Read it — again and again. Then you will know what God expects from the body of Christ today.

Byline #164

The urgency and vitality of faithful church attendance

Hebrews 10:25: Not forsaking the assembling of ourselves together, as the manner of some is; but exhorting one another: and so much the more, as ye see the day approaching.

It is reported in some quarters that faithful church attendance is dwindling in America. Apparently, to some, Sunday is just "another day of the week." That is a tragedy, not to mention an affront to God, who has commanded us to remember the Sabbath and keep it holy. It should be noted here that some will respond, "But Sunday is not the Sabbath; Saturday is." If you are still living in the Old Testament, you're right; but since the resurrection of our Lord Jesus occurred "on the first day of the week," as Scriptures report to us, Christians for the most part have observed Sunday as the Lord's Day.

Many folks will look you right in the eyes and declare, "I don't need to be in church." That's rather like saying you don't need to eat, or go to a doctor, or take care of your body. The souls of these people must be starving. Why go to church, indeed? There are many eternally valid reasons to be a faithful attender: to participate in corporate worship of our Lord, to enjoy the fellowship of other believers, to have our faith lifted by hearing the Word of God faithfully proclaimed from the pulpit, to participate in giving so that others may have access to the gospel. It's not just an "occasional" visit to God's house either; it's that constant, life-long habit of faithful adherence to God's command to not forsake "the assembling of ourselves together."

No matter how one rationalizes lack of attendance in God's house, the practice harms the soul and doubtless grieves our precious Lord, whom, we learn in Ephesians, "loved the church" (Eph. 5:25). Not appreciating a particular church or fellowship, or failure to like its pastor, does not eliminate our need to be in God's house as often as humanly possible. We have folks who drive 50 miles or more (each way) to be in our church every weekend. When I press them for reasons why they drive so far, they respond, "Being in God's house is what keeps us alert, spiritually alive, and fed." I encourage you to be in church this weekend — make it a faithful habit. Find a good, Bible-believing congregation where the pastor truly feeds nourishing spiritual food, and become a strong attender and advocate of it. You will be a much stronger Christian!

Prayer: O God, I truly do thank You for the Church. Please bless all congregations who will honor You this weekend. Let Your anointing flow upon them. ***Amen.***

A QUARTERBACK FUMBLES THE BALL

Ecclesiastes 1:14: I have seen all the works that are done under the sun; and, behold, all is vanity and vexation of spirit.

During the late summer of 2007, America's sports pages were filled with a tragic story. It was the sorry tale of a sports figure who "had it all" and lost it. It was the fall of the Atlanta Falcons star quarterback Michael Vick. His personal empire collapsed virtually overnight because of alleged dog-fighting activity.

The player's fortune came from several highly lucrative sources. Not only did Vick make an annual fortune in salary from throwing a football (and superbly running with it, as well), he made yet another fortune as a television spokesman for various products, such as Air Tran. When the dog-fighting charges surfaced, those companies dropped Vick faster than a sizzling-hot horseshoe. Paul Swangard, managing director of the Warsaw Sports Marketing Center, said, "Michael Vick stands as the crowning achievement of brand destruction." What a condemnation![1]

Vick allegedly leaves in his wake a number of maimed or dead pit bulls and answered to charges that he personally executed some of those animals that did not fight up to his expectations. A *USA Today* sports columnist suggested, when commenting on Vick's situation, "We're not the civilized society we think. Sometimes, collectively, we're ignorant."[2] What would motivate this blessed, rich, talented, charismatic, and highly popular quarterback to just pitch it all because he pitted dogs against each other? Money? My goodness, he already had all the money in George. Stupidity? Arrogance? Who knows? No one but God can read the heart of a man. One thing is sure: it doesn't take much to jeopardize a lifetime of achievement.

Will Vick ever play another game in the National Football League? Maybe, although it is quite doubtful. Vanity of vanities, all is vanity, lamented King Solomon (Eccles. 1:2). Vick may have a long, long time in the Gray Bar Hotel to consider that awful reality.

1. Gary Mihoces and Kevin Johnson, "Vick Agrees to Plead Guilty to Dogfighting Charges," *USA Today* (8/21/07).
2. Jon Saraceno, "In End, Even Vick Can't Scramble from Legal Heat," *USA Today* (8/21/07).

Prayer: O God, give me the wisdom to live my life in a way pleasing to You, avoiding all those many pitfalls along the way. I ask the Holy Spirit to quicken my mind so that the thoughts I think, the things I do, and even the words I say are always pleasing to You and benefit mankind. Amen.

ROBOT SEALS AND PEACE OF MIND

John 14:27

Peace I leave with you, my peace I give unto you: not as the world giveth, give I unto you. Let not your heart be troubled, neither let it be afraid.

The Japanese have done it again! They have developed "mental commit" robots that provide psychological, physiological, and social effects to human beings through physical interaction. A friend of mine, who has the U.S. franchise for these robots, brought one in to me just this morning. It looks and feels for all the world like a baby harp seal, so soft and cuddly. The "seal" quickly learned my voice and began to respond while cradled in my arms. It would open and shut its eyes, wag its little tail, and even — at my suggestion — close its eyes and go to sleep. This six-pound creature of delight made me laugh and relax as it wiggled and made all kinds of cute "seal" sounds.

Most hospitals don't allow animals in the rooms (many care facilities do

Byline #166

not either) because medical personnel are concerned about negative effects such as allergies, infection, bites, and scratches. But the robot seal has none of those detriments, and you don't have to clean up after them. At the moment, these creatures are still somewhat expensive, but the developers are confident that as they become accepted coast-to-coast, the cost will diminish substantially. I hope so, because I'd really like to have one. I've often told my wife somebody should start a rent-a-dog company. When I get home at night and turn on the news, I'd love to have a little dog in my lap. But within an hour, I want him to go away. And I truly do not want to have to take him for his morning and night "walk."

I think these robots will catch on because people are desperate for peace of mind. Jesus committed himself to provide such peace for those of us who would put our faith and trust in Him. Yes, I enjoyed the robot seal, but I might tire of it rather quickly. But I've known Jesus for, well, nearly 60 years, and He grows sweeter day by day. And no replacement batteries are necessary, for He is *the life*.

PRAYER

O God, I do thank You for peace of mind. Even when all is in turmoil, there is the sanctuary of Your presence. I can sing as the song writer, "It is well with my soul!"[1] That reality is more priceless than gold. Thank You! Amen.

1. Horatio Spafford and Philip Bliss, "It Is Well with My Soul."

PERSPECTIVE ON LIFE ON EARTH FROM THE MOON

Psalm 8:4: What is man, that thou art mindful of him? and the son of man, that thou visitest him?

During the last year of his administration, President George W. Bush challenged Americans to once again explore the moon within the next decade or so. As you are well aware, 12 of our brave astronauts have already walked on the lunar surface. Several of those men, including a Christian, Colonel Jim Irwin, have passed away in the intervening years. Two recent films have been produced that feature the remaining astronauts, with the exception of Neil Armstrong, the first human to set foot on the moon, who is notoriously camera-shy. In these films, the astronauts converse off-the-cuff about the miracle of actually landing and walking on the moon.

One of them, Ed Mitchell, reported the three-day flight back to earth as his "highlight." He said he looked out the window of the space capsule and "saw the Earth in this tiny little perspective in the huge cosmos and thrilled at its beauty." Mitchell concluded, "Earth is a little oasis in this vastness of space."[1] King David certainly never walked on the moon, yet he wrote, "What is man that thou, O God, art mindful of him?" Both the astronaut and the king pretty well put life in perspective, don't you think?

Our life circumstances look pretty huge to us sometimes. They are often all we can see. But if we could take a good look at our lives with the same viewpoint as God, our responses to those circumstances would certainly be altered. For one thing, we would view them from an eternal perspective. Friend, stop to consider that one million years from now you will be more alive than you are at this very moment! The trivia of life, those things that will not last past our lifetimes, cannot be the driving forces of our day. Someone has observed, "Only what's done for Christ will last."

Well now, that person was right!

1. Traci Watson, "Astronauts Recall Time as Men on the Moon," *USA Today* (9/7/07).

PRAYER: O God, if I could see for 30 seconds my life and world as You see it, how differently would I live and think? I would observe, as did the astronaut, that You are very big, and I am not. So I put all my faith in You this day and rest in the reality of Your promise to never leave nor forsake me. Amen.

Staying the course

2 Timothy 4:7: I have fought a good fight, I have finished my course, I have kept the faith.

It is hard to comprehend how large Russia is until you actually visit there. The sun never sets on that nation; when it goes down over the Finnish border in the west, it is just rising over Vladivostok in the east. I dearly love Russia and its people. Any day I can spend in Moscow is a joy to my soul.

On our last trip there, Darlene and I drove about 20 miles into the countryside through a magnificent forest. Near Gorki, we found a lovely rural estate, once turned over to Vladimir Lenin by a fellow Communist sympathizer. Lenin, without question one of the most influential figures in the 20th century, lived there until his death in 1924. The rather surprising factor to me was the modesty of the place. Lenin had overthrown the Romanov czars who lived in palaces beyond words to describe. If you are in St. Petersburg, be sure to visit both the summer and winter palaces. In each of them you will find opulence beyond description. In Czar Nicholas's days (the last of the clan overthrown and executed by the Communists), 85 percent of Russia had no electricity and almost 90 percent of the people were illiterate. The czar could not possibly have cared less, but Lenin was passionate about their cause. I sat at his desk in that country villa home and tried to imagine what it would have been like those nights he was joined by Joseph Stalin and Leon Trotsky and others. Those men were consumed by one thing: to change the course of humanity in Russia and, they hoped, the entire world. They were successful in their enterprise in that they put almost half of humanity under their hammer and sickle.

Do we Christians have the same intense purpose? Do we get easily sidetracked on peripheral issues that don't really matter much? Our task is to tell the world about Jesus. That's the Great Commission from our Lord. Lenin let nothing deter him from his purpose. Can we, as followers of Christ, do less? Energized by the Holy Spirit, let us refocus on our purpose. We are going to be held accountable one day. In God's eyes, will we have been successful? That's the eternal question, isn't it?

Prayer: O God, may I be able to say, as Paul, at the conclusion of my life that I have finished my course. If unregenerate men and women can be so committed to their cause, how can I be less committed? Help me today, I pray! *Amen.*

A TALE OF
TWO TOMBS

Byline #169

Matthew 28:5–6

I know that ye seek Jesus, which was crucified. He is not here: for he is risen, as he said. Come, see the place where the Lord lay.

Red Square in Moscow is a must-see for world tourists. It is not named "Red" for any connection with the Communist "Reds." Rather the word "Red" comes from an old Russian term for "beautiful." Red Square truly lives up to its name in that regard. In the center of the square is the mausoleum that houses the mummified body of Vladimir Lenin, the Communist tyrant who overthrew the czars and put in place the brutal regime later headed by Stalin. It was on top of the mausoleum, a dark marble block of a building, that Stalin and Khrushchev and Malenkov and other Soviet leaders stood for so many years to watch the famous military parades.

Inside the mausoleum lies the body of Lenin, who died in 1924 after a series of strokes. The lines of tourists waiting to see him are still long. You can wait for hours for your brief and very brisk walk through the tomb, or you can find an English guide, give him ten bucks, and go directly to the head of the line. That may be one of the best ten-spots you ever invested. No one is allowed to take anything inside, not a purse, not a camera — nothing. And you have to keep moving! You may be inside for two minutes, total. But there he lies: Vladimir Lenin, dead as a beached carp.

Compare that to the marvelous announcement of the angel at the tomb of Christ: "He is not here: for he is risen!" A short 72 hours or so is all our Lord spent in His earthly repose before He was quickened by the Holy Spirit and resurrected. Ephesians 2:1 reminds us that we, too, have been quickened (resurrected from spiritual death) by the same Holy Spirit. We receive life through our Lord Jesus! Now — which tomb makes your heart beat a little faster? The full one? Or the empty one?

PRAYER

O God, how grateful I am to know and understand that quite empty tomb just north of Jerusalem's Damascus Gate. Your Son lay there once, for a short time, but death could not hold Him. Jesus was the prototype, the first-fruit, of all of us who will be quickened by Your Spirit! We encourage and comfort each other because of this promised future. We bless Your name for this reality. Amen.

DOES YOUR CHURCH HAVE A MOTOR?

Acts 13:4

So they, being sent forth by the Holy Ghost, departed unto Seleucia; and from thence they sailed to Cyprus.

With those words, Christ's Great Commission of going into all the world to preach the gospel to every person began to be fulfilled. From that anointed church in Antioch, Paul and Barnabas were sent to foreign soil.

For decades now, the "motor" of our church has been its annual missions convention. This nine-day convocation has revolutionized our congregation and brought upon it the blessings of God. Every other activity in our church and school is discontinued as we give preeminence to the task of missions.

Why is this week, this "motor" of the church, so urgent? In the decades of pastoring our church, I have been blessed to see many miracles of God's provision. Every one of those miracles, yes, every single one of them, is attributable directly or indirectly to missions! It is often difficult for me to convince church leaders of other congregations to accept this reality. But the thousands who attend here, as well as our board of directors, will attest to the role of missions among us. This is much more than an issue of money. It is a matter of commitment of ourselves in every way to global evangelization. Over 50 of our church people now serve in some way on the mission field at home or abroad. Several hundred of our folks take short-term missions trips year after year.

Twenty years ago, our church stood on the brink of bankruptcy and disintegration. God impressed upon my heart to turn our attention to the mission field. We obeyed Him. Words cannot adequately express to you how much we as a fellowship have been blessed again and again. Yes, missions is the motor of our church. So — let's crank it up again!

Byline #170

PRAYER

O God, we believe You were serious about this matter of impacting the world for Jesus. We do not consider the Great Commission a suggestion, but rather a commandment. As we obey it, You bless us. Help us always to be obedient to Your call and vision. Amen.

FATAL OVERSIGHT

Proverbs 3:1: My son, forget not my law; but let thine heart keep my commandments.

It has not been all that long ago that Americans were stunned by what came to be known as 9/11. Hijacked airplanes crashed into the World Trade Center, the Pentagon, and a field in Pennsylvania. Thousands of Americans died, and the entire population was shaken. In recent days, several major newspapers have carried editorials calling for us to "just let it go," that is, get over the tragedy. Stop talking about it. Stop remembering. What calloused and cold editorials! One of the writers informed us, "Grief has its limits." Oh, really? Tell that to the family of the victims.

People somehow have the propensity to forget. Here is a classic example: On September 1, 1923, one of the most devastating earthquakes in history rocked Japan. In the city of Yokohama alone, over a hundred thousand people either died or were severely injured or maimed. Out of this inferno of human tragedy came a frantic plea to America for assistance. Our nation responded by sending entire fleets of supplies and food to that devastated nation. Japan's emperor cabled our president with this promise: "America, we will not forget." Just 18 years later, the Pacific sky over Pearl Harbor was buzzing with Japanese warplanes bombing and strafing our navy forces. It was a horrendous and savage attack, completely unprovoked. Japan . . . had forgotten.

The night before our Lord Jesus was crucified, He asked His followers to observe communion, breaking the bread as His body would soon be broken, and drinking the cup symbolizing His shed blood. "This do in remembrance of me," He asked (Luke 22:19). We must never forget the horrors of Calvary. The concerns of ordinary life can cause the memories of Golgotha to fade from our conscious awareness. This must not happen! "Lest I forget Gethsemane; lest I forget Thine agony; lest I forget Thy love for me; lead me to Calvary."[1]

Prayer: O God, so great was the eternal trauma of that day when Christ died that the sun turned away. How it must cause pain in Your heart when You see humanity spurn the very sacrifice that cost You so much. We will always and ever keep Calvary before us, as well as the empty and open tomb. And with our remembering will come the deepest and most heartfelt thanksgiving for Your great love. Amen.

1. Jennie Evelyn Hussey and William J. Kirkpatrick, "Lead Me to Calvary."

Byline #172

Gospel geek squads

Luke 24:45: Then opened he their understanding, that they might understand the scriptures.

The CBS television show *Sixty Minutes* recently had a segment on geek squads. This term is in no way derogatory. The geek squads are made up of brilliant young people who know computers inside and out and offer repair service. Technology is growing so fast that there is hardly any way most of us golden oldies can keep up with it. Frankly, I never have known much about these machines, although I use them every day.

Are you aware that you can now purchase a refrigerator that is totally computer controlled? It keeps inventory on what food you have in it and when you run out of certain items, the refrigerator computer calls a local grocery store and orders those foods supplies for you (which are then delivered to your front door). Now, friend, that's just a bit scary.

I have a couple of computers, one in my church study and another in my study at home. I use them primarily for word processing. I also browse the Internet for news and sports. Both of these machines take great delight somehow in driving me crazy. For example: I have tried on occasion to change settings, but to no avail. The screen tells me to read the manual. Hey, have *you* ever tried to read a computer manual? It is written in computerese that bears little or no resemblance to any language spoken by normal human beings. So . . . I need those geeks.

Sometimes we in the church make the gospel about as complicated as computers. We speak in terminology that the unchurched can't begin to understand. The gospel should be kept simple. John 3:16, the most beloved verse in the Bible, is made up for the most part of single-syllable words. The Holy Spirit kept it simple, so why can't we do the same for other folks?

I'd write more on this page but my computer screen just informed me that I need to install a new gazorninwhatzits. Or something.

Prayer: O God, in my communicating the gospel to others, please make me keep it simple so everyone can understand. I need Your help with this! *Amen.*

THE BIBLICAL PREMISE OF FAITH PROMISE GIVING

Proverbs 11:24: There is that scattereth, and yet increaseth; and there is that withholdeth more than is meet, but it tendeth to poverty.

It was the missions legend, Dr. Oswald J. Smith, of the People's Church in Toronto, Canada, who drummed this scriptural truth into me when I was just starting to pastor. I didn't know anything about faith promise giving. Frankly, I'd never heard of it. I knew God had impressed upon me to have our first missions convention in the tiny church we had just started. But I didn't know how, when, or where. The Lord impressed upon my spirit to have a full week for the convention (in the fall during the agricultural harvest in our area), to invite Dr. Smith to be the preacher, and to learn how to operate in finances God's way.

Smith, not the easiest man to please, transformed our church in those precious days — and me! Our tiny congregation, numbering fewer than 100 (this goes back to the mid-60s), was going broke. Our annual budget for everything was a mere $16,000 annually, a little over $300 per week. We weren't even coming close to our need. We had been attempting to finance our church man's way. Smith taught us to do it God's way. The offering for missions that final Sunday was $32,000! Twice our annual budget! So where did the money come from? Smith taught us faith promise giving, that is, making God the source for our provisions, depending, of course, upon our commitment to His work, which is redemption. Immediately the general fund doubled in our church. We began to buy up property around us for cash, not loans. Our church, numbering 90+ on Sunday mornings, was now bursting with hundreds of people within a year of that first missions convention. I contend there are no money problems in God's church, only ministry and priority problems. Jesus taught us to seek His kingdom first and then all the other things would be added. I believe it. And practice it.

PRAYER: O God, I do thank You so much for bringing that grand old man into my life early in the ministry. I can sing from experience, "'Tis so sweet to trust in Jesus / just to take Him at His word!"[1] I thank You for every missionary around the world and that through Your provision You allow us to be their missionaries of supply. Let us always be so faithful. **Amen.**

---

1. Louisa M.R. Stead and Wm. J. Kirkpatrick, "'Tis So Sweet to Trust in Jesus."

HONORING
SPIRITUAL
VETERANS

1 Timothy 5:17

Let the elders that rule well be counted worthy of double honour, especially they who labour in the word and doctrine.

Someone asked me the other day what I would do differently if I could live my life over. Easy. I would have spent time in the U.S. military. It was never a matter of evasion of duty; it was always a matter of timing. Each time I am in a gathering where our veterans are honored, I always feel such a sense of loss. God bless our veterans and those who serve now! We must always honor them.

While paying respect to these worthies, let's call attention also to the veterans of faith we sometimes call "aged ministers." Note Paul's words in the text at the top of this page. I often stop to thank God for the pastors who preceded me in this church. I am the 11th pastor in our church's 65-year history. On several occasions we have honored previous pastors by bringing

Byline #174

them in to say "thank you." Several of them have gone home to glory. When I was just a kid, my pastor was a man named A.M. Alber. How I loved him! In the 1980s, I heard that he was very ill and in a nursing home in Friend, Nebraska, just west of Lincoln. I took a couple days off and drove to the little town, found the home, and was told where his room was. But I was warned, "He is in a coma." My goodness, there he was, that once-strapping man, now so tiny. He lay unconscious in a fetal position. Miraculously, he awakened and we talked for nearly an hour before he slipped back into the coma. I had time to thank him for all his messages, for his encouragement to me to be a reader, for spending time with me when I was just a smart-aleck kid. And I had time to tell him that I loved him. Several months later, Pastor Alber went home to be with the Lord. I cannot imagine where I would have been without his involvement in my life.

Today, why not find one of the great spiritual veterans who has influenced your past and give him or her some verbal appreciation. Make their day! They deserve it!

PRAYER

O God, I bless those gracious and gallant heroes of the faith who so blessed my life. I pray for their health and well-being. May I always be grateful for those pioneers of the faith who have preceded me and made my life so much easier and more productive. Amen.

VICTORY OVER DEPRESSION

1 Kings 19:4

> But [Elijah] himself went a day's journey into the wilderness, and came and sat down under a juniper tree: and he requested for himself that he might die; and said, It is enough; now, O LORD, take away my life; for I am not better than my fathers.

Consider the prophets such as Isaiah, Ezekiel, Amos, Samuel, Zechariah, and so many others. Yet Jesus said flatly that the greatest prophet of them all was John the Baptist. It was John who introduced Jesus and who pointed a finger at King Herod Antipas and brought to light his illicit liaison with Herodias. It was John who waded into the swirling Jordan preaching repentance and baptizing converts. Yet after some time in Herod's filthy, rat-infested dungeon at Machaerus, John sent word quietly to Jesus, "Are you the one who was to come, or should we expect someone else?" (Matt. 11:3; Luke 7:20; NIV). John the Baptist felt the pangs of depression, as did Elijah (see text above) after Jezebel threatened his life.

It is believed by medics that at least 21 million Americans suffer from depression. Many of those victims are followers of Christ. Don't let Satan besiege you with guilt if you are melancholy. Many creative people are, to one degree or another.

One way to combat depression is to withdraw for a time. Jesus often went away from the crowds. Someone has suggested, "Come apart before you fall apart." Paul gave us yet another insight into the battling of depression: "Bringing every thought into captivity to the obedience of Christ" (2 Cor. 10:5; NKJV). Don't allow yourself to mentally wallow in what Bunyan aptly called "the slough (or swamp) of despondency."[1] Paul wrote to the Philippians, "Whatever is true . . . noble . . . right . . . pure . . . lovely . . . admirable . . . think about such things" — the best, not the worst (Phil. 4:8; NIV). But the best way to combat depression is to talk to Jesus about it. Remember the old hymn: "And since He bids me seek His face, believe His word and trust His grace / I'll cast on Him my every care."[2] There is so much help in Scripture for those who know the reality of depression. Check it out.

PRAYER

O God, I look to You to enable me to be of sound mind and uplifted spirit. I will not succumb to the guilt trip of Satan but instead will look unto Jesus, the author and finisher of my faith! I rejoice that by Your power I do not have to be a victim of depression or any other thing thrown my way. Amen.

1. John Bunyan, *The Pilgrim's Progress* (Green Forest, AR: Master Books, 2005).
2. W.W. Walford and Wm. B. Bradbury, "Sweet Hour of Prayer."

"Jell-O, Folks . . . this is Jack Benny"

Matthew 5:16: Let your light so shine before men, that they may see your good works, and glorify your Father which is in heaven.

I suspect a person would have to be post-60 years old to remember that famous line, for years the opening sentence in a comedian's radio show. It got started in October of 1934. General Foods became the sponsor of the then-new Jack Benny radio show. (In fact, radio itself as an entertainment medium in this country was only about ten years old.) General Foods had introduced a gelatin dessert they called Jell-O. We remember, don't we, that it came in "six delicious flavors." The problem was, nobody much was buying it. Did you ever hear of Knox Gelatins? No? Well, that was the big-selling dessert during the early part of the Great Depression.

Almost in desperation, General Foods decided to sponsor the Jack Benny radio show and feature Jell-O as their product. The bigwigs at GF panicked when Benny constantly made fun of their gelatin on the air. But Benny knew how to market, and they did not. Both Benny and Jell-O caught on big-time. Jell-O became so famous that it ended up the "generic name" of such desserts. As Benny recalled, "People liked it [Jell-O]. The mountains of unsold Jell-O disappeared and even the warehouses ran out of supplies. People kept buying it. The more we kidded it, the more they bought." Within three years, Benny had the number-one show in broadcasting, and Jell-O sold as fast as grocers put it on display. Hence, the power of advertising.

"So what?" you may ask. If you live in a pretty good-sized town at all, the chances are that most of the people in your neck-of-the-woods have never heard of your church and couldn't find it if they had to. Most congregations inadvertently keep their churches as some deep secret. Jesus told us to let our lights shine to all people. Yes, I know that meant the way we live and personally represent the Master. But it does no disservice to the verse to apply it to our churches. Let's get the word out! We have a better product than Jell-O!

Prayer: O God, forgive us for allowing Your house to become mere private country clubs for believers rather than hospitals for the lost and hurting of the world. Teach us how to evangelize our communities! They will thank us for it. ***Amen.***

LIVING FROM THE LIFE OF CHRIST

Galatians 2:20: I am crucified with Christ: nevertheless I live; yet not I, but Christ liveth in me: and the life which I now live in the flesh I live by the faith of the Son of God, who loved me, and gave himself for me.

It appears that the American public may see our national history and our origins as a nation in a severely different light than the courts or the press. According to columnist Andrea Stone, "Most Americans believe the nation's founders wrote Christianity into the Constitution." She quoted a recent survey that indicated that 55 percent of those polled believe that the Constitution established a Christian nation. The columnist then added her two cents' worth and wrote, "They believe this erroneously." That was Ms. Stone's opinion, not an historical reality.[1]

Fifty-eight percent of those Americans polled said teachers in public schools should be allowed to lead prayers, a number that is increasing, by the way. Half those polled said teachers should be allowed to use the Bible as a factual text in history class. Rich Green of Wall Builders, an advocacy group that believes the nation was built on Christian principles, says the poll does not mean a majority of Americans favor a theocracy (God rule). "But," he said, "I would call the Constitution a Christian document just like the Declaration of Independence."[2]

Well, it will require more than a poll or an advocacy group to turn this nation back to God. Government-enforced edicts will not succeed either. A national revival will require those who are followers of Christ to live as He lived so that a watching world can actually see in real life the saving life of Christ. There's an old chorus with this prayerful lyric: "Let the beauty of Jesus be seen in me / All His wonderful passion and purity / Oh, thou Spirit divine all my nature refine / 'Til the beauty of Jesus be seen in me."[3] If the citizens of this nation could see, lived out in practical ways, the beauty of Jesus, the turn-around would be astonishing.

Prayer: O God, it has been so long since there was an authentic, nation-changing move of the Holy Spirit upon our nation. How urgently we need You today. But You will need to change us as individuals before the nation can be enhanced. So I repeat the musical prayer, "Let Your beauty be seen in me today." Amen.

1. Andrea Stone, USAToday.com, 9/11/2007.
2. Ibid.
3. Words by Albert Orsbon, "Let the Beauty of Jesus."

WHY SOME CHRISTIANS LACK FAITH

Romans 10:17

So then faith cometh by hearing, and hearing by the word of God.

Without any question, I declare as a lifelong pastor that the most needed area in ministries today is solid Bible training. Paul instructed his young pastor friend Timothy to preach the Word. The lack of biblical knowledge among today's believers is astonishing. And, at the same time, it appears that there is a great "want-to" to learn the Word. Our greatest church crowds during the week are not for concerts but for the Wednesday night Bible training. On those wonderful evenings, I have the joy time to do nothing but teach the Word. I usually put together a 10- to 15-page syllabus on the subject being taught, usually systematically through a book of the Bible. I just know people want to learn the Word. That puts the responsibility directly on church leadership to provide the training.

Why is such training important? Because, according to Hebrews 11:6, we cannot please God without faith. Where does this faith originate? Read again the Scripture that adorns the top of this page. Paul wrote it to the faithful saints in Rome, many of them living actually in Caesar's household. They desperately needed supernatural faith. This goes beyond "saving faith." The more of Scripture a person truly knows (and I do not speak only of Scripture memorization here, but also understanding what the Bible teaches), the more faith is generated in his or her heart. Much of today's Church is geared to music "worship," often indicating that when the singing stops, the worship stops. But, my friend, when your life hits the wall, you're going to need a whole lot more than a catchy melody and clever lyric to see you through. You are going to need faith, and faith comes from hearing the actual Word of God.

Check the electives in your Christian education program to see how many are Bible-based as opposed to sociologically oriented. You might be surprised. As I think you would be if your pastor sprang an unannounced test on Bible knowledge next Sunday morning. I wonder just how many of our congregants could pass it? Such a showing might well indicate why some folks are having a problem with their faith.

Byline #178

PRAYER

O God, Your Holy Spirit moved upon some 40 people over 1,500 years to give to us Your holy and inspired Word. Forgive me when I do not dwell on it more, passing it over for the local newspaper or best-selling novel. I urgently need divine faith. In Your word I know where and how to get it. Thank You. Amen.

BACK TO BASICS

Luke 6:48: He is like a man which built an house, and digged deep, and laid the foundation on a rock: and when the flood arose, the stream beat vehemently upon that house, and could not shake it: for it was founded upon a rock.

Paul stated flatly in 1 Corinthians 3 that the foundation of our lives must be Jesus. Isaiah reminded us in 55:11 that God's Word will never return to the heavens void. There you have it: the basics of our faith. God is committed to His Word, and Jesus paid the price for its redemptive application. Yet often in church we are given less promising menus for consideration. Music is fine, as are needed buildings. Church government is described and required in Scripture, to be sure. The fellowship of the believers is a gracious activity. God bless all these things. But what about the actual impartation of God's Word itself?

How long do you suppose the typical Christian can converse about the contents of the Bible? How long could that person describe God without repeating a thought? Two minutes? How much does the average churchgoer know about the great Old Testament patriarchs? Or Israel's kings? Or the prophets and priests? Could that person tell how many missionary journeys Paul took or describe what happened on each one, and where? Can the average Christian discuss the Book of Revelation with any credibility? Can a pew-sitter give a true synopsis of the life and teachings of Jesus? If the answers to these questions are "no" or "maybe," then maybe we need to get back to the basics.

Here is a revolutionary thought: Let's shorten the preliminaries in our services, dismissing interminable announcements, and cut back singing of choruses, and give the pastors and teachers more time to impart the Word. Let's start highlighting the urgency of Sunday school and Christian education. If we do not attend to this, we are short-circuiting the very thing God has committed himself to honor: His Word! And we will certainly be less than effective in "making disciples," which Jesus commanded us to do.

PRAYER: O God, how often we set aside the "best" for merely the "good." We are fascinated by the wooden chest, and not the treasure that it contains. Help us to return to the basic faith of our fathers. Amen.

Blessed friendship

Proverbs 22:11: He that loveth pureness of heart, for the grace of his lips the king shall be his friend.

Oscar Wilde wrote of George Bernard Shaw, "Shaw hasn't an enemy in the world. But none of his friends like him."[1] When I read author Jeremy Thorpe's misquoting of a Bible concept, I must admit it struck me funny. Here it is: "Greater love hath no man than this that he lay down his friends for his life."[2] Unfortunately, there are some folks who would actually abide by that fractured command. Someone else once ventured, "A friend in need . . . is a pest!" Ah, but a real friend — now we're talking!

We all have acquaintances that we appreciate and enjoy. But a friend goes beyond that into another dimension. A friend is someone who has been at your side through the proverbial "thick and thin" for years. That friend knows you on your good days and bad ones, can almost detect your unspoken thoughts, yet never varies in his or her appreciation of you. You can probably count the number of those friends on your fingers, especially if the duration of that friendship has been for decades.

I am so blessed to have such friends. My oldest and dearest friend has held that place and trust in my heart since we went to high school together in the early 1950s.

The best friend you have, of course, is Jesus, who has promised never to leave, never to forsake you. Unlike Thorpe's misquote, Jesus actually did lay down His life for His friend. That friend is you! Lyricist J.C. Ludgate wrote, "A friend when other friendships cease, a friend when others fail, a friend who gives me joy and peace, a friend who will prevail! Friendship with Jesus, fellowship divine! O what blessed sweet communion, Jesus is a friend of mine."[3]

Our walk with the Lord is not a religion. It's a friendship. And such a blessed one.

1. Stanley Weintraub, *Shaw: An Autobiography* (New York: Weybright and Talley, 1969).
2. Quoted in D.E. Butler and Anthony King, *The British General Election of 1964* (New York: St. Martins Press, 1965), chapter 1.
3. Joseph C. Ludgate, "Friendship with Jesus," published 1898.

Prayer: O God, I thank You for the closeness, the walk, the talks, the awareness of Your presence. A cold dogma or liturgy cannot comfort me in the dark hours. But You can. And You do! Today, may I consciously draw even closer to You, knowing that in so doing, You will draw closer to me. How I thank You! ***Amen.***

THE NEARLY FORGOTTEN
TREASURE CHEST

Byline #181

> And when they had sung an hymn, they went out into the mount of Olives.

There are two books that will strengthen your theology. Theology, of course, means the knowledge of God. These two books will supply you with all the spiritual vitamins you need. The main one is your Bible. The second is a good hymnal. In my study, I have an entire shelf consisting of hymnals from the past 100 years. I often refer to them when needing a lift or a shot of spiritual adrenalin.

If the hymnal has a topical index, you can easily find the song you need for any particular occasion. I hold before me, as I write this, a hymnal titled *Hymns of Glorious Praise*. The index gives me a cornucopia of greatly needed subjects such as The Trinity (featuring such songs as "The Church's One Foundation"); Testimonies ("It Is Well with My Soul"); The Bible ("Break Thou the Bread Of Life"); Prayer ("I Must Tell Jesus"); The Second Coming of Christ ("Is It the Crowning Day?"); Redemption ("There Is a Fountain Filled with Blood"); The Resurrection of Christ ("Death Hath No Terrors"); Missions ("Rescue the Perishing"); Jesus ("Glory to His Name"); Divine Guidance ("Lead On, O King Eternal"); God ("A Mighty Fortress"); Heaven ("When We See Christ"); Holiness ("A Glorious Church"); Comfort ("Near to the Heart Of God"); Consecration ("I Surrender All"); Assurance ("My Anchor Holds"); Adoration ("Joyful, Joyful We Adore Thee"); and the list of these treasures goes on and on.

The hymnal is a veritable fountainhead of help and inspiration. When is the last time you were given such a buffet of musical help in your church? For many, probably, a long time. Many of today's worship leaders are caught up in the latest catchy tunes, exchanging the theological treasure chests for them. I encourage you to go online or to a good Christian bookstore and buy a hymnal packed with these great songs of our faith. Along with your Scripture readings, go through the lyrics. You'll be strengthened and blessed.

PRAYER

O God, Your church is growing weaker in some areas because of the lack of spiritual food and vitamins. Lead us back to the mainland of scriptural stability. It is more than noteworthy that in the Upper Room, Your Son led His men in . . . a hymn.
Amen.

VIGILANCE, THE WATCHWORD FOR THE HOUR

Matthew 24:42

Watch therefore: for ye know not what hour your Lord doth come.

On a bitterly cold day, with the temperature far below zero, I stood on Moscow's Red Square looking over the top of the brick wall to the massive government building behind it. There, Russian President Vladimir Putin was preparing the way to dissolve his parliament in a bid to retain power even after his terms of office expired. There were police everywhere. Some of the liberties I had enjoyed there in previous visits were conspicuously missing. Freedom of the press originating in that nation, and especially in Moscow or St. Petersburg, has been obliterated. The Putin government is in no way friendly toward evangelicals. The door for preaching the gospel that was opened wide after detente is appearing to close, inch by inch.

Ezekiel 38 has never looked closer at hand than it does today. In that chapter, the great prophet foretold a day when an amalgamation of nations, led, I believe, by Russia (Gog, Magog, Meshech), would militarily invade tiny Israel. Despite the tearing down of the Berlin Wall and some other developments in Russia that have momentarily caused us to believe the Russian dove of peace might be spreading its wings, I still am convinced that Russia will lead the invasion of Israel. Some theologians link this invasion with the second seal of Revelation 6. One thing is sure: more than ever we need to be aware of prophecy and the return of Christ. Vigilance is critical in this hour. No church, no believer, can adopt a "whatever will be will be" stance.

The cry from many alleged believers today is, "Entertain me!" The cry from the prophets is, "Jesus is coming!" And the challenge from Christ is, "Occupy 'til I come." Our prayer must be, "O Lord, in the light of all that is occurring around us, what can I do today that will honor and please You?"

Byline #182

PRAYER

O God, awaken the Western-world church from our ecclesiastical impression of Rip Van Winkle. Open our eyes to see the rapidly declining civilized world around us and the rise of those forces that would even deny us freedom of our worship. And in all this, cause us to be aware of Your imminent return. Awaken Your people, I pray, and cause us to be vigilant! Amen.

MY FRIEND, "CALIGULA"

Philippians 4:22: All the saints salute you, chiefly they that are of Caesar's household.

Hollywood's first Cinemascope production was the classic film *The Robe* (1953). It starred Richard Burton, Victor Mature, and Jean Simmons. It was the story of the Roman soldier (Burton) who oversaw the crucifixion of Jesus and later became a devoted follower (according to the film) of Christ. In his devotion to Christ, he came afoul of the vicious Roman Emperor, Caligula. In the movie, Jay Robinson, who later reprised the role in *Demetrius and the Gladiators*, played the emperor. Robinson's portrayal was one of the most stunning in Hollywood history. Many years ago, while watching the movie on TV late one night, the Holy Spirit impressed upon me to call the actor. I had no idea how to reach him but finally got a "possible" number in Sherman Oaks, California. I dialed the number and heard the voice of Caligula respond, "Hello!" It was Robinson. I said, "Mr. Robinson, my name is Dan Betzer and. . . .""Who?" he asked. "Uh . . . Dan Betzer, and. . . .""Dan Betzer? Are you the Dan Betzer who is my radio pastor on the *Revivaltime* broadcast?" Needless to say, I was shocked. He told me of his conversion to Christ and his deliverance from a demonic influence following those films that convinced him he actually was Caligula. I asked him to come to our church the following Palm Sunday to give his testimony of meeting Jesus as Savior. I also requested that at the end of his witness he give once again that amazing soliloquy near the end of *The Robe* where he sentenced Christians to death. He said he would.

Before a packed crowd, Jay gave his incredible testimony of finding Christ. "Now," he said, "I promised your pastor I would reprise that part of the film where, as Caligula, I sentenced believers to the archery range for death." He began the chilling lines, "Senators, Tribunes, Romans . . . there exists today in our Empire . . . a secret party of seditionists who call themselves . . . Christians. . . ." Suddenly Jay's face clouded and he turned to me and said, "Pastor . . . I'm sorry. I just can't do that anymore. I am a follower of Jesus now." Oh, my friend — the power of Christ's life within us! What a change!

Prayer: O God, I am grateful for my friend Jay. Even in the death of his precious wife Pauline, he remained faithful, unmovable, always abounding in Your work. I am thankful our paths crossed so I could see firsthand once again the power of the Cross in a person's life. Bless all those who are seeking You today. Amen.

Thoughts on the death of a lion

Matthew 6:26: . . . your heavenly Father feedeth them. Are ye not much better than they?

My friend Donavan trains wild animals for movies and television . . . everything from monkeys to the big cats. We have many times presented a stage presentation of *Noah and the Ark* in our church, one year to over 23,000 people. I play Noah, and I always have Donavan play Noah's son Ham, because we use his animals. On the stage with us are chimps, snakes, zebras, a leopard, kangaroos, giant turtles, exotic birds, camels — you name 'em. I want Donavan nearby in case the animals get — uh, hungry.

Until recently, Donavan had a gorgeous five-year-old male lion. Majestic creature! One Christmas, Donavan and his wife had their Christmas card picture taken with the lion right between them, their arms draped around his neck. Recently, I asked him about the lion and Donavan's countenance dropped as he mumbled, "He's dead." I responded, "What? How?" He replied, "He got hold of something and ate it. A lion's digestive system is so delicate that it doesn't take much to kill them. When I got to his cage one morning, there he was — dead." I thought about that lion the other day when I ate some old, and very bad, yogurt. I didn't die. I just wanted to.

If something pretty slight in a lion's digestive system can kill that noble king of the beasts, what do you think will happen inside you spiritually if you ingest Satan's garbage? Small wonder that Paul wrote to the Christians in Philippi and instructed them, "Finally, brethren, whatsoever things are true, whatsoever things are honest, whatsoever things are just, whatsoever things are pure, whatsoever things are lovely, whatsoever things are of good report; if there be any virtue, and if there be any praise, think on these things" (Phil. 4:8).

There is so much spiritual junk food around that we need to be careful what we "eat." We may think, *Well, just a little taste of this will be all right.* Listen, you have more nobility in your little finger than a pride of lions has in their whole group. So watch what you eat — mentally and spiritually. And stay alive!

Prayer: O God, help me be very careful what I take into my brain and heart today. Teach me to discern good from evil. And please keep me spiritually well. ***Amen.***

HALLSTATT — PARADISE IN AUSTRIA

1 Corinthians 2:9 Eye hath not seen, nor ear heard, neither have entered into the heart of man, the things which God hath prepared for them that love him.

In the early 1980s, my wife and I were taken by a missionary to visit the dazzling lakeside village of Hallstatt, Austria, a couple hours drive east of Salzburg. I have no way to adequately describe the wondrous beauty of this place. We arrived after driving through a tunnel deep inside the glorious Alps a quarter-mile or so, at the end of which the landscape plummets to a spot far, far below to one of the bluest lakes I have ever seen. The reflections of the mountains that encircle the water stop you dead in your tracks. The mountain sides are so steep that it appears the buildings of the village are built on top of each other. We know for a fact that the town has been inhabited since the early Iron Age, about 800 B.C. Through the intervening years, Darlene and I had determined to visit the town once again during our 50th wedding anniversary, which took place in 2006. We secured lodging well in advance in a several-hundred-year-old hotel called the Gruner Baum. The suite boasted a large balcony hovering over the lake. I spent literally hours on end sitting at the edge of that balcony, my feet perched on the railing, just watching the water and the boats scooting here and there. It was all so very quiet. Across the lake, a passenger train arrived every hour or so and a little boat ferried across to pick up the newly arriving guests. Hey, look it up on the Internet for yourself. You will say, "Thank God!" as you peruse the magnificence of the town, mountains, and lake. And you'll probably want to go there.

Paul reminds the Corinthians that no matter what we had ever seen on planet Earth, it could not compare to the beauty God has prepared for eternity for those who love and serve Him. We read about gold and precious stones in heaven. That doesn't much light my fire. I want to see mountains and streams and waterfalls and a profusion of flowers and fir trees. The poet wrote that only God can make a tree. Okay, throw in a few oaks and maples while we're at it. And birds and deer and green grass. Listen, only God could create the hollow in the Alps known as Hallstatt. See for yourself!

PRAYER: O God, in this long lifetime, You have allowed me to see so much of the grandeur of Your creation. Words cannot describe the wonder You have made. So what will heaven be like? For one thing, Jesus will be there. And that may be all the beauty I can handle. At any rate, thanks for reserving me a place. Amen.

JOGGING THROUGH PANTHER COUNTRY

1 Peter 5:8

Be sober, be vigilant; because your adversary the devil, as a roaring lion, walketh about, seeking whom he may devour.

Several years ago, my wife and I vacationed for a week with my brother Ben and his wife Linda in a little cabin, deep in the Ozarks wilderness near the Arkansas-Missouri state line. They are both retired from the banking business. I love my brother dearly, but years ago he developed this strange habit of jogging. The guy runs five or six miles each night. I have tried to explain the concept of cars to him, but he's slow to catch on. I am not a runner. Never was and never can be. I have knees that will sing an aria if I even attempt it. But I do love to walk. Slowly. "Sauntering" is the word I'm looking for here. So Ben humored me, and every night we would amble along for four or five miles.

One morning we were driving down the trail toward a restaurant, pretty much along the path that Ben and I had

Byline #186

been walking each night. Suddenly, sauntering across the road right in front of us was a full-grown, tawny panther! I kid you not! I suspect the cat was just marking his trail in quest of his late-night dinner. Well, Ben and I are smarter than the average cat, and the next day the two of us looked for a gymnasium where they had treadmills inside. I can tell you right now that had the two of us known there were varmints like that prowling through the darkness in those heavy woods, we never would have been doing our near-midnight constitutionals.

It reminds me of Peter's warning in one of his epistles in the New Testament that Satan goes about as a lion, seeking whom he may devour. I don't know if you are aware of this or not, friend, but being consumed by any carnivore is pretty much considered fatal! Having your life snuffed out by Satan is not only tragic but also completely unnecessary. Stay away from Satan's turf. Be alert in your daily walk. Yes, there are dangers, but you don't have to be eaten by any of them. David told us in the Psalms so many times that the Lord was His defense. So if you walk through life in places that you know God will walk with you, why, you'll be just fine.

PRAYER

O God, I pray that You will prod me to stay alert in this jogging track of life. Keep me away from the pits and let me hear the snarl of the waiting lion. And most of all, may I always look to You for protection. Amen.

EVER BEEN DISAPPOINTED?

Proverbs 15:22

Without counsel purposes are disappointed: but in the multitude of counselors they are established.

A person doesn't get too far along in life without realizing that disappointments are a part of life. Life is not one big fairy tale, is it?

Just up the road a mile or so from our house is the winter home of the great inventor Thomas Edison. His laboratory is still there as well. I've been through both of those facilities several times, and it was always encouraging. I have heard, although I cannot attest to it being a fact, that Edison made over a thousand experiments before he got an electric light to work. One thing is sure: he didn't succeed on the first attempt. We baseball fans remember with joy the great "Sultan of Swat" Babe Ruth, who for years held the major league home run record of over 700 round-trippers. (My father actually saw him hit one of those homers.) But what we don't remember about Babe Ruth is that for every home run he smacked, he struck out twice! In my own life, there have been some resounding victories, but I must tell you I have also struck out any number of times. Bitter losses! Dim paths ending in the swamplands of life.

A person has to make a decision. Am I going to allow disappointments to earmark my life? Or will I make these "failures" nothing more than iron sharpening iron? See, everyone will have disappointments. They are, quite frankly, inevitable. But it is how we react to those disappointments that mark us as failures or winners. The champions will make bitter seeds yield fragrant flowers later on even while others will allow those unfortunate days to negatively mark their lives forever. We each make our own call. I am not a counselor, but I believe some of the best advice I could give a "valley walker" is this: Get over it! Get on with life. As long as there is still breath in your body, the fight is still on!

PRAYER

O God, as I read Your Word, I am struck by the number of times Your great heroes of faith had bitter disappointments. But they overcame those obstacles to win life's battles for You. Help me in my down times to keep my eyes upon You and continue striving for the prize of my high calling in Christ Jesus. Amen.

Agreeing to disagree

Acts 28:25: And when they agreed not among themselves, they departed, after that Paul had spoken one word, Well spake the Holy Ghost by Esaias the prophet unto our fathers.

For 30 years I had the joy of being the speaker on network radio and television programs for my denomination. Our programs went all over the world. During that time, I received over 1.3 million pieces of mail plus phone calls and e-mails. Now I am sure this will not come as a shock to you, but not every person who contacted me agreed with what I had said or written. One e-mailer let me know, "I continue to disagree with you." Well, you know what? That's fine. What a dull world this would be if we all thought the same thing.

Disagreement is acceptable, providing we understand *how* to disagree. I must tell you that I have often had correspondents let me know in some pretty un-Christian ways they thought I should be put out to pasture. Or committed somewhere. But most of those who have disagreed with me have been kind and considerate in their responses. I learned a great deal from them, facts I did not know or understand, or opinions I had never considered before.

As brothers and sisters in Christ, we should not expect everyone in the Lord's army to agree on everything. We will never all agree on church music, for instance. We probably won't get a unanimous vote on the way church polity is run or who the pastor is. That should not deter us in our work for the Lord. On the contrary, the disagreements should make us a more interesting group of people on their way to heaven. Diversity! There's the word. God made the turtle, but He also made the cheetah. Go figure. One is so awfully slow, while the other is the fastest creature on earth, yet they both had the same Designer.

So let's agree to disagree on those issues that are, at best, peripheral. But let's remain united behind our lovely Lord and the Cross.

Prayer: O God give me wisdom and understanding with those whose points of view differ from mine. Let me learn from them. And when I still believe I am right, may I stand on my perspective with dignity and Christian grace. *Amen.*

DOING BIG THINGS FOR GOD IN SMALL PLACES

Acts 9:32–35: And it came to pass, as Peter passed throughout all quarters, he came down also to the saints which dwelt at Lydda. . . . And all that dwelt at Lydda and Saron saw him, and turned to the Lord.

In Peter's day, Lydda was just a wide spot in the road. Today, known as Lod, the area boasts the gorgeous new Jerusalem International Airport. It is a thriving metropolitan part of Tel Aviv. God led the apostle Peter to the early site where, despite its small size, there was a great revival. You don't have to be in a metropolis to see big things happen for the Lord. I write this because I often have folks, both laity and clergy alike, tell me they would like to have major ministry for Christ in their community, but they just don't have enough people. My wife and I spent the first 20 years or so of our ministry pioneering churches in northern Ohio. We started one of those congregations with only 16 people in the basement of our home. Our resources were always less than minimal. Still, God helped through His creativity to launch major enterprises for the Kingdom.

In one of those home missions churches, we formed a drama repertory company. During December, the cast would take a play on the road before presenting it in our church. One year we did an adaptation of Sheldon's classic book *In His Steps*. A dear friend of mine, now with the Lord, was the British stage and screen actor John French. Billy Graham personally led John to the Lord in the '50s in a hotel room in London. Our little church asked John to play the lead in the play and actually direct it, which he did. Looking back on that repertory company from the perspective of time, it just was not possible for our little church to do that kind of thing. But we did! God calls us to impossible feats for Him. I often wonder how many spiritual breakthroughs churches miss because they rationalize, "We could never do thus and so." But the Bible says, "I can do all things through Christ which strengtheneth me" (Phil. 4:13). Yes, even in small places.

Prayer: O God, let me see You, not my circumstance, when confronted with Your challenge for ministry. If I keep my eyes on You, then truly I'll be able by Your Spirit to accomplish Your work in a way I have never before dreamed. And I will most surely give You all the glory. Amen.

MAYBE WE WEREN'T SUCH NERDS AFTER ALL

1 Corinthians 3:16

Know ye not that ye are the temple of God, and that the Spirit of God dwelleth in you?

In 1947, Merle Travis wrote a song for singer Tex Williams that became the first million seller for Capitol Records, "Smoke, Smoke, Smoke That Cigarette." Today local governments are making it tougher and tougher for smokers to do that. For example, recently in California, several city councils voted to ban smoking inside apartments and condos. It is reported that their actions have triggered death threats against the council members. The smokers apparently resent having their "rights" violated, even though those "rights" might infringe on the physical welfare of innocents around them.

Health officials in about 30 states now promote the health and economic benefits of non-smoking rules, including reduced fire risk and lower clean-up costs for multi-unit housing.

Byline #190

Tens of thousands of such units have gone smoke-free in the past five years. The surgeon general has informed the public that no level of secondhand smoke is risk free. It makes absolutely no sense whatsoever to smoke. Critics of civic officials moan and groan about these restrictions. One condo owner said, "You should be able to do as you wish in your own home." That's nonsense, of course, if, in fulfilling your own personal desires, you infringe on the welfare of those around you.

Now I can remember clearly my junior and senior high school days decades ago when, if you didn't smoke, you were a nerd. It was somehow a mark of distinction, we were told by our peers, to fill your lungs with cancer-inducing smoke and blow it out your nose. I am so very thankful that I had parents who did not countenance such nonsense and for a pastor who warned against smoking. Yes, we may have been nerds in *those* days, but in *these* days we're quite healthy nerds, thank you very much. I recently received a list of those who graduated from high school with me who are now dead. How incredibly sad. And how unnecessary.

PRAYER

O God, You have given us our bodies that You call temples of the Holy Spirit. We have an obligation of what we put in them, yes, even including food. I ask Your forgiveness for each time I have treated Your temple with contempt by not taking care of this precious gift. Amen.

RAVENHILL

1 Samuel 9:6: And he said unto him, Behold now, there is in this city a man of God, and he is an honourable man.

Leonard Ravenhill was a beacon light to me and to more ministers than I can count! Ravenhill, who went to be with the Lord in 1994 at the age of 87, was one of Britain's foremost outdoor evangelists. He was a pillar of the Christian renewal movement and one of the greatest authorities on revival. But, as stated in the Wikipedia Encyclopedia, ". . . his message of radical holy living was considered extreme by some mainstream Christian ministers." To me, he was a prophet sent from God, a mentor, a second father, and a stabilizer in my life. His classic books, which I have read over and again, fill my bookshelves, such as *Why Revival Tarries, Revival Praying,* and *Meat for Men.*

Ravenhill and his wife, Martha, now also with Christ, were often guests in our home, and my wife and I had the joy, the privilege, of being their guests in their Texas home several times. I saw firsthand Ravenhill's prayer life, usually six to eight hours a day. While his message was strictly no-nonsense, both in pulpit and books, he was a sheer delight to be around. He had a bright spirit and a sparkling sense of humor.

When I was a young pastor, Ravenhill took me aside and said, "Dan, preach the eternities!" He added, "If Jesus had preached the same message that many ministers preach today, He never would have been crucified." He certainly followed his own advice. I heard him preach for over two hours one night in a large Methodist Church on the Judgment Seat of Christ. He never raised his voice but kept 1,500 people riveted to their pews. When he suddenly stopped preaching, a lady sitting right in front of me jumped to her feet and cried out, "No, please don't stop now!" The altars were jammed that night, including my own son David, who committed his life to ministry and has spent the last many years in Africa as a missionary. The Book of Ephesians teaches that God gave the church prophets. Ravenhill was one!

PRAYER: O God, how I thank You for putting giants of the faith in my path so I could observe and learn from them. Ravenhill was certainly Your divine gift to me so many years ago. I bless his memory and the legacy he left to so many of us still on the front lines today. Amen.

The lessons of Pearl Harbor

Psalm 91:5–6: Thou shalt not be afraid for the terror by night; nor for the arrow that flieth by day; Nor for the pestilence that walketh in darkness; nor for the destruction that wasteth at noonday.

While on business in Honolulu, Hawaii, not long ago, I caught a cab from my downtown hotel and was taken to Pearl Harbor. There on December 7, 1941, a Sunday morning by the way (8:00), the Japanese Air Force pulled a surprise and very successful attack on our U.S. Navy. If you have ever visited this site, which I passionately suggest, you are aware of the exposure and vulnerability of our ships there that morning. You are perhaps also aware that about eight months earlier, two senior officers, one army and the other navy, drew attention to the possible danger to which the base was exposed from a carrier-borne aircraft attack. The warning, for some reason still not fully understood, was disregarded.

Japanese Vice-Admiral Nagumo was given a task force of 321 planes, two fast battleships, three cruisers, nine destroyers, three submarines, and eight tankers to refuel his ships at sea. On that fateful morning, the United States had 70 warships and 24 auxiliaries in the harbor. Apparently no one suspected what awaited them. Pearl Harbor was still asleep in the morning mist. It was calm and serene inside the harbor. In fact, vital U.S. naval vessels of the Pacific Fleet were strung out and anchored, two ships side by side, in an orderly manner. The initial Japanese concentration was on the seven U.S. battleships moored alongside Ford Island. Within two hours, most of our ships were sunk or severely damaged and about 2,400 of our valiant men had died. Why did U.S. leaders neglect the warning of the previous months? Who was asleep at the switch? All these decades later, we still have no satisfactory answers.

But then, how many times have *you* heard about eternity? How many times have *you* been told of the coming of Christ and the judgment to follow? I can only pray that you are prepared spiritually for that which is to come. Otherwise, you are in for a spiritual Pearl Harbor of a dimension you can't even begin to imagine.

Prayer: O God, may we not neglect our souls in these days before Your Son returns. May we learn spiritual lessons about adequate preparation from historic tragedies. May we hear the prodding in our souls from Your Holy Spirit today. *Amen.*

A MOST IMPERFECT JUSTICE

In the 1960s, I was pastoring a small church that my wife and I had planted in northern Ohio. We didn't live far from Cleveland. An autoworker there was suspected of being the notoriously brutal Nazi guard known as Ivan the Terrible in the Treblinka, Poland, death camp during World War II. A series of hearings and trials took place, but it was not until 2002 that the man, John Demjanjuk, lost his U.S. citizenship. A subsequent hearing determined that the alleged former Nazi be deported to his native Ukraine. The case was even more puzzling when one remembered that Demjanjuk was sent to Israel in 1977, tried, convicted, and sentenced to hang. But the Israeli Supreme Court found that someone else was apparently the evil Ivan and Demjanjuk was returned to America. It was a terrible ordeal for all those who lost family members and friends in the death camps, having once again to at least mentally relive the Holocaust. But it was also a most difficult time for Demjanjuk's family. Was the man actually guilty of all those atrocities? Or was he not?

Mankind attempts some kind of justice system, but it's all so terribly flawed. Every other month I spend a day in Florida's Death Row. During the years I have been doing this, there have been men actually found innocent of the crime for which they were convicted and walked out the front gate free men. They could have gone to either the electric chair or the lethal injection table, even though actually innocent. But there will come a time when all mankind will stand before God. At that eternal bar of justice there will be no conjecture about the verdict. The Book of Revelation informs us that "the books will be opened." What books? The telltale records God keeps on our lives. So is our case hopeless? Not at all. The precious blood of Jesus Christ cleanses us from every sin, and even the memory of the transgression is erased from God's mind. Our most elaborate systems aren't perfect. But God's is.

A COLD AND FRIGHTENING NIGHT AT AUSCHWITZ

Genesis 12:1–3

Now the LORD had said unto Abram, Get thee out of thy country, and from thy kindred, and from thy father's house, unto a land that I will shew thee: And I will make of thee a great nation, and I will bless thee, and make thy name great; and thou shalt be a blessing: And I will bless them that bless thee, and curse him that curseth thee: and in thee shall all families of the earth be blessed.

It was 6:45 at night as Darlene and I drove our rented car to the gate of Birkenau, a part of the Auschwitz Nazi killing center in Poland. It is located on the outskirts of the city of Oswiecim. As we walked alongside the infamous railroad tracks to the gate, a guard met us to say it was closing time. We begged him to allow us entry, which he did, asking us only to pull the gate locked behind us when we left. It was growing dark, chilly, and drizzling as we ventured to the spot where the trains bearing tens of thousands of Europe's Jews stopped, where they were met by the evil Dr. Josef Mengele, S.S. guards, and snarling dogs. Women and children, for the most part, were directed immediately to the gas chambers, and men who could work had their lives temporarily spared as they were assigned barracks and work. Some of those barracks still stand. They were built to hold 200 inmates, but they were usually packed with up to 2,000, sleeping on lice-infected bunks and eating daily tiny bowls of swill. The four Birkenau crematoria were dynamited by the retreating Nazi SS; however, their ruins are clearly visible. The visitor can still enter an underground chamber where several million victims were asphyxiated on Zyklon B gas.

Darlene and I stayed as long as we could, fairly warm in our appropriate clothes, but remembering the thousands who froze to death or were worked into extinction by Nazi guards who had lost all semblance of humanity. By late April of 1945, the Germans had been defeated by the Allied powers. Hitler was dead by his own hand, as was Himmler, the mastermind of the death camps. Germany was left a wasteland that took several decades to rebuild. As we left the horrors of Birkenau that night, we reflected on God's promise to Abraham, "I will bless those who bless you (the Jews) and curse them that curse you." My friend, read your history books. God has never been mocked.

Byline #194

PRAYER

O God, help us as a nation and as individuals to never forget Your divine promise to Abraham. Then may we live accordingly. Amen.

THE ROLE OF A PASTOR

Jeremiah 3:15: And I will give you pastors according to mine heart, which shall feed you with knowledge and understanding.

The very word "pastor" has its roots in Eastern understanding. "Pastor" actually means "shepherd." The true pastor must protect and feed his sheep. It is my personal feeling that there can be no greater honor or responsibility than this. It was my privilege to serve in such a role for 34 years.

I always felt my primary role as a pastor/shepherd was to feed and guide the flock entrusted to me. But I had the dual responsibility of equipping the saints for ministry and leading them to worldwide effectiveness in evangelism. This is not an easy assignment, given that the balance between strong leadership and dictatorship can be razor-thin and the saint being equipped doesn't then understand his or her ministry role.

Many issues in the churches I pastored were quite frankly of only passing interest to me. For example, I could not have cared less about the color or style of carpet, or the design of the pews or chairs, or even the layout of the Sunday bulletin or weekly mailer. Even when I founded home missions churches, those issues were not of supreme urgency to me. What *did* concern me was what I delivered from the pulpit, what biblical content was being taught by our Christian education and Sunday school staffs, attitudes and ministries of our musicians, and whether the altars were utilized or not. I cared about the goals set before us by the Holy Spirit. I cared desperately about how effectively the church ministry was positively infiltrating every strata of our community. It is so easy for a pastor to care for the *good* responsibilities while neglecting the *best* ones.

It requires a firm but gentle hand at the helm of a church. Without the guidance of the blessed Holy Spirit, leadership is impossible. But with His direction, pastoral leadership is blessed, fulfilling, and exciting. I speak from experience. Over three decades of it.

Prayer: O God, I do thank You most sincerely for nearly a half of my lifetime spent in the role of a pastor. I thank You for every person won to Christ and guided into strong discipleship. It has been my honor and privilege! I am grateful. Amen.

Mediocrity in the house of God

2 Samuel 24:24: And the king said unto Araunah, Nay; but I will surely buy it of thee at a price: neither will I offer burnt offerings unto the LORD my God of that which doth cost me nothing. So David bought the threshingfloor and the oxen for fifty shekels of silver.

Every time you see the famous picture of Jerusalem, featuring that spectacular golden Dome of the Rock, you are looking generally at the place where the Great Temple of Solomon was constructed. This is the property purchased by David in the above 2 Samuel text. David, offered the property by its owner free of charge, countered, "No, I'm not going to give an offering to God that costs me nothing!"

In all too many churches today, giving God less than our best is the accepted norm. The bar of excellence is set very low. W. Somerset Maugham observed, "Only a mediocre person is always at his best."[1] I've heard it again and again, "That's good enough — it's just for the church." In the cause of Christ, it's never good enough until you have gone the last mile and given His work the best that is within you. My late, great mentor, Dr. Oswald J. Smith, quoted an old hymn: "Lord, I give myself to Thee / Friends and time and earthly store / Soul and body Thine to be / Wholly thine forevermore."[2]

I recently attended a Christian Education conference in which our instructor said, "Our goal should always be to teach a halfway decent lesson." My wife had to hold me back from taking a run at him. "Halfway decent? For the King? Are you joking?" Have we never read *My Utmost for His Highest?* How many times have you heard a singer in church apologize first by muttering, "Pray for me . . . I haven't had time to practice." No? Then get off the platform. What do you think this is, God's karaoke hour? Oh, Christian friend, let us care about the quality of God's work everywhere. At every level of service to the King, let's improve our quality. We cannot make up by singing praise choruses for our lack of commitment to excellence for the Master.

1. http://quote.robertgenn.com.
2. William McDonald, "I Am Coming to the Cross."

Prayer: O God, forgive me for every time I have sloughed on You service that reeked of less than my best. You have given me the very best You had in Jesus Christ. Can I then offer You that which costs me nothing? No, a thousand times no! I renew today my commitment to excellence in my service for You. *Amen.*

DO WOMEN HAVE A PLACE IN MINISTRY?

Hebrews 11:8: By faith Abraham, when he was called to go out into a place which he should after receive for an inheritance, obeyed; and he went out, not knowing whither he went.

Let's think about Abraham for a moment or two. This man of faith lived for 175 years. From his 75th year, when he left what we know today as Iraq until the death of his wife, Sarah, 62 years later, Abraham conducted a vigorous life for his Lord. When Sarah died, Abraham lived another 33 years. During that time he married again and sired more children. But, as I was studying Abraham's life from Scripture, it suddenly hit me the other day that there is not one biblical record of Abraham's having any special communication from God, or performing any act of significance for his family or nation. Let that sink in for a moment. For 33 years, until he died, Abraham became just another man. What tremendous impact Sarah had in his life! Small wonder then that Abraham spent 400 silver shekels (about $200,000 in our current money) to properly bury her in the Cave of Machpelah in Hebron, Israel.

Writer Shlomo Riskin summarizes: "Apparently Abraham was the rabbi in no small measure because Sarah was the rabbi's wife."[1] It certainly bears our attention to the biblical detail that Abraham spent a whole lot of time and money sending out his assistant Eliezer to a far country to find his son Isaac a wife of Sarah's status and spiritual stature. He knew full well what Sarah had meant to him and he wanted the same help for his son Isaac. The importance of women in ministry, to their spouses and their congregants, is underestimated by many. I have some male minister friends who take a very restrictive position on the subject. I believe Abraham might want to refute their position. He might even put Sarah on the platform and say, "Take a good look at that woman! She made me what I am today, a man of faith!"

I personally have been positively impacted for Christ by some women ministers. Several of them have founded and still pastor very large, spiritual and missions-minded churches. What's your take on this subject?

1. Shlomo Riskin, "Deeds Rather than Words," *Jerusalem Post* (11/21/03).

PRAYER: O God, I pray that You will anoint every handmaiden who carries forth Your Word to a lost, dying, hopeless world. May they have Your protection, provision, and care. May they be 21st century "Sarahs." Amen.

IT ONLY
HURTS WHEN
I LAUGH

Proverbs 15:13

A merry heart maketh a cheerful countenance: but by sorrow of the heart the spirit is broken.

Few advertising geniuses have so impacted media selling as has Stan Freberg. In his autobiography, *It Only Hurts When I Laugh*,[1] he tells about proposing an advertising approach to a major aluminum foil distributor. The campaign resulted in 43,000 new placements in stores across America. But the successful advertising push nearly got stopped at its inception by an executive in the foil firm. The company man, a bean-counter if ever there was one apparently, could not conceive of such "off-the-wall" advertising. But Freberg was right and the executive was dead wrong.

Freberg reported, "If I seem unduly harsh on rigid ad executives, it is because I am angered and depressed that people like that in advertising, or any business, stand in the way of progress with horse blinders on their heads. In their rigidity they attempt to thwart creative people to communicate with consumers in a more effective way on behalf of the products they been entrusted to sell." Freberg should know. He's a genius. And he knows his businesses.

But you should know that this negative mentality comes to the top in church work, too. Contrary to some opinions, Americans are very reachable with the gospel, especially as it relates to the real Jesus from Scripture. Holy Spirit-anointed initiatives can impact any town anywhere. But then you hear that plaintive and pathetic plea, "But we've never done it that way before!" God's people should maximize every resource our Father has made available. We should be "cutting edge" creatively. So what to do about those who stand in the way of progress? Pray for them, of course. Still love them. But get on with the project God has entrusted to you. No, you cannot always please people, but you *must* please God.

1. Stan Freberg, *It Only Hurts When I Laugh* (New York: Times Books, 1988).

Byline #198

PRAYER

O God, enable me by Your Holy Spirit to always be fresh and creative in my work for You. May Your anointing rest upon me as I labor on Your front lines. I may not reach every person for You, but help me so I don't bore them to death either. Amen.

THE UNREASONABLENESS
OF FEAR Byline #199

Years have passed now since the nation suffered through its paranoia with Y2K. Remember the dire predictions on the part of many who truly thought the world would end as January 1, 2000, dawned? Their reasoning, if it can be called that, was that computers were not geared for a millennial change. They believed that all earth's computers would shut down, that planes would fall out of the sky, that starvation would cover the planet like a suffocating blanket. None of those things happened, of course.

What surprised me so much was that many church people joined the neurosis that gripped the world. I know of churches that shut down their New Year's Eve services for fear people would not be able to get home. In the church I pastor, we actually saw some folks leave the church because I refused to encourage folks to start stockpiling food and supplies for the supposed "terror that awaited us." There was just no reasoning with such frightened people. All the assurances and logic I applied to them simply bounced off like raindrops on a windshield. Like Chicken Little, they just "knew" the sky was falling. Now, all these years later, it does not seem possible that this time of fear actually happened, that so many could have been so paralyzed by it.

The Bible teaches us clearly that fear does not come from God. Our Heavenly Father never meant for His children to walk in a mental valley where the shadows are long and spooky. The apostle John encouraged us to "walk in the light, as He [Jesus] is in the light" (1 John 1:7). Y2K never happened. Logic spoke eloquently that it never could. Those things we fear rarely materialize. Yet many people make tons of money from those whose minds feast on the fearful. God calls us to a higher plane of life. One free from goblins, "what-ifs," and fright. Perhaps today you are challenged to a new and exciting level of life, yet the enemy of your soul keeps pestering you with doubts. God's perfect love casts out all fear. Walk in the light, good friend. There are no shadows there.

PRAYER

O God, David wrote so long ago that not even the valley of the shadow of death could bring us fear. You are with us. Banish all fears by Your over-shading love, I ask. And oh, how much I thank You for such victory from darkness. Amen.

Enjoying our measure of health

Isaiah 58:8: Then shall thy light break forth as the morning, and thine health shall spring forth speedily: and thy righteousness shall go before thee; the glory of the LORD shall be thy reward.

The annual time for my physical has just rolled around and so I have spent a couple of days in various doctors' offices. Nothing serious, thank God, just routine. Two things have struck me rather forcefully: (1) magazines remain readable even though they were printed shortly after World War II, and (2) there are surely a lot of people with major medical problems. Coming to my study today, I drove by a radiology facility. Cars jammed the parking lot as well as the streets around it, and yes, even on the lawns.

It is a sad thing to lose your health, when that cheek with vital glow turns wan and cold, when the sparkle leaves the eyes. Succeeding years take their toll on these bodies of ours, don't they? Well, we can do one of several things: we can moan and groan about youth-lost or we can thank God for the strength and health we do retain and maximize

it. It is interesting how some of my acquaintances have done so.

A friend of mine celebrated his 80th birthday by learning to water ski. Another dear friend, on his 94th birthday, bought (and learned to operate) his very first computer. Colonel Sanders, whom I met, was 65 when he kicked off his finger-lickin'-chicken career. Grandma Moses was 80, I hear, when she hit her stride painting. Every second of life we possess is a treasure, and it is also a sacred responsibility. Yes, I frankly have a few aches and pains today. You, too? So what do we do, just collapse in a chair and bemoan our passing years? Or do we say, as Caleb at age 85, "Give me this mountain"? (Josh. 14:12). I'm going to be thankful to the Lord for the health I enjoy today. I am going to rejoice that I'm getting in a full day of work instead of convalescing in a hospital somewhere. How about you?

Prayer: O God, all life comes from You. I am grateful that I can lift my hands and voice to You today and cry from the depths of my soul a resounding "thank You" for this precious gift of "being." Please help me to maximize my health today by bringing You great joy in Your own creation. *Amen.*

LEST WE FORGET

Joshua 4:6–7: That this may be a sign among you, that when your children ask their fathers in time to come, saying, What mean ye by these stones? Then ye shall answer them, That the waters of Jordan were cut off before the ark of the covenant of the Lord. . . .

Our nation is at war. I do not speak of some Middle-East battle, but rather a war of will. A struggle of the human will. The evil abroad on this planet is choking the present and future of humanity.

I was not much more than a toddler in the late 1930s, but I can still remember (oh, yes, I can!) the disintegration of peace around the world and America's struggle about whether to get involved in the European conflict. In fact, civil liberties and freedom were at stake not only there but also in the Far East. The dictatorships of Hitler, Mussolini, and Tojo, not to mention Russia's Stalin, were of a magnitude never before experienced on earth. Woodrow Wilson's League of Nations had fizzled its mission. All Britain was in peril. Their prime minister, Sir Winston Churchill, declared, "I have nothing to offer but blood, toil, tears, and sweat." That was hardly an attractive offer to a free world that wanted to eat, drink, and be merry. When on September 1, 1939, Hitler's Nazis invaded Poland off the shores of Gdansk, President Franklin Roosevelt used his growing influence to further the cause of the beleaguered Allies abroad. Many well-known Americans fought our involvement tooth and nail until that horrible day of December 7, 1941, when the Japanese surprised Pearl Harbor with a lethal attack that left thousands dead or maimed. Within hours, Congress had declared war on Japan, Germany, and Italy, the "Axis" powers. It was a brutal war that cost nearly 60 million people their lives. I can still remember. Can you?

It is urgent that those of us who remember continue to tell the story of the price that was paid for this wondrous nation of freedom we so enjoy. This liberty did not just "evolve." In the Revolutionary War, World Wars I and II, Korea, Vietnam, the Gulf War, Iraq, and others, men and women laid down their lives for us. God help us lest we forget.

Prayer: O God, I bless the memory of these heroes now gone. Give us the courage to always strive for liberty of mind, body, and soul! Amen.

PLAYING GOLF IN RUSSIA

Genesis 2:2

And on the seventh day God ended his work which he had made; and he rested. . . .

On my last trip into Russia, I was happily surprised to hear of golf course construction there. Granted, the golf season is not all that long, five or six months at best. Plus the fact that the severity of the former Communist regimes and the resulting poverty of the people precluded anything so "materialistic" as golf. There is still economic chaos in much of Russia, but at least in major metropolitan areas, there is growth. Hence the new construction of golf courses. In 2004 there were a mere 27 holes total in that entire nation. Now some fine 18-hole public courses are available. But here's the stinger: a green fee will still be $100 or even higher because of the shortness of the season.

There are some civilized countries in which golf is little-known. Israel, for instance, has but one course near the Mediterranean coastline at Caesarea. I have never played it, but I have walked around the course. It's beautiful. South Africa, on the other hand, has some of the world's great championship layouts, including Sun City (a Gary Player course) and Leopard Creek at Kruger Park (pro golfer Ernie Els has a beautiful home along one of the fairways there). I played Leopard Creek not long ago and counted five elephants, four hippos, and a number of crocodiles. One does not go wandering into the rough there in pursuit of errant Titleists. (Well, not more than once.)

Golf is a great game. I've been playing it for over 50 years — not well, mind you. I've never had a hole-in-one, although I've had a number of lakes-in-one. Golf is at its best when you're playing with close friends. It's the camaraderie, the give-and-take, the delightful competition. You may not golf, but you ought to have something in life that gives you relaxation. Yes, of course, we all work hard, but there's nothing wrong with resting. God did.

Byline #202

PRAYER

O God, I am grateful for work that provides not only sustenance for my family, but also contributes something worthwhile to humanity. Yet I need to remember that this body You gave me is finite. It needs rest and tune-ups occasionally. Help me exercise good sense in "the care and feeding" of this body. By Your grace, may it last for a long, long time. Amen.

JUST A BIG BALL OF STRING

JAMES 4:14: Whereas ye know not what shall be on the morrow. For what is your life? It is even a vapour, that appeareth for a little time, and then vanisheth away.

My friend President Dr. Don Meyers (of Valley Forge University) told me the story of Frances A. Johnson, who at 46 years of age started tying pieces of bailer twine together. He had always been a collector of junk, such as string. Reportedly, he never dated, stayed single, and finally died in his mid-80s. Back to the bailer twine: Thirty years of collecting this string resulted in a huge ball, 13 feet high, 44 feet in circumference, and weighing 21,000 pounds. Unraveled, it was long enough to stretch from the collector's front yard in Minnesota to the Gulf of Mexico. The massive ball brought a certain amount of fame to Johnson, as it got him into the Guinness Book of Records.

Now here's the kicker to this story: Near death, Johnson was quoted as saying, "I still like to look at it (the string). It's the greatest thing I ever did." Dr. Meyers concluded his story, "Over 80 years of living and the high-water mark of his entire life was a smelly ball of twine that could be gone in a moment with one match." I thought as Meyers told it to me of Peggy Lee's classic pop hit, "Is That All There Is?"

So what do you figure is your greatest accomplishment in life? I've asked myself that question a number of times. I suspect it's the Children's Bible, 125 Bible stories I recorded (in stereo with all original music and sound effects) with my ventriloquist dummy Louie in the "Dan and Louie" series. Two generations of children have now learned the Word of God through these CDs. I am told that up to a million kids have heard these stories. Funny how things we consider inconsequential become mountaintops in life while, conversely, issues we once thought so important now look like — well, like a big ball of string.

PRAYER: O God, help us to see our lives and this world through Your eyes. May Your value system become our value system. As the songwriter reminded us, "The things of this world grow strangely dim in the light of Your glory and grace."[1] I certainly want more to lay at Your feet than just a big ball of string. Amen.

---

1. Helen Howarth Lemmel, "Turn Your Eyes Upon Jesus."

Hey! What's happened to Sundays?

John 20:1 The first day of the week cometh Mary Magdalene early, when it was yet dark, unto the sepulchre, and seeth the stone taken away from the sepulchre.

Our Lord Jesus was resurrected from the tomb early Sunday morning. That is why most churches celebrate the first day of the week (Sunday), rather than the seventh (Saturday), as the day to worship. In days gone by, Sundays were considered sacred, with most businesses closing and schools not imposing their will. Not any longer. Now even the local sports world claims this day. The Associated Press issued a 2004 column with this headline: "Churches Want Their Sundays Back!" Absolutely! With weekend sports growing in popularity, schedules have stretched into hours that were once the exclusive domain of churches. Now, league directors and coaches, who often themselves have little or no interest in church, schedule games for kids during church hours and expect — demand! — all the players to miss their religious services to hit or catch a ball.

I feel for Jewish families, too, whose kids want to be in synagogue on Shabbat and keep their holy day. There are some ball players in the major leagues who absolutely refuse to play on religious sacred days. Good for them. They can get their way because of their greatness on the field or court. But what about the players who cannot make any demands? There still must be that day of the week that is set aside for the things of God to be first and foremost. The AP reports that it's not uncommon in churches now to see kids sitting in pews dressed in sports uniforms so they can rush right from the sanctuary to the ball field.

At what point did we put a ball over the Creator? Who or what is more important than God? A soccer game? Smacking a Maxfli down a fairway? Stuffing a round ball in a basket? Is that what Jesus demanded? No. His demands were to seek first the kingdom of God and His righteousness (Matt. 6:33). Thank God there are still some stars and even a few coaches who believe in doing just that. I have even heard there are some church leaders who still believe in the sanctity of the Lord's Day.

Prayer: O God, it must grieve Your heart to see us so callous about setting aside a day just for Your glory. Forgive us for putting nonessentials above and beyond our worship of You. May we truly seek You first and foremost. *Amen.*

WAS IT THE "GREAT COMMISSION" OR THE "GREAT SUGGESTION"?

Byline #205

> **Acts 1:8**
> But ye shall receive power, after that the Holy Ghost is come upon you: and ye shall be witnesses unto me both in Jerusalem, and in all Judaea, and in Samaria, and unto the uttermost part of the earth.

Why should we, as followers and servants of Jesus Christ, be involved in world missions? First, it's a matter of *obedience*. The commission issued by our King to evangelize the world was not a suggestion! Singing choruses in church and making some Sabbath pretense of faith will make precious little impact on the divine throne if the believer has disobeyed the very Lord he or she professes to worship. Second, the subject of missions is a matter of *spiritual concern*. Joel wrote, "Multitudes, multitudes in the valley of decision . . ." (Joel 3:14). Does that line pierce your soul? Does it make you even blink? Do you wonder what your responsibility is in this matter? Third, involvement in world missions is a matter of *fairness*. Why should you, or I, or anyone else, have the privilege of hearing the gospel twice when so many in the world have never heard about Jesus once?

Fourth, as Paul writes in Romans, missions is a matter of *logic*. "How then shall they call on him in whom they have not believed? And how shall they believe in him of whom they have not heard? And how shall they hear without a preacher? And how shall they preach except they be sent?" (Rom. 10:14–15) Fifth, participation in missions is *evidence* that we believe in heaven and hell. If we truly believe that there is a heaven to be gained and a hell to be shunned, how can we not give and go? Sixth, faithfulness in missions is a matter of *divine supply*. Jesus promised signs and wonders to those who believe (see Mark 16). This applies to those who are obeying His divine command. God will be no man's debtor, my friend.

These facts are so biblical, so simple, and so understandable. Yet there are many Christians and church leaders who act as if the missions command doesn't even exist. Yet they still ask God for His blessings. Small wonder they get confused at unanswered prayer.

> **PRAYER**
> O God, You have but one plan for global evangelism, and "we're it!" May we ever, always, totally be faithful to the Great Commission by giving or going. Amen.

AUNT PAULINE

Judges 21:24

And the children of Israel departed thence at that time, every man to his tribe and to his family, and they went out from thence every man to his inheritance.

Pardon me while I write about my family for a few moments. I got the news by e-mail from a relative that my dear Aunt Pauline had died in Moville, Iowa. She was 88. I had a double-grief at the news — her death and the fact that I couldn't make it to the funeral in the old Methodist Church up there. I had visited Aunt Pauline a few months earlier. She wasn't well and was on oxygen, but was still fiercely independent and determined. I so much enjoyed our visit in her immaculately maintained house at the edge of the northwest Iowa town.

There were four children in my mother's family: Mom (Roberta, the eldest), then Pauline, then Richard and Rex. Only Uncle Rex remains. My grandfather's name was Prince. Prince Harshfield. I love that name! Grandma Harshfield's first name was Mabel. For years grandfather operated a farm between Moville and Bronson. I remember a lot of happy days as a small kid spent on that farm, especially playing in the hayloft in the old, rickety barn. (Which, last I saw, still stands!) When farming got too tough for grandfather physically, he took a job driving a grader on those old gravel country roads. The Harshfields were never well-off financially, although the kids did well enough after they left home. Please pardon my rambling on about my family, but I loved them all so much — yes, even the distant cousin I had who was hanged for horse stealing in the late 1800s. True. Hey, nobody's perfect.

You know, "family" was the first institution God created, followed by the state and the church. I am grateful for my immediate family today, all these long years later. Our four kids and many grandchildren are scattered literally around the world. Your family is precious, good friend. I hope you realize that. And I hope you tell them so.

Byline #206

PRAYER

O God, help me to understand that those around me, especially my family, are jewels. Help me to treat them so. I want to be a good husband, father, and grandfather. Let me leave a spiritual heritage for those who will follow me. Amen.

JAWS

Romans 10:11: For the scripture saith, Whosoever believeth on him shall not be ashamed.

While surfing the TV channels recently (you know us men — we like to do that!), I happened upon an old James Bond movie in which the villain was Richard Kiel. Do you remember him? The guy with the steel teeth? Jaws! I have had the delight on several occasions of spending time with Richard. He has given his remarkable testimony in our church.

He is 7 feet 2 inches tall. His wife is only 5 feet 1. The Kiels have four children, last I heard. Now I have a picture of Richard and me, his hand on top of my head. His thumb hits one of my ears and the tips of his fingers touch my other ear. Is that a huge hand or what? Put your hand on your own head and check it out. But this man who appears so menacing on the screen is actually one of the most gentle, soft-spoken men I have ever known.

Richard gave his heart to Christ when he was only nine years old. But it wasn't until he was in his 30s that he began to realize his full potential in God. When offered a lucrative job in a beer TV commercial, he turned it down. He said beer offended his beliefs. One of Richard's passions is praying for the sick. He spent hours at our altars praying for anyone and everyone. There were some who testified of being healed. My point is this: don't judge anyone on first sight or by temporary circumstances. Neither you nor I really know what's in the heart of someone else. Jesus made it a flat command: "Judge not" (Matt. 7:1; Luke 6:37). But we like to anyway, don't we? Sometimes perhaps it makes us feel superior or more spiritual. The very fact that we disobey our Lord and judge others anyway is a clear indication we're not so spiritual after all. Next time you see Richard on the screen, pray that God will continue to use him in a part of society that you or I can never touch.

Prayer: O God, I do thank You for the servants You have placed in such strategic places, yes, even in Hollywood, major league sports, government, and music. Let us be lights unto all mankind, not just a few choice corners of society. Amen.

Holyfield

1 Samuel 17:45: Then said David to the Philistine, Thou comest to me with a sword, and with a spear, and with a shield: but I come to thee in the name of the LORD of hosts, the God of the armies of Israel, whom thou hast defied.

No, I don't equate David with Evander Holyfield. David became a king while Evander became the great heavyweight champion of the world. On the wall of my study hang two boxing gloves with the autograph: To Dan Betzer from Holyfield. When he gave them to me, he said, "From one fighter to another." I laughed.

Every fight fan remembers the classic first bout between Evander and Mike Tyson. Holyfield had offered me front-row seats, but I couldn't go. Ah, but I saw it on television! A month or so before the battle, Evander was a 25-1 underdog. Just before the opening bell, he was listed at 6-1 odds against him. No one gave the then-33-year-old warrior a chance against Tyson, the raging bull. But it became obvious in the first round that Tyson was not going to push his opponent around. Evander won the first four rounds on most cards, and midway through the fight he decked Tyson with a vicious body shot. In round 11 he had the champ out on his feet and the referee stopped the bout, awarding Holyfield the TKO (technical knock-out) victory, and for the third time, he was the heavyweight champion of the world.

At the close of the fight, the "boxing doctor" (as he's known to TV fans) Ferdie Paccheco interviewed Holyfield and was somewhat perplexed and not-a-little miffed when the champ would only talk about Jesus. Paccheco couldn't get Evander's thoughts back to the fight, only the Lord. Interesting. Evander has had his ups and downs since that historic sports event, probably more "ups" if the truth be known. But I'll never forget his determination to speak of the Lord at the highest moment of his professional career. There are some who call on the Lord in time of trouble, but in times of success can't quite remember His name anymore. Listen, God is your God in good times and bad. Holyfield knew that. Let's you and I remember it, too.

Prayer: O God, I will acknowledge You in my life at all times, good and bad. Your power and dominion do not diminish or increase according to my personal circumstances. No matter what happens, You are still God and I praise You. ***Amen.***

SOME THOUGHTS ON OUR FUTURE BODIES

1 Corinthians 15:42–44: So also is the resurrection of the dead. It is sown in corruption; it is raised in incorruption: It is sown in dishonour; it is raised in glory: it is sown in weakness; it is raised in power: It is sown a natural body; it is raised a spiritual body. There is a natural body, and there is a spiritual body.

As a pastor, I am often asked how a follower of Christ should be buried and if cremation is ever justified. Only a couple decades ago, about one American in ten chose cremation. Now it's one in four. It is estimated that there will be about a million or more cremations in this country this year. In my own state of Florida, those figures have already hit peak figures with a couple hundred crematories and nearly half of our population opting for cremation. I understand the highest percentage is in Hawaii, with 65 percent.

There are battles royal in some places where crematories are scheduled to be built. Someone has said, "The dead may rest in peace, but their bodies are causing quite a stir." Theologically, I don't suppose it matters a whole lot whether a person chooses burial or cremation. Now psychologically there may be a different story. Somehow there needs to be "closure" with friends and close family. However, the bottom line to this story is the coming resurrection. Every person who has ever died will be raised to life, according to Scripture, whether that person was good or bad, born-again or non-redeemed by the blood of Christ. The resurrection will be divided: those who are resurrected to eternal life and those who are resurrected to divine judgment.

The Bible tells us of glorified bodies for God's saints never again subject to disease or decay. Those bodies will know no time or space limitations. Think of it! This opens up to us believers a fascinating array of possibilities. One thing is sure: death is not a terrifying issue for a follower of Christ. Whether buried or cremated, that redeemed person will spend eternity with God. No wonder Christians get excited about "the joy set before us."

PRAYER: O God, I know that 100 years from now I will be vitally alive in Your presence, as I will be a million years from now. Eternal life is Your promise to those who follow You! I bless You for the comfort in knowing what awaits me ahead. Amen.

HOW THE RED-LETTER EDITION OF THE BIBLE CAME TO BE

Matthew 5:1–2

And seeing the multitudes, he went up into a mountain: and when he was set, his disciples came unto him: And he opened his mouth, and taught them. . . .

Louis Klopsch was pretty excited when he received the letter on White House stationery from President Theodore Roosevelt. "Mr. Klopsch, please have dinner with me." A few days before that Klopsch had received a telegram of congratulations from the king of Sweden. Pretty heady stuff for a man who served as the first editor of the *Christian Herald Magazine*.

Klopsch was born in 1852 in Germany and studied journalism at the school that later became Columbia University. He rose from stock boy to editor and finally, owner of the *Christian Herald Magazine*. He attended Brooklyn Temple where T. DeWitt Talmage was the minister.

One day in 1899, Klopsch was reading Jesus' words from Luke 22:20: "This cup is the new testament in my blood, which is shed for you." Klopsch thought, *The blood of Jesus — the red blood of Jesus.* And the thought came to him, *Why not an edition of the Bible where Jesus' words were all printed in red?* And so it came to be. The first printing of a red-letter Bible numbered 60,000 copies. The demand for them was overwhelming. Presses were run day and night to supply the demand. The Bibles were read by even the president of the United States and the king of Sweden and many other notables as well. At his death in 1910, the *New York Tribune* reported, "He will not easily be replaced. He lived and died by his own motto: 'Do all the good you can for all the people you can.'" To this day I love those editions of sacred Scripture in which the words of our Lord are printed in red. And we have the good editor of the *Christian Herald* to thank for it.

Byline #210

PRAYER

O God, Your Word is so precious to us, whether the ink used is black, red, or some other color. If we would live by the words of Jesus, what a different world this would be! Quicken Your Word to us, O God. But in order for You to do that, we must read the Scriptures and see for ourselves the plane of holy living You require of us. May we faithfully study Your Word, this marvelous light unto our pathway. Amen.

THE 12 MEN OF JESUS WHO CHANGED THE WORLD

Byline #211

Matthew 10:2–4

Now the names of the twelve apostles are these; The first, Simon, who is called Peter, and Andrew his brother; James the son of Zebedee, and John his brother; Philip, and Bartholomew; Thomas, and Matthew the publican; James the son of Alphaeus, and Lebbaeus, whose surname was Thaddaeus; Simon the Canaanite, and Judas Iscariot, who also betrayed him.

Did you ever wonder how much the average Christian knows about the 12 men Jesus chose to be His disciples, the men who would be entrusted with His message of redemption to the world? They had no media, no printing presses, no computers, no modern transportation — only themselves, energized by the Holy Spirit. Yet these somewhat ordinary men turned their world upside-down.

When contemplating them, one of them a devil (Jesus' own words), we can get easily sidetracked. We hear of *Saint* James or *Saint* Peter and our minds conjure up a group of unusually gifted, exceptionally talented, deeply religious, and quite naturally saintly men. Not true. With the possible exception of Nathaniel (Bartholomew), they were common, hard-working, live-by-the-sweat-of-their-brow men with instincts that often were far from any spiritual inclination. Yet they allowed Jesus to so mold their lives that their impact is felt even today, 2,000 years later, by a third of the world's population.

Today's Christian world needs to see again the commitment of these early church leaders. We need to understand the price they paid in their zeal and love of the Master. Most of these men died martyrs' deaths. Andrew, Bartholomew, James the Elder, James the son of Alphaeus, John, Jude, Matthew, Peter, Philip, Simon, and Thomas, all sinners saved by grace and endued with supernatural power by the Holy Spirit. You and I need to understand that they were just people like us in abilities and sinful natures. But God touched their lives, just as He touches ours. We, too, can change our world. It depends upon our level of commitment and love of the Master.

PRAYER

O God, we love to study the lives of these ordinary men who became extraordinary as they accompanied Jesus. How magnificently You used them. You are no respecter of persons and You will use us, too, as we commit our ways unto You and Your divine purpose. To that end we pledge ourselves today. Amen.

Jack

Ephesians 4:11: And he gave . . . evangelists. . . .

The year was 1950. I was a 13-year-old kid, growing up in a Christian home. One Sunday our pastor announced that our congregation would participate in something I'd never heard of, a city-wide crusade in the gorgeous new downtown auditorium. Everyone in our little church was somewhat taken back. You mean, meet with Baptists and Methodists and Presbyterians and Evangelical Free and all those other types? Yes, that is exactly what our pastor had in mind. The meeting, scheduled for two weeks, began with a soft thud. Maybe 300 people in that huge arena. But the preacher was Evangelist Jack Shuler. To this day, nearly 60 years later, Jack was the greatest preacher I ever heard. The crowd grew to 500, then to 800, and past 1,000. By the scheduled end of the meeting, the arena was packed with thousands of eager hearers. The revival continued another two weeks. On the final night, the crusade was moved to the baseball park. The stands were jammed, with hundreds more sitting on the field.

It was on the first Thursday night of Shuler's preaching that I went forward during the invitation and gave my life to Christ. Jack himself prayed with me in the prayer room. Although I grew up in a Christian home and knew the Bible well, I had not had a time when I actually gave my heart, soul, and life to Jesus.

Looking back on that eventful week, I am so thankful for the vision of my pastor and a few other clergymen in the city. They did something that had never been done. They did not get discouraged when the crusade did not start well. They believed something extraordinary would happen and dared to act on their faith. I often thank the Lord that my path crossed that of Jack Shuler. He died in 1963, far too young and far too early. All of Christendom lost a gift . . . a great evangelist.

Prayer: O God, You have graced my life with men and women who were standouts in Your divine army. I am so grateful. To this day when I listen to recordings of Jack, I am still deeply moved in my spirit. As my pastor and the evangelist impacted me, may I impact others in the time You allow to remain in my life. ***Amen.***

OLD ABE

Romans 13:3: For rulers are not a terror to good works, but to the evil. Wilt thou then not be afraid of the power? do that which is good, and thou shalt have praise of the same.

It is a story that somehow never grows old to us Americans. On the morning of February 12, 1809, Tom came out of his cabin to the road where he stopped a neighbor. He asked, "Please tell that granny woman that my Nancy will need her help now." The "granny woman," the midwife, arrived and before long Tom and Nancy Lincoln welcomed into the world (in the words of Carl Sandburg) "of battle and blood, of whispering dreams and wistful dust a new child, a boy." Someone asked old Tom what he was going to name his son. "Abraham," was the answer, "after his grandfather."[1]

Over 100 years later, Congressman Homer Hock of Kansas stood in the House of Representatives to say, "There is no new thing to be said about Lincoln. There is no new thing to be said of the mountains, or of the sea, or of the stars. The years go their way, but the same old mountains lift their granite shoulders above the drifting clouds; the same mysterious sea beats upon the shore; the same silent stars keep holy vigil above a tired world. But to the mountains and sea and stars men turn forever in unwearied homage. And thus with Lincoln. For he was a mountain in grandeur of the soul, he was a sea in deep under voice of mystic loneliness; he was a star in steadfast purity of purpose and serve. And he abides."[2]

The legend of Abraham Lincoln continues to loom before us today as each year we celebrate the birth of this man whom many consider the greatest president of them all. If he was not the greatest, then certainly he was one of the true high-watermark leaders of our history. We must always cover our leaders in intercessory prayer, whether we are subscribers of their political party or not. Anyone can criticize or poke fun; it takes quite another person to undergird our leaders before the throne of God. And it requires a "giant" to fill the shoes of Lincoln.

Prayer: O God, America is in turmoil at home and around the world. We pray for those currently in authority over us and ask that You somehow lift them to the status of true "states-persons" of dignity, effectiveness, and godliness. At this stage of our American history, we can afford no less standard than this. Amen.

1. Carl Sandburg, *Abe Lincoln Grows Up* (New York: Voyager Books, 1975), p. 32–33.
2. http://thelincolnassociationofjerseycity.com_wsn/page3_html.

A CLOUD LIFTS OFF EUROPE

Genesis 19:28

And he looked toward Sodom and Gomorrah, and toward all the land of the plain, and beheld, and, lo, the smoke of the country went up as the smoke of a furnace.

In the late '40s, Bing Crosby had a hit song, "Faraway Places With Strange-soundin' Names." He sang about islands of the sea and far-off continents, and I used to think, *Boy, I'd like to see some of those places*. Well, God has been very good to me, and I have traveled or ministered in over 60 nations, including the continent of Europe 40 or 50 times, I suspect. I have always been bothered in Europe by the fact that you have to wade through billows of choking, asphyxiating cigarette and cigar smoke. But several years ago, that atmosphere began to be cleared.

Ireland is banning smoking in pubs and restaurants, leading the way in Europe's crackdown on tobacco. Norway, Holland, and Greece are supposedly next. In

Byline #214

Britain, some restaurants, such as Pizza Hut, have gone smoke-free throughout the country. Among the efforts: cigarette packs in all European Union member nations now carry health warnings such as, "Smoking can cause a slow, painful death." Tobacco companies no longer can call their cigarettes "light" or "mild," because all cigarettes are deadly. Cigarette ads in newspapers, on billboards, on the Internet, and at sporting events were all banned in 2005. There are teeth in those restrictions, too. Lawbreakers will be subject to fines of $3,700 for each offense.

In the United States about a fifth of our citizens smoke. In Europe the figure is closer to the mid-30 percent range. So is everyone happy about the new restrictions? No, of course not. The folks who cough a lot are not happy. Those whose fingers are yellow and have breath like a farmyard aren't thrilled. They like their coffin (coughin') nails. But everywhere else people are singing, "Somewhere Over the Rainbow." Smoking is deadly, and no one has the right to impose their filthy air on another person. Now . . . if we can only get rid of cell phones in public places!

PRAYER

O God, You have created these bodies of ours that Scripture calls "temples of the Holy Spirit." Sometimes we abuse those bodies through all sorts of malpractice against them. Forgive us and help us tend to our bodies in the way that is beneficial and pleasing to us and You. Amen.

GOD HELPS THOSE WHO HELP THEMSELVES

Daniel 8:24: He shall . . . prosper, and practice. . . .

Yes, yes, I can hear you from here: the title of this page is not in the Bible, and I have taken the Daniel passage out of context. I admit it. But hear me out:

When I was a youngster, I lived in a house that had 800 square feet. One of my mother's priceless possessions was a huge upright piano that pretty much filled the front room. It was her desire that I learn to play it and frankly, I was willing to give it a try. However, I had a dear aunt who made the word "super-spiritual" an understatement.

My auntie came to me and said she had had a dream. In her nighttime visit, she got the impression that God told her that He was going to wake me up one night and in just a few short minutes, teach me to play the piano. I would come out for breakfast one morning, sit at that yellowed old keyboard, put my fingers on the keys, and *voila!* I would make Dino sound like Grandpa Jones. Or something. Mom bought into the dream and hoped it would happen. Every morning I would dutifully sit at those keys, place my little fingers on them, and the result was always "klunk-klunk-klunk." But despite my daily failings, we kept hanging on to the dream, or nightmare, or whatever it was.

Yes, I know, I should have said, "You know, Mom, this just ain't workin'! I'm going to take lessons." But, no, dear auntie had this dream and sometime or other it would come to pass. As I write this, I'm pressing close to 72 years of age and the miracle better happen pretty fast. I surely wish I had taken lessons. Yes, I know it's not a Scripture, but I do believe the Lord helps those who help themselves. Last I heard, learning how to play the piano was not provided in the atonement at Calvary. See, I could have been playing a pretty mean piano by now, 60 years later. So, good friend, do you want to achieve something worthwhile in life? Then do a little work. Take a lesson. Practice. I wish I would have.

PRAYER: O God, teach us how to separate theology from old wives' tales and quit blaming everyone else for our shortcomings. But, to paraphrase Teyve from *Fiddler on the Roof*, "Would it spoil some cosmic plan if You would touch my fingers and. . . ." Sorry I brought it up again. Amen.

Gary changes the face of Africa

Matthew 16:19: . . . whatsoever thou shalt bind on earth shall be bound in heaven: and whatsoever thou shalt loose on earth shall be loosed in heaven.

Africa! It's called the Dark Continent. Spiritually, there are bright lights springing up, south, east, and west. The north has yet to be strongly penetrated. Sadly, AIDS has settled on the land like a thick, choking cloud. In some nations, it is killing one in five persons. For example, the average life expectancy in Swaziland is currently 36.

My dear friend, Canadian Gary Skinner, was called by God to work in Uganda. He and his wife journeyed there when Big Daddy Idi Amin was the vicious dictator of the land. It was made very clear to Gary that he could work for the Lord with children, but not with adults. Amin is long since gone and thousands upon thousands now attend Skinner's church in Kampala. Those children have grown up to become some of the nation's leaders. Gary and his church family have attacked the AIDS virus with a passion. They feed, house, clothe, and care for hundreds upon hundreds of victims, and joined by others in the struggle, they are seeing a change in the health climate of that nation.

Our son David and his family live in South Africa. For many years they have led a rescue operation for children whose parents have died of AIDS. They bring these children to the Lighthouse Children's Shelter in the city of Rustenburg, operated by David and his wife, Janis, and their staff in conjunction with the medical community of that area. Many of these children are brought back to health, unless, as babies, they nursed from their HIV-stricken mothers. These latter cases usually end in the death of the child. All of these doctors, nurses, and missionaries put their own safety and health on the line every day. They know about sacrifice. Each of them will testify that he or she is there because of "want to," not "have to." Some truly good things are beginning to happen in the emerging nations of Africa. May God grant a full victory over these horrible diseases.

Prayer: O God, keep our hearts tender toward those who suffer all over the world. Forgive us for any judgmental attitudes we have and teach us the compassion that Jesus showed on this earth each time He confronted human suffering. Bless those who labor so long and hard on the front lines today. And keep them safe. ***Amen.***

THOUGHTS ON GROWING OLD — FROM AN OLD PERSON

Deuteronomy 31:2

And he said unto them, I am an hundred and twenty years old this day. . . .

Shortly after President John Kennedy was assassinated, his brother Bobby, then Attorney General of the United States, appeared as a guest on the Jack Paar show. Paar asked him, "What do you consider your brother's greatest legacy to Americans?" Bobby Kennedy's answer, "He made Americans feel young again." This is not my personal endorsement of, or critique of, that president's policies or politics, but merely a recital of the attorney general's opinion about his brother. I believe Kennedy was not speaking of physical youth but an inner youth, a state of mind.

I look for that in any leader, whether political, social, or spiritual. Where is that man or women who can stir my soul to its youthful vigor and vision? Joshua's leadership made 85-year-old Caleb a champion once again. Read that amazing story in the Old Testament Book of Joshua. Where is that leader whose very words fire my imagination and stimulate my strength of mind and heart? What person, still with spring in his or her step, wants to hear mere recitations of old issues or the continual harping of problems and shortcomings? An auditor can give that dull report. But a true leader soars above and beyond it and makes people feel young again, makes them feel able to achieve once more, and perhaps above all, instills a "want-to" spirit within them.

Nowhere is this needed today more than in Christ's church, where the message remains a constant, but the impartation of eternal truths must stay as up-to-date as tomorrow. Bobby Kennedy's words keep running through my mind: "He made Americans feel young again." The Church must never be allowed to grow old in spirit. Or old in concepts. This body of mine is far from young — and keeps reminding me of it. But my mind and heart? Well now, that's a whole different matter. Strike up the band, friend, and let's march!

PRAYER

O God, I thank You today that I have a rational mind. Help my body keep up with my spirit. If it is indeed true that as a person thinks, so is she or he, then straighten up my brain. Let me see the wisdom You have imparted to me and not the wrinkles; the experience, not the energy loss. And use me once again today for You, I pray. Amen.

ARE YOU A SPIRITUAL PERSON?

Galatians 6:1

Brethren, if a man be overtaken in a fault, ye which are spiritual, restore such an one in the spirit of meekness; considering thyself, lest thou also be tempted.

What is there about that verse that so many believers can't quite understand? It says very emphatically that folks who are truly spiritual are "restorers" of those whom life has "overtaken" in one way or the other. The essence of the word "restore" means "to bring back from virtual extinction." Thus, the holy Scriptures command us followers of Jesus Christ that if we are truly spiritual people, we will bring back from virtual extinction those of Christ's flock who have been overtaken in a fault. Or to put it bluntly, they have sinned.

Strange as it may seem, obeying this command of the Lord requires uncommon courage. It frankly requires a pretty thick hide, not to mention a strong degree of spiritual security of the believer.

Byline #218

Why is this so? Because some in our flock of sheep would rather ostracize or put away that one who has brought reproach to Christ and His people. In so doing, we conveniently forget that Scripture says, "We all, like sheep, have gone astray, each of us has turned to his own way; and the LORD has laid on him the iniquity of us all" (Isa. 53:6; NIV).

Now, friend, I did not write this Galatians 6:1 requirement. It comes from the Holy Spirit himself. Think of the ramifications of our obedience to it. If a church could somehow round up all the people in its town who have fallen away, if we could "restore" these brothers and sisters in an attitude of love and respect, why, we would not have room enough in our churches to house them all. I cannot tell you in this short space how many of these "fallen" have told me, "Pastor, I would love to come home to Father's house, but I am afraid of the rejection of the people." This attitude ought not to be anywhere apparent in the house of God. Restoration is the sincere and magnificent work of love in the life of a follower of Christ. So, then, are we spiritual? Well, do we restore? That's one of the simplest tests.

PRAYER

O God, forgive us for being so judgmental, for shooting our own wounded and for forgetting that we, too, are sheep who have gone astray. Teach us to restore others even as You have so graciously restored us. Amen.

SUCH LOVE!

1 John 3:1: Behold, what manner of love the Father hath bestowed upon us, that we should be called the sons of God: therefore the world knoweth us not, because it knew him not.

I can still remember it from decades past. Our pastor would stand in the pulpit and say, "Now turn to page 300 in our hymnal and let's sing that great old song, 'Such Love!'" Oh, how I loved those lyrics, yes, even then as a little boy: "That God should love a sinner such as I, should yearn to change my sorrow into bliss!" The chorus closed with, "That God should love a sinner such as I, how wonderful is love like this!"[1]

Have you ever loved someone so much that your chest sometimes constricts and it's hard to breathe? Where the vision of that someone's face is always present on the screen of your mind? Have you ever loved someone so much that in moments of being apart you have spontaneously wept? Or, strange thought, just laughed out loud for joy? Where the very sound of that person's voice filled you with more joy than you felt you could contain? And against all odds, that love grows and grows through the years, deeper and faster so that it becomes an almost exponential emotion of fulfillment? Have you ever loved someone so much that you would gladly lay down your life on your lover's behalf and consider it a joy and honor?

Then, my friend, you truly know the emotions that ran through Jesus' heart as He gave His life for you and me on Calvary. All the nails possessed by the Roman Empire could never have held God's Son to a cross. It was His love that held Him there, pinioned against that rough plank of suffering. A songwriter has penned that Christ's love for us has been written in red, the red being His precious blood. He gladly laid down His life for us, paying the penalty once and for all the sins of mankind. Why would He do such a thing? Such love, such wondrous love! I proclaim to you once again the never-ending love of the Savior. The price for such exquisite treasure has been paid in full. Jesus loves you, this I know, for the Bible tells me so.

1. C. Bishop and Robert Harkness, "Such Love," 1928.

Prayer: O God, sometimes in the pursuit of our days, we temporarily lose sight of the magnificence of Calvary, of Your eternal love for us. We often feel unloved and unwanted. But if we would just remember Calvary, such selfish thoughts would vanish like fog in the morning sun. Thank You for loving me today. And every day. Amen.

God's commitment to Abraham

Genesis 12:2–3: And I will make of thee a great nation, and I will bless thee, and make thy name great; and thou shalt be a blessing: And I will bless them that bless thee, and curse him that curseth thee: and in thee shall all families of the earth be blessed.

A careful study of history shows clearly that God meant what He told Abraham. He has fulfilled His commitment. Despite the pogroms, despite efforts at genocide, despite the worst of Auschwitz, Treblinka, and Buchenwald, God's chosen people, the Jews, have shown remarkable courage and blessing to the world.

In his excellent book *The Jewish Phenomenon*, Steven Silbiger reminds us of key facts that everyone should know: Jews make up only 2 percent of the total U.S. population, yet 45 percent of the top 40 of the Forbes 400 richest Americans are Jewish. One-third of all American multimillionaires are Jewish. Twenty-five percent of all American Nobel Prize winners are Jewish. The percentage of Jewish households with income greater than $50,000 is double that of non-Jews. Twenty percent of professors at leading universities are Jewish. Forty percent of partners at leading New York and Washington, D.C., law firms are Jewish.[1] Think of all the medical breakthroughs that have come through the brilliant minds of the Jews. God has certainly fulfilled His promise made so long ago to Abraham.

But God also warned that while He would bless nations that blessed His people, He would curse those nations that did not. Any glance at history would show you the result of those nations who have attempted to obliterate the Jews, while at the same time here is America, bountiful and blessed, known historically to be a friend of the Jews. God made a promise. He is not slack concerning His Word. How then should we live with our Jewish neighbors? I am privileged to have the rabbis in our county as very good friends. I have on several occasions been honored to speak in their synagogues on Shabbat. Oh — one thing more: my Savior, Jesus Christ, was a Jew.

1. Steven Silbiger, *The Jewish Phenomenon* (Atlanta, GA: Longstreet Press, 2000).

Prayer: O God, history makes a clinical case for Genesis 12. You meant what You promised to Abraham. May I, as a follower of the Jew Jesus Christ, always treat Abraham's progeny with the dignity and respect they deserve. You expect it of me. Your blessing on my life is indication once again of Your promise to Abraham. *Amen.*

POST VICTORY DANGERS

Joshua 7:5: And the men of Ai smote of them about thirty and six men: for they chased them from before the gate even unto Shebarim, and smote them in the going down: wherefore the hearts of the people melted, and became as water.

Mighty Israel, following a stunning military victory at Jericho, suffered a humiliating defeat in the tiny Israeli mountain village of Ai. History shows there were similar losses to other nations prior to that and countless more since.

The German conquest of France in the spring of 1940 is a profile of miscalculation. Despite the fact that it was generally believed the French had the strongest army on earth at that time, the Nazis overcame their enemy in a mere five-week stretch. Why? How? Historians agree on three general principles that brought about the French defeat: (1) France planned a defensive war. The thought was to keep the Germans out, rather than marching on Berlin as she had in World War I. France never planned to defeat Germany, only keep Germany from defeating her. French Defense Minister Andre Maginot had devised the defensive front line called "The Maginot Line." (Wonder where they got that name?) It was a line of deeply entrenched gun emplacements that could hold up to a million soldiers. The German Wermacht made mince-meat of it in days. The church of Jesus must never adopt that fateful malaise of just "holding the fort" against Satan. (2) France underestimated Germany. Her commanders believed they could still win with cavalry and horses. But Hitler had the best tanks of those days, the Panzers. Does the church underestimate our enemy? Frankly, yes. (3) A spokesman for France said, "The main reason we lost in such swift fashion is this: we suffered from a terrible disease. That disease was *victory in the previous war*. A previous victory is usually the weakest part of any nation."

After every spiritual victory, we must be keenly aware of a fresh attack from Satan. We are extremely vulnerable at that moment. France probably could have ended Hitler's dream of European conquest in the late 1930s when the Nazis invaded Czechoslovakia. But she did nothing and lost the war. So, is Christ's church on the march today? Or just dreaming of past victories?

PRAYER:
O God, keep us, Your church, on our spiritual toes constantly. May we never be taken by surprise! Holy Spirit, guide us day by day. Amen.

SORRY, MISS RAND, THERE IS NO VIRTUE IN SELFISHNESS

2 Peter 2:10

But chiefly them that walk after the flesh in the lust of uncleanness, and despise government. Presumptuous are they, selfwilled, they are not afraid to speak evil of dignities.

In 1964, a collection of essays by Ayn Rand appeared in book form called *The Virtue of Selfishness*. Her thesis was the validation of egoism as a rational code of ethics. This byline is not a condemnation of the late Miss Rand, for I have read every book she ever wrote and enjoyed them thoroughly. It's just that I disagree with her on just about everything. See, Miss Rand's writings stand in direct antithesis to Christ's Sermon on the Mount, found in Matthew 5, 6, and 7.

To be perfectly fair, Rand did not define selfishness as that brutal "me first in everything" philosophy of life. Her definition had more to do with fulfillment of one's dreams and talents. However, that lofty ambition all too often gets lost in the swamp of "I want my own way!" For example, recently on an airplane the stewardess made the standard announcement that all electronic devices had to be turned off before the plane could take off. The lady across the aisle from me just kept yakking away on her cell phone while the man in front of me continued pecking on his laptop. Twice the stewardess called for appliances to be turned *off!* The two ignored her again. Finally the pilot came on the intercom: "To the man who continues to use his laptop and to the lady still talking on her cell phone, if those two devices are not shut off in 30 seconds, I will personally come out there and take them away from you." The rest of us applauded. Reluctantly, Chatty Cathy and Computer Carl obeyed the edict. They were thinking only of themselves, not the safety of the other 150 passengers.

Selfishness, as normally defined, is not a Christian characteristic. Jesus always put other people before himself to the extreme point of His crucifixion. As His followers, it only stands to reason that we are to offer the same perspective in our own lives: Christ first, others second, ourselves dead last. Remember the Golden Rule is do unto others *as* you would have them do unto you, not do unto others *before* they do unto you.

Byline #222

PRAYER

O God, I need to relearn that principle every day of my life. Help me to learn the joy of giving . . . of giving myself. Amen.

CHRIST AND
THE COMEDIAN

Mark 2:14

And as he passed by, he saw Levi the son of Alphaeus sitting at the receipt of custom, and said unto him, Follow me. And he arose and followed him.

There is no limit to whom our Lord may call. Levi, in the verse above, was Matthew, a dreaded tax collector for the Romans.

I ran into Jim the other night in the gym — Jim Labriola. He is a professional comedian. His career began in New York's famous "Catch a Rising Star" Comedy Club. From there he went on the road to become a favorite in comedy clubs across the nation. Then he got a real break by getting the part of Benny on the hit television show *Home Improvement*. Jim also appeared in Disney's huge holiday film, *The Santa Clause*.

But even though his career was riding high, Jim felt empty and noticed the personal problems of so many of the famous people around him. He has since dedicated his life to Jesus Christ, has gone through a discipleship program, and is a faithful attender of his church. He travels the nation, speaking at churches, concerts, and outreach events, as well as appearances on television and film.

"So how's it going, Jim?" I asked him. "Great," he responded, sweat dripping down his face. "Physically and spiritually it's great." He seemed to have it all together. There have been changes in his life since making Jesus his Lord. For instance, he won't do raunchy humor any longer, yet he remains as funny as ever. He won't take part in films that require him to swear or compromise his witness to the Lord. Yes, good friend, I am sure that has narrowed his course of options professionally. But Jim considers that a small price to pay for the joy that now fills his life. As many others, he has found that all that thrills his soul is Jesus. He's never been happier, nor has he ever been more proficient in his work.

PRAYER

O God, please keep Your hand upon all those who turn to You. May they never turn aside. Keep them true, Lord Jesus. Keep them true. Amen.

I have met strong followers of Christ in every walk of life — sports, politics, films, writers, butchers, bakers, and candle-stick makers. Jesus touches us all if we'll let Him.

Don't judge the herd by one hog

Job 15:34: For the congregation of hypocrites shall be desolate. . . .

I wish I had that proverbial dollar for everyone I have invited to church who has responded with, "Ah, too many hypocrites in the church." I usually tell them that if a hypocrite is standing between them and God, the hypocrite is closer to God than they are.

But I could also tell them this little parable (not one Jesus told, by the way). A certain hog farmer refused to have anything to do with the local church because all he thought he ever saw there was a bunch of hypocrites. He could even tell you their names. One day the pastor of the church came by to purchase a hog from him. After looking over the farmer's entire swine herd, the pastor pointed to a scrawny, sickly little runt and said, "I want that one." The farmer remonstrated immediately and vigorously, "Oh no, Preacher, you don't want that one! Why, he's the scrawniest runt I ever saw. Look, here are some fine hogs — much better ones." "No, that's all right," said the preacher, "I still want that skinny one."

After the purchase was completed, the farmer asked, "What in the world are you going to do with that runt?" The pastor replied, "Now I'm going to haul this pig all over the country and tell everyone that's the kind of hogs you raise." The farmer protested, "No, preacher, that's just not fair! I raise fine hogs. An occasional runt like the one you've chosen doesn't ruin my whole stock." The pastor explained, "Sir, I am only following your example of condemning a whole church because of the stunted spirituality of a few of its members."

The farmer got the point. You know, I run into hypocrites who work at my local grocery store and pharmacy. But I don't stop shopping in those places. My favorite baseball team is full of hypocrites who think they can play the game, but they can't (although they still draw down the big bucks). But I still root for them. So why do people isolate the church for their "hypocrite" game?

Prayer: O God, I guess I pray first that I won't be a hypocrite myself, that I will always live what I preach. But I pray also for those who get sidetracked when their eyes get on people instead of Christ. People will usually fail. Jesus never does. So help us all keep our attention on the One who is our example. ***Amen.***

THE PASSION OF CHRIST

LUKE 23:27–28: And there followed him a great company of people, and of women, which also bewailed and lamented him. But Jesus turning unto them said, Daughters of Jerusalem, weep not for me, but weep for yourselves, and for your children.

Mel Gibson's film *The Passion of the Christ* swept across America with unusual intensity. Keith Fournier wrote, "One scene in the film has now been forever etched in my mind. A brutalized Jesus was soon to fall again under the weight of the cross. His mother had made her way along the Via Dolorosa. As she ran to him, she flashed back to a memory of Jesus as a child, falling in the dirt road outside of their home. Just as she reached to protect him from the fall, she was now reaching to touch His wounded adult face. Jesus looked at her with intensely probing and passionately loving eyes (and at all of us through the screen) and said, 'Behold, I make all things new.'"[1]

I have seen the film a number of times and my impression has been this: few people can even begin to comprehend the violence of a crucifixion. Most Hollywood films try to make the passion of our Lord real, but they miss the boat by "patty-caking" around it. Gibson did not. He had done his homework. He showed Roman crucifixion for what it was: brutal!

The reality of Jesus' savagely beaten body being nailed — hear that verb *nailed* — to a timber takes on a whole new dimension to me now. We sometimes sing in church services, "He Was Nailed to the Cross for Me," while in our minds we are wondering if the person sitting next to us is singing off-key on purpose or just plain can't sing, or how long the service is going to last, or if we will beat the other churches to the restaurant. The Christian world is indebted to Mel Gibson, not only for the untold multi-millions of his own dollars he invested in the film, but also for his strong adherence to the scriptural narrative and the passion he brings forth from all of us. The old songs "At Calvary" and "The Old Rugged Cross" will never be the same for me again.

1. www.catholic.org/featured/headline.php?ID=345

Prayer: O God, we need to be reminded again and again, as we always are at communion, of the incredible price You paid for our redemption. Isaiah wrote that it's our sins He was dying for, this horribly marred human figure writhing on the cross. May I never forget history's horror picture, the death of Your Son on Calvary. And may I ever be thankful in words and by the way I live. Amen.

LIKING GOD? OR YEARNING FOR HIM?

Psalm 141:8

But mine eyes are unto thee, O GOD the Lord: in thee is my trust; leave not my soul destitute.

His name was Edwin Hatch, a high school principal who lived well over a hundred years ago. He gained most of his fame, however, as a church historian and theologian. Accolades directed his way were pretty meaningless to him; his passion was God. It was his intimate walk with the Lord that charmed him most. He wrote a great hymn that has long been one of the cries of my own heart:

> Breathe on me, Breath of God / Fill me with life anew / That I may love what Thou dost love / and do what Thou would'st do / Breathe on me, Breath of God / 'Til I am wholly Thine / until this earthly part of me / glows with Thy fire divine.

Only a person who really knew God could ever write such a lyrical prayer and still maintain a clear conscience. The whole song is the overflow of a heart that yearned for the Creator. There is a difference between "liking" God and "yearning" for Him. David wrote, "As the deer pants for streams of water, so my soul pants for you, O God" (Ps. 42:1; NIV). That expression of desire comes from a person in travail, from one who has somehow captured a brief glimpse of the majesty of God and who wants the fullness of the Creator in his or life at any cost.

Do we have such seekers today? Or is God only a vague concept, you know, as in "somebody up there likes me"? To some, God is "an ever-present help in time of trouble," "the man upstairs," an abstract entity, some mystical being of Mount Olympus legend. But to a man like Edwin Hatch, God was his dearest, closest companion, his confidant. Can we pray his prayer today, "Breathe on me, breath of God"? If so, God will hear. And answer.

Byline #226

PRAYER

O God, let not my walk with You be a passive one. I do not follow You just to miss the flaming licks of hell, but rather because to know You is the fulfillment of everything I was ever created to be. You are the joy of life. My greatest love. And I do yearn for a closer relationship with You today. Amen.

IF WE ALL WILL PULL TOGETHER . . .

Acts 2:44 And all that believed were together. . . .

I remember a children's chorus of years and years gone by, "If we all will pull together, together, together, if we all will pull together, how happy we'll be." We used to sing that in our old Iowa church.

Recently I was in a church where the folks were all "pulling together." Over 150 of them gathered in work clothes, with tools, paintbrushes, vacuums, cleaning rags, shovels, rakes — you name it. After a rousing fellowship breakfast at 7:30, those 150 saints put in four hard hours, doing everything you can imagine as laid out for them by the church administrator. I did not see one person goofing off. Think of it: a total of 600 hours of volunteer work all in one morning, and I mean really hard work. What a transformation in that church facility! At even a few bucks an hour, the church would have had to lay out thousands of dollars for the same manual labor.

You see, we have a choice as church members. We can complain about the landscaping, the paint work, lights that have burned out, dust on the piano, etc., or we can pitch in and do something about it.

By noon, those dear people were pretty tuckered and a huge meal was waiting for them in the gym. They stacked their plates high, and while they ate, they laughed and talked, all of them getting better acquainted. They just had a good old time. Yes, that old chorus is prophetic in a sense: "If we all will pull together, how happy we'll be." And the church and adjacent grounds will surely look better. That's a testimony to the neighborhood and community. The last I heard, those folks had such a good time they were planning to do it again next month, and maybe the month after that. Why, there's no telling what that church will look like before those folks get done with it. Of course, they could have chosen the other route and just sat around . . . complaining.

PRAYER: O God, all of us, Your children, need a keener understanding of our responsibilities to Your house of worship. Of all the buildings in town, Your house should be the cleanest and best cared for. Forgive us please if we neglect Your house in our desire to make our own house look better. Amen.

Jesus commanded us to do . . . what?

Matthew 5:23–24: Therefore if thou bring thy gift to the altar, and there rememberest that thy brother hath ought against thee; Leave there thy gift before the altar, and go thy way; first be reconciled to thy brother, and then come and offer thy gift.

Jesus gave us a high standard of conduct, didn't He? He commanded us to love our enemies. You know, if everyone in the world obeyed that principle, every nation on the planet could cut its defense spending. Law enforcement agencies would be reduced to helping little old ladies across the street and plucking cats out of trees. I remember hearing President Ronald Reagan once say that if everyone obeyed the principles of the Bible, there would be worldwide peace.

Jesus' words were shocking for both His day and ours. "Love your enemies! Do good to those who hate you! Pray for the well-being of those who curse you!" (See Matt. 5:44.) Christ preached forgiveness. That subject was at the heart of His message. He fulfilled His own directive when He forgave the Roman soldiers who nailed His body to a cross.

Say what you want, but the Christian message includes the loving of one's enemies. Yet it is directly opposite of what far too many of our Lord's professing followers often practice. Sometimes we just don't want to forgive. We claim that it's too difficult. It is easier by far to strike out at that person and wound the one who has wounded us. Forgiveness of our enemies sounds like an invitation to disaster. Yet forgiveness is precisely the way God deals with us. He forgives us and teaches us to forgive ourselves and those around us. This degree of forgiveness is the dynamic of change, both spiritual and social. Still, it's not a virtue the world holds in much regard today. We would too often rather be avengers. We reason that forgiveness, as taught by our Lord, is not much of a tool for survival in our current world. Yet it is exactly that — a God-given tool for survival and progress.

Prayer: O God, if Jesus could look down at the men who whipped Him and crucified Him and say, "Father, forgive them," then none of us anywhere or any time have the right to hold grudges against those who have grieved us. Forgive us for not obeying Your instructions for proper social behavior. Live through us this very day so that we may treat others as You would treat them. ***Amen.***

THE HISTORY OF THE JEWS PROVES GOD EXISTS

Byline #229

Thirty-five hundred years or so ago, Moses led the Children of Israel, the Jews, out of Egyptian bondage. The legendary film *The Ten Commandments* of Cecil B. DeMille fame somewhat adequately depicted the parting of the Red Sea. An interesting question is: how many Jews were liberated? The Bible records that there were 600,000 Jewish males between the ages of 20 and 60 who left Egypt. Accounting for women, children, and the aged, one could estimate that a possible three million Jews left the land of the Nile for the Promised Land of Israel.

We don't know what the population was in the golden era of Kings David and Solomon. It was Jewish practice at that time not to make a census. In fact, David was punished by the Lord for even attempting to do so. It is believed that there were as few as 42,000 Jews in Israel when Ezra actually rebuilt the Temple in Jerusalem, following Babylonian captivity about 450 B.C. But let's bring this to modern times. Fifty years ago, an Israeli prime minister said that when the State of Israel was home to five million Jews, it would be secure. I am afraid the government leader was not much of a prophet. Israel has passed this population benchmark, but security is still a major problem.

The gist of this story to me is this: the Jews have survived the most diabolical attacks on their very existence of any race under the sun. Pogroms, forced emigration, and efforts at actual genocide from Haman to Hitler have held down the population without question. It is amazing that the Jews have prospered, even as God told Abraham and Jacob they would. If you are not convinced the Bible is true, then study the history of the Jews. Their very existence today is verification that there truly is a God.

ECCLESIASTICAL HIRELINGS

John 10:12

But he that is an hireling, and not the shepherd, whose own the sheep are not, seeth the wolf coming, and leaveth the sheep, and fleeth: and the wolf catcheth them, and scattereth the sheep.

Recently on a syndicated radio show I spoke on the subject "The Workers Are Few." On that broadcast I decried the "package" preachers, those who are willing to work for the Lord provided "the package" is right. Translate "package": salary and benefits. The response to that broadcast was pretty strong. Several e-mailed me, taking me to task for my belief that when we are called into the ministry we do it for the Lord and have faith that He will care for us. "Pretty 'old-school,' Dan," one wrote. But the overwhelming response was, "Dan, you're absolutely right! We are weary of the hirelings." Apparently, from the words of Jesus at the top of this page, so is He!

I received a lengthy response from a denominational district superintendent. He opened his e-mail with these words: "Thank you, thank you, thank you!" And he continued, "As a district superintendent, I am faced with 'the package preachers' all the time. I routinely dismiss their resumes. One young minister wrote to me to say, 'Don't send my resume to any church that won't pay at least $85,000 a year.'"

Every person I personally know who has been successful in God's work has started at the bottom. One irate pastor, apparently a "package" preacher, wrote me, "I don't believe you when you say you've never asked for a dime to minister anywhere." Well, I'm very sorry he didn't believe that, but it happens to be a fact. I am not for hire. God takes care of those who take care of His business. It's just that simple. If you are in the ministry full-time and plan to work 20 or 30 hours a week in His vineyard, you'll probably never do very well — spiritually or materially. But if you give our King the best you have, He will most certainly reciprocate. As my mentor, the late Oswald J. Smith, used to tell me, "God will never owe you money." That's the truth, my friend. Live with it.

Byline #230

PRAYER

O God, I thank You for Your faithfulness to me and my family over all these decades of ministry. We always had "enough." My wife and I, our four children, and seven grandchildren say to You from our hearts, "Thank You!" Amen.

THE FUTILITY OF FEELING SORRY FOR YOURSELF

1 Kings 19:10: And he said . . . I, even I only, am left; and they seek my life, to take it away.

The great prophet Elijah was feeling sorry for himself. It is interesting to observe what happens to not only a person but a civilization of people who follow suit. Who invariably blame others for their problems. Columnist James Pinkerton brought this to my attention with a recent article on Iraq. Here is some of his opinion:

Iraq and the entire Fertile Crescent ". . . gave the world its first writing, its first literature, the first laws, the first prayers, the first songs. . . . How could this place . . . fall so far? . . . According to a recent UN report, Iraq and other Arab states are clustered toward the bottom of almost every international ranking, from economic growth to literacy to life expectancy."[1]

Pinkerton made me think about the dozens of times I have visited the Middle East through the past almost 40 years. I think the newspaper man is right, for I have heard the same old excuses for their plight over and over: "It was the Crusades!" "It was colonization by the West." The main miserable theme, "It's the Jews!" That's all nonsense, of course. No, this whining doesn't come from everyone there, just a very large percentage. What has happened in those countries, to my thinking, is the mindset of people who believe they have no personal accountability, that all their misfortunes are the result of actions of others. They are thus ruled by a deadly fatalism, a passivity, the defeat of something inside a person that makes one believe personal actions can make life better. While it's true that where there's a will there's a way, it's also true that *where there is no will there is no way*. What a tragedy for anyone who spends a lifetime blaming others for his or her own situation. Jesus told the man at the Pool of Bethesda, "Take up your bed and walk" (John 5:8; NKJV). But doing those things requires both faith and action. Whole societies seem to lack those ingredients in these days. As an individual, don't feel sorry for yourself. It's so counter-productive.

1. James P. Pinkerton, "The Decline of Iraq Offers US a Lesson," *Newsday* (June 22, 2003).

Prayer: O God, Elijah went from victory to depression almost overnight. You had not changed; he had. I don't want my circumstances to dictate my thoughts and actions today. Help me with this today, Lord. Through You I am an overcomer. Amen.

The most difficult exercise of all

Psalm 131:1: . . . neither do I exercise myself . . .

Okay, okay — I've taken that verse out of context. But stay with me a minute to see where I'm going with this. On the advice of my good doctor, I have taken up going to the gym several days a week. I thought I would dislike it intensely. But you know what? I was right. But I feel better. That encourages me to keep exercising. My trainer puts me through various and sundry movements, some aerobic and some weight lifting and a whole lot of treadmill work. I must tell you that most of the effective exercises are somewhat painful, or at least uncomfortable, at first.

However, there is one exercise that is the most painful of all. It causes me to groan in agony. It is that exercise that makes me get out of my La-Z-Boy recliner at home and go to my car, put the key in the ignition, and drive to the gym. But it's the strangest thing — as soon as I have driven out of my driveway, the pain of that effort goes away instantly, and I am filled with gratification. Sometimes even delight. (Boy, I hate to admit that.) I tell you, friend, I dread no exercise as much as I dread that one of leaving the house! Pile the weights on, increase the time on the treadmill, put me through the ordeal of those muscle stretches; but please, *please*, don't make me leave *Wheel of Fortune* and get into my gym outfit and head for the car! Oh, the agony!

Now I know I am reaching someone who goes through this same ordeal. Many times in our lifetimes we find that it's not the actual effort or activity that causes pain or stress, it's the thinking about it beforehand. You know . . . like going to church. I cannot tell you how many people have told me at the close of a service, "You know, pastor, I didn't want to come today, but I'm surely glad I did." Well, just stop fretting about it and get up and go! You're going to feel so much better. And think about exercising!

Prayer: O God, sometimes my "get-up-and-go" has just "got-up-and-left." That person You want me to speak to or visit, that service I really need to attend, that time spent in Your Word and with You . . . the enemy tries to keep me away from involving myself in those blessed pursuits. Please forgive my laziness in this regard. By Your convicting Holy Spirit, spur me on to new activity for You. ***Amen.***

JEWS, JESUS, AND GENTILES

Romans 3:9: What then? are we better than they? No, in no wise: for we have before proved both Jews and Gentiles, that they are all under sin. . . .

I was thrilled! Ecstatic! The sun was shining that day! The conservative rabbi had just left my study. During our time together he said to me, "Dan, have you seen Mel Gibson's film *The Passion of the Christ*?" "Indeed, I have," I replied, expecting perhaps a frown to cross his face. I was shocked at the next words out of his mouth.

"Dan," he inquired, "would you be willing to come to my synagogue on Shabbat and enter into a dialogue with me and my entire congregation about the crucifixion of Christ?"

"What did you just say?" I replied, a bit stunned. He repeated the invitation. This was a conservative rabbi, not a reform one. When I got my breath back I said, "Yes, sir, I most surely would. How soon do you want me there?"

I have always had the best of relationships with the Jewish community and have done everything I know to be open and respectful of them and their faith. On several occasions it has been my desire to address their congregants in synagogue. (In fact, one rabbi once gave me an hour in synagogue to explain, "Why we talk about Jesus all the time!") Then the rabbi in my study told me the most wonderful story of the divine healing of his son. He said, "Dan, we prayed for him three times a day and God has delivered him completely from his life-threatening illness."

By the time the night had come to meet with his people, another rabbi had joined us and we had quite a time before a packed-out synagogue! It was just simply exhilarating. Now here's our options as followers of Christ: we can throw stones at those people of different beliefs or we can build bridges. Someone said you can collect more bees with honey than you can with vinegar. As we parted at my office door, my rabbi friend gave me a bear hug (the guy is huge!). Do I water down my faith? Absolutely not. Not in my lifetime, friend. But I can reach out with gentleness, patience, love, and goodness. Last I heard, those virtues were fruit of the Holy Spirit.

PRAYER: O God, I pray fervently that I may always be a help and not a hindrance to everyone around me, whether atheist or saint, whether Jew or Gentile, whether Muslim or Methodist. If You reached out to those of Your earthly society, can I do less? Help me, Lord, just please help me in this light and salt business. Amen.

SISTER AIMEE

Joel 2:28

And it shall come to pass afterward, that I will pour out my spirit upon all flesh; and your sons and your daughters shall prophesy. . . .

In September of 1944, the legendary evangelist and pastor Aimee Semple McPherson died. She was only 54. How I would love to have met her! Her son Rolf, at this writing, is still alive and in his 90s, I suppose. We have talked on several occasions about his remarkable mother. In fact, Rolf gave me a number of recorded sermons she preached in the 1930s. Sister Aimee, as I recall, built the second great commercial radio station in the Los Angeles area. Her equipment was so good that those old recorded sermons Rolf gave me sound as if they were just recently recorded. Her church was Angeles Temple. Out of her ministry came the great Four Square denomination. My wife's mother, and all her family, were converted to Christ on the night Angeles Temple opened on January 1, 1923. Oh, the stories they have told me about her.

Actor Charley Chaplin called Sister Aimee the greatest actress of his generation. Anthony Quinn wrote in his autobiography that it was Sister Aimee who kept Hispanics from starving during the Depression. When she passed away, there were over 400 churches in her fellowship plus hundreds of others, birthed by her, that belonged to other denominations or fellowships. Biographer Edith Blumhofer wrote, "Her relentless pursuit of her dream brought [McPherson] personal notoriety as well as fame; it also captured the deepest religious longings of common people and articulated them in a popular idiom that both bound her to others and set her apart from them. . . . she reveled on the mountaintops but also walked through deep valleys spiritually, emotionally, and physically, both privately and publicly."[1]

How I would love to have known this remarkable woman, to have been in her dramatic divine healing services, and to have sat under her anointed teaching. God bless her memory. The effects of her life continue among millions even today.

1. Edith L. Blumhofer, *Aimee Semple McPherson: Everybody's Sister* (Grand Rapids, MI: W.B. Erdmans Pub. Co., 1993), p. 382.

Byline #234

PRAYER

O God, Joel was right when he prophesied that You would use women in these last days. Thank You for giving each one of us, whether men or women, the opportunity to be of ministry to You in so many arenas of life. Let us never forget the impact of Your handmaidens on our spiritual lives. Amen.

JANICE, BRING LIGHT TO THE DARKNESS

Byline #235

Early this morning an e-mail came across my computer screen. It came from the far northeast corner of South Africa, just north of Kruger Park. The sender was Janice Cole, a member of our church. This truly lovely woman is a fully accredited nurse. She could probably do anything in life she wanted. She has outstanding talents in so many areas. But God has called her to Africa, where she has been a great light for humanity and the gospel for a number of years. She works among the poor, the naked, the hungry, and the HIV-infected natives of that area. The youth of our church raised the funds to buy her a 4 x 4 SUV that she has since called "Princess."

In her e-mail she reported, "Without the 'Princess,' our ministry of Mercy Medicine with Children in Crisis would not be possible. Dan, you know this area, as you have traveled through it on occasion. I drive on roads that only a 4 x 4 could travel, through mud, over dusty rocks and potholes big enough to hide a child. This vehicle allows me to network among groups of individuals to provide services and food for the women and children of those remote villages. The locals cannot afford the bus fare to take them to grocery stores, so 'Princess' and I load up and take the food to them. The vehicle even transports some of the members of the village church to do home visits to the sick."

Janice is a woman who could accomplish anything in life she wanted. Yet she spends her life in a snake-infested, semi-forest area where I have personally seen leopards along the road at night and elephants over twice the size of her 4 x 4. What compels her to do these things? The same force that compelled the apostle Paul who wrote, "The love of Christ constraineth" (2 Cor. 5:14) me to do this and that. And Janice certainly fulfills our Lord's command to be light in the darkness. I asked her how long she planned to keep going. She replied, "As long as there is life in my body. Any other questions?"

Rules to live by
— kinda

Proverbs 10:21: The lips of the righteous feed many: but fools die for want of wisdom.

My friend Larry gave me a set of "rules to live by." Go ahead and read them, but honestly, I would really pray about actually trying them.

Let's start with a tip for leaders: "If you are riding ahead of the herd, look back every once in a while to see if the critters are still there." (Well, that one isn't bad, come to think of it.) And for those whose heads get turned by shallow compliments: "A person who agrees with everything you say or do is either a fool or is getting ready to skin you."

A similar bromide: "Never take to sawin' off the branch that is supportin' you unless you're being hung from it." You know, the closer I'm looking at these rules, the more sense they make. Let's try on one more: "Don't get mad at somebody who knows more than you do; it ain't his fault."

Now those "rules" are what we Germans call "practical." We're not much on theory. And in the Christian walk, it is vital for me to know what works and what doesn't. I have found that what has been successful in one person's life, if I can't find it in the Bible, it may not work for me. It's that "Saul's armor" thing.

There are so many "how-to" books today that you could build a house with them. We get inundated with these manuals in everything from our own personal lives to church leadership. The problem is, we're not all alike. God didn't create a bunch of robots. The urgent thing in each life is to hear from the Master Designer who built us in the first place — and made each of us unique. We don't think alike, act alike, and respond alike. So I need to hear from the Lord what will work in *my* life. Everything written in Scripture is there to help me. I should know what the Bible says and observe the admonitions. But suggestions from other sources? Be careful. Well, as one old trailhand observed, "You cain't never tell which way a pickle will squirt." That's not in the Bible.

Prayer: O God, You designed each of us the way we are for a reason. You created a whale, and You also made an amoeba. Help me to learn from You and Your divine manual, the Bible, what You want from me. And increase my faith to obey what You say. **_Amen._**

MORE THAN ONE ISRAEL?

Revelation 12:13: And when the dragon saw that he was cast unto the earth, he persecuted the woman which brought forth the man child.

Here's the cast of this drama: (1) the dragon — Satan; (2) the woman — Israel; and (3) the man child — Jesus Christ.

Before entering the ministry, I spent a number of years as a TV/radio newscaster. I know the media news business somewhat well. That's why I am confused about today's media journalists. It appears, from listening and watching them, that there are *two* Israels rather than just *one*. There is the Israel described to us by the self-appointed consciences of the world at CNN, NBC, ABC, CBS, and the BBC, as well as much of the print media. They paint vivid pictures of mayhem and violence in Israel and have their stories sanctioned by the U.S. government, which issues dire travel warnings. So there is one of the Israels. But I have been going to Israel virtually every year since 1971, and I see a land there that is quiet, where kids go to school, where people go about their work, where families observe Shabbat together, where the tourism business, as I write this, is flourishing to record levels, and where I have traveled the land from far north to far south. Are there occasions of trouble and tension, and even bloodshed? Yes, quite frankly, there are. But have you glanced at the United States in recent years? If you are just looking for trouble spots, look no farther, my friend. We have them here aplenty. Yet we continue our daily lives.

On another note: I met an Iraqi in Israel recently who told me, "Mr. Betzer, the overwhelming number of Iraqis bless the United States and what they have done to help our beleaguered nation! Thirty million Iraqis say, 'Thank you!'"

Seems the news media haven't picked up on that story either. I have to ask myself as a former practitioner, "If today's media are so haywire on this aspect of world affairs, is it possible they are skewed in other news as well?" My suspicion is in the affirmative. In the meantime, God remains in charge of it all, and our hearts need not be troubled.

Prayer: O God, bless Israel and bring peace to the land. I pray that You will also touch all peace-loving Palestinians and may they work diligently as well for peace. How urgently they all need the Prince of Peace in that ancient land! Amen.

MAKING GOOD USE OF GOD'S MONEY

Luke 16:2

And he called him, and said unto him, How is it that I hear this of thee? give an account of thy stewardship; for thou mayest be no longer steward.

Let's say you have tons of money. Should you flaunt it? Not according to a lot of millionaires who were interviewed by author Thomas Stanley for his book *The Millionaire Next Door*. Stanley wrote about frugal rich people who lived far below their means.

Through surveys and interviews, he found that people who *earn* their millions rather than *inheriting* or *winning* them live relatively simple lives. They often drive used cars, clip grocery coupons, and live in middle-class homes. They shun debt and credit cards and they choose Seiko watches over Rolex showpieces. Over two-and-a-half million people have purchased Stanley's book to learn about people with values, not just megabucks. His book tells the story of people who are comfortable with themselves rather than enamored by their bank accounts.

As a pastor, I often encountered people who believed if they have made a dollar, they should really spend a dollar and a dime. Then they wonder why they struggle with money problems. My wife and I have watched our money very carefully over the past over-half century of marriage. We pay the Lord His 10 percent *first*! Make no mistake about that priority. God must come first in our finances. We give another 10 percent (in fact, a great deal more than that) to missions. We pay Uncle Sam his due share and do so with gladness. We pay ourselves 10 percent for a rainy day. And we live on the rest. Our house is over 50 years old. Our clothes are not fancy. But we know who we are and are most comfortable with that reality. We are not trying to keep up with the Joneses (whoever they are) or impress anybody. We don't have those millions of dollars that Stanley wrote about, but we know we've been good stewards of God's money. I cannot tell you how good that makes us feel. We are ready for the coming eternal audit.

Byline #238

PRAYER

O God, You have always promised to take care of us. We have willingly and happily put You first in our lives. We have always had what we needed in raising four children, who now pursue the same course they learned from us. I cannot express to You adequately my gratitude for Your loving care. Thank You! Thank You! Amen.

SEND THE RAIN, O LORD!

1 Kings 18:45: And it came to pass in the mean while, that the heaven was black with clouds and wind, and there was a great rain.

Our beloved southwest Florida often hits precipitation extremes: either drought or floods. Not long ago we went through an extremely dry spring. Our aquifers were choking dust and almost any spark could set off a grass or timber fire, even in the Everglade Swamps. I saw the smoke from one such fire 60 miles away (remember, south Florida is as flat as a pool table), as over 1,500 acres were destroyed by the inferno. That very weekend I boarded a plane for the Midwest, leaving my parched county behind. As the plane climbed higher and higher, I looked down on the grim visage of baked soil beneath.

I returned four days later, during which the skies had unzipped and dropped nearly a foot of rain on that needy soil. What a difference the moisture had made! Now, on my return flight, as I looked down from the plane, I saw green fields and full streams. That's what the rain of the Holy Spirit does in a dry and barren life. The formerly dry church or family or individual takes on new vitality and joy.

We often sing in our church circles, "Oh, Lord, send the rain!" We are singing of the rain of God's presence and Spirit, of His anointing. As a pastor, I sensed more and more, year after year, my desperate need for the anointing of the Holy Spirit. I no longer have the responsibility of leading a church, but even in this pseudo-retirement (still laboring in God's fields) I continue to need the rain of the Holy Spirit in my life. I cannot function without Him. All the best programming or preaching or music we can produce will leave nothing but parched, burned-out lives unless the Holy Spirit refreshes it. But what a difference when we ask Him to have His way in our churches, our lives, our homes! Our spiritual aquifers fill quickly, the empty river beds are overflowing with fresh water from heaven, and we become productive and alive once more. O Lord, send the rain! Not just a sprinkling, but a deluge we cannot contain.

PRAYER: O God, today I gratefully acknowledge my complete need of You in all facets of my life. Your touch, Your anointing are the very source of true living. You are always faithful when we pray for that which we need. So, Lord, please send the rain! **Amen.**

America, the beautiful

Numbers 34:12: . . . this shall be your land with the coasts thereof round about.

In the summer of 2004, America lost two landmark personalities, one in politics and the other in show business. One of our greatest presidents, Ronald Reagan, passed away after an epic battle with Alzheimer's disease. The nation mourned for many days. On a somewhat lesser note (and this is not a play on words), we also lost Ray Charles. I was a fan!

After I first heard Charles sing "America the Beautiful" many years ago, I thought perhaps no other person could sing the song with such poignancy. Same for "Georgia on My Mind." I attended a heavyweight title boxing match one night where I first heard Charles sing "America the Beautiful." I must tell you I wept as the King of the Blues sang, ". . . for purple mountain majesties above the fruited plain. . . . God shed His grace on thee . . . and crown thy good with brotherhood from sea to shining sea." Ray Charles had not seen this land since he was a little boy. He had his sight until he was five or six,

then his blindness overcame him. So when he sang about this nation, he was seeing long-past images. His treatment of the great song moved me so deeply, I suppose, because I have had the privilege of ministering in every one of our 50 states. I've been on Mount McKinley in Alaska to the Florida Keys and from San Diego to the farthest reaches of Maine. What a magnificently beautiful land this is! And it's not just the geography to which I refer. The people are beautiful, every color, every conceivable kind of background, enjoying the precious and blessed liberties with which we are divinely blessed, paid for in patriots' blood.

I have ministered now in 60 countries, but the United States stands alone in my heart. I wish I could watch and listen to Ray Charles again sing, "O beautiful for patriot's dreams . . . thine alabaster cities gleam undimmed by human tears." Yes, I would probably weep once again.

Prayer: O God, we take this incredible nation of the United States for granted, I fear, until we see through our own eyes other lands and people far less blessed. Thank You for every inch of our country and for every law-abiding, America-loving person in it. And thank You for blessing us, from sea to shining sea. *Amen.*

RONALD REAGAN AND THE HYMNS OF THE CHURCH

Byline #241

It was heavenly to hear them again. I had not heard most of those songs of our faith in years. Great hymns such as "I Need Thee"; "Abide with Me"; "Softly and Tenderly"; "Just as I Am"; "Jesus, Lover of My Soul"; "Rock of Ages"; "God of our Fathers"; "My Faith Looks Up to Thee"; and "Jesus Savior, Pilot Me." And there were even more of the classic songs than I have listed here. I listened to the memorable melodies and the brilliant lyrics and more than one time my eyes moistened with tears of delight and mind pictures of years gone by.

No, I wasn't in church. You seldom hear those songs in churches anymore. No, not in these days when there are church leaders who literally boast that they have done away with such "songs of the past" and hymnals are relics gathering dust in the basement. No, I heard these great classic hymns of the faith at the televised funeral and burial services of President Ronald Reagan. TV commentators told us several times that the president had personally chosen each of the songs before he was diagnosed with Alzheimer's disease. The great preponderance of the nation was moved in heart and soul during the Reagan memorials, and the hymns played an integral part of that emotional process.

The question begs an answer: Why can we not hear these songs anymore in our churches? At what point did the hymnals, the greatest repository of theology ever given to mankind outside of the Bible, become anathema? When was the decision made that arbitrarily removed these songs from our singing worship experience and who made the decision for all the rest of us? Are praise and worship choruses valuable? Of course they are. But so are the hymns. President Reagan left so much to this nation. The gift of the hymns at his homegoing was a part of that legacy.

PRAYER

O God, I thank You for the legacy, the stability, and the majesty of these great songs in my life as a youngster. Even now, decades later, I find myself singing them again and again. I bless the memory of each one of them. Amen.

A RESPONSE TO THOSE CRITICAL OF MISSIONARIES

Mark 16:20

And they went forth, and preached every where, the Lord working with them, and confirming the word with signs following. Amen.

Critics of missionaries are usually people who don't know Christ personally, or don't give to missions themselves, or who have no idea what missionaries really contribute to a society. Recently I read a newspaper column written by a non-Christian who does not believe in missionaries and called for their eviction from all nations. He wrote, "For centuries (the tribes) have been served quite well by Buddhism, animism, ancestor worship, or other combinations thereof." Charis Crowley, whose family has long been involved in Cambodia, responded in an issue of the *Touchstone* magazine. She wrote: 'Have you ever attended a tribal funeral? The sick child becomes worse and the family sacrifices (to their gods) from their pitiful funds, first a chicken, then a pig. The child worsens and the family sacrifices a water buffalo to those spirits that fill their lives with

Byline #242

fear. And then the child dies, often from a very treatable condition. The funeral begins. The wailings and sobs haunt me. These people live in fear of starvation, fear of sickness and death, fear of the spirits who rule their lives and soak up their small supplies of rice and animals for futile sacrifices. Would you deny them change if they desire it? Would you deny them freedom from their bondage? They may smile for your camera, but I lived with them. We preach the gospel to save souls from dying eternally. There are no 'head games' involved. Buddhism, animism, and other religions have not served them well. They have no peace and yet it is peace they seek. They say, 'Help us! We are sick and dying and in fear of the demons who make our lives a living hell. Won't you please help us?'" So wrote Charis Crowley.[1]

The questions require answers. Good answers! Will we help them? Does your church emphasize missions? Do your church leaders make global evangelism a priority? The questions require answers. Will you do something to lift the hands of the eternally dying? Or are you and your church just too busy, unwilling to part with money or time?

1. Charis Crowley, "Cambodian Call," *Touchstone* (May 2004).

PRAYER

O God, You have one plan for mankind's redemption and that plan requires a delivery system. We are Your delivery system. If we fail to distribute the gospel, people will perish for all eternity. May we never fail You! Amen.

FISHING FOR MARLIN AND MEN

Hosea 5:14: . . . and none shall rescue him.

Several years ago, some friends of mine invited me to join them on their boat for the blue marlin fishing tournament in the Bahamas. The winning catch was a near-ten-foot behemoth weighing 780 pounds. No, we did not catch it on our boat. In fact, we didn't catch anything at all. We plied those azure waters hour after hour, our outriggers trailing four delicious-looking baits that we just knew would make any self-respecting marlin positively salivate. We were wrong. Like Peter and his crew, we toiled fruitlessly for hours and had the Master asked, "Have ye any fish?" we would have had to report, "Uh — no." But I can promise you it was not for lack of trying.

Now not all my fishing trips have been like that. It wasn't that long ago when I landed two tarpon in one three-hour stretch, one of them well over 100 pounds. Not bad, if I do say so myself. See, sometimes you catch 'em, and sometimes you just don't. But those of us who love to fish keep working at it. We never know when that rod will bend over double and the reel will scream out that wondrous sound, "Zi-i--i-n--n-n-g-g-g-g-g," the most beautiful song a fisherman can hear. The fish are in the sea; you just have to go after them. They are not coming to the fisherman. Very seldom does a bass knock on my door and ask, "Got a hook I could bite?"

Yet we fishers of men toil in waters where all too often there are seemingly no fish. Or if we get skunked on a particular mission for Christ, we give up fishing for the souls of humanity, mumbling, "Well, I guess I just don't have the gift of evangelism." Yet you and I work under a divine commission, a mandate, a direct order from Christ himself to take the gospel everywhere. Jesus never promised we would always be "catchers of men," but He did require that we fish for them! The perishing must be rescued! What if there is no one to do so?

Prayer: O God, there is no thrill like that of bringing a lost soul to You, of seeing that precious person find salvation through Jesus, the forgiveness of sins, and the weight of the past lifted off his or her shoulders. Spirit of God, sharpen my "fishing" skills that I may bring You a great catch. Amen.

The deadly trap of debt

Romans 13:8: Owe no man any thing, but to love one another: for he that loveth another hath fulfilled the law.

Let's discuss borrowing money. As a newlywed husband, well over a half-century ago, I learned firsthand the heartbreak of debt. I experienced what a deadly trap it can be. I don't care what the advertisement promises, *there is no such thing as an easy payment!* Once my wife and I were back on an even financial keel, I vowed to never again borrow money unless it was for a house mortgage. Even then, the deal had to be in my best interests, not the lending institution's.

Among the vital lessons of life our Lord Jesus taught us through Scripture is that of never consuming more than you produce. I don't want you to skip over that line, so here it is again: Never consume more than you produce! Why not? That's how you get into debt. The Bible equates debt with slavery. Proverbs 22:7 teaches, "The rich rule over the poor, and the borrower is servant to the lender" (NIV). The moment you borrow, someone else owns part of you. Debt also violates James 4:14 and 15,

which teaches against presumption. "You ought to say, 'If it is the Lord's will, we will live and do this or that'" (NIV). Borrowing presumes that you will earn enough in the future to pay the debt of today. And finally, debt can persuade you from seeing the provision of God. Philippians 4:19 promises us that God will supply all our needs according to His riches in Christ Jesus.

Again and again I have seen the Lord's hand in provision by simply trusting Him instead of running to a lender. Some things in life don't exist: the Loch Ness Monster, California's Big Foot, a recent World Series victory for the Chicago Cubs, and an easy payment. It is the world's system to borrow money, not the Christian's. Seek first the Kingdom of God and His righteousness and then all the other "things" will come in their proper sequence. A Christian must be a faithful steward of God's provision. Flagrant borrowing of money is contrary to that responsibility.

Prayer: O God, I am truly thankful that in Your lavish love for us, You provide what we need. We don't have to run to the nearest lending institution for provision. I pray for those who are in the bondage of debt today. Help them, Lord, to satisfy their lenders and learn their lessons well — to never borrow again. *Amen.*

SUNRISE, SUNSET

Genesis 45:10: And thou shalt dwell in the land of Goshen, and thou shalt be near unto me, thou, and thy children, and thy children's children, and thy flocks, and thy herds, and all that thou hast.

My good friend Gary S. Paxton once wrote a song with the question, "How did I get so old so fast?" On a summer Sunday in 1986, I preached a radio sermon on the worldwide *Revivaltime* network called simply "Brittany." It celebrated the advent of our first grandchild, born to our missionary son David and his wife, Janis. Now Brittany is all "grown up," and married! How did that happen? Where did those years fly by? And how can it be we have two of our four children now pushing the 50 mark? Wasn't it just recently when they were born? Surely it wasn't a half-century ago!

I remember the night when Darlene awakened me in the wee small hours to say it was time to go to the hospital . . . the baby was coming. David was born almost immediately upon our arrival there. We brought him home a couple days later. I remember he cried (make that "screamed") all the way home. I thought about taking him back to the hospital, but Darlene said we had to keep him. Good move on our part! Despite dire prediction about his future from some of his teachers, and the fact that he loved to bring home frogs, puppies, and snakes, David was always a delight to me. Now he has a daughter who's been married for a couple years. What has happened to the time? How did it pass by so quickly? What was it the old woman of Tekoah told King David? Oh yes, that our lives are like water spilled on the ground that cannot be gathered up again. That's a sobering thought, isn't it?

Reminds me that I played in a Pebble Beach golf tournament recently with my friend Joe. He was so healthy! We will bury him this Friday. Sunrise, sunset, quickly through the years. . . . James asked in his little epistle, "What is your life?" (James 4:14).

Short. That's what it is.

PRAYER: O God, bless our children and our grandchildren. Keep them safe by night and by day. Give them the wisdom to make sound decisions. May they always be in love with You! May they always know how dearly we love them. **Amen.**